Campus
Landscape

Campus Landscape

FUNCTIONS, FORMS, FEATURES

RICHARD P. DOBER, AICP

JOHN WILEY & SONS, INC.

New York • Chichester • Weinheim • Brisbane • Singapore • Toronto

This book is printed on acid-free paper. ∞

Copyright © 2000 by John Wiley & Sons. All rights reserved.

Published simultaneously in Canada.

This publication is designed to provide accurate and authoritative information in regard to the subject matter covered. It is sold with the understanding that the publisher is not engaged in rendering professional services. If professional advice or other expert assistance is required, the services of a competent professional person should be sought.

Library of Congress Cataloging-in-Publication Data:

Dober, Richard P.
   Campus landscape : functions, forms, features / Richard P. Dober.
      p. cm.
   Includes index
    ISBN 0-471-35356-6 (alk. paper)
     1. Campus planning—United States.   2. Landscape design—United States.   3. Universities and colleges—United States.   I. Title.

LB3223.3 .C26 2000
712'.7—dc21

                                                                                    99-056351

Printed in the United States of America.

10 9 8 7 6 5 4 3 2 1

For Kevin, Phoebe, and Michael

University of British Columbia
Photo: University of British Columbia; Courtesy University Architect.

CAMPUS LANDSCAPES

Campus landscape is an art of multiple and overlapping designs. A variegated pattern of landscape types and visual effects is evident at institutions such as Cornell University and the University of British Columbia, honored for their campus design. At Cornell, for example, the intersection of a pedestrian circulation network is configured as an informal gathering area that incorporates a celebrated vista to Lake Cayuga. At the University of British Columbia, a small garden is situated adjacent the main campus walk. Enclosed with a stone wall constructed with traditional regional university building material, the visual experience and memory of place is heightened by the contrasting view of the façade of the late-twentieth-century library.

Cornell University
Photo: © Charles Harrington/Cornell University Photography; courtesy John Ullberg, ASLA.

CONTENTS

SOURCES AND ACKNOWLEDGMENTS

My interest in campus landscape began with childhood experiences in Philadelphia—Franklin Park, schoolboy trips to the museums along the Benjamin Franklin Parkway, and visits to the University of Pennsylvania campus. Engagement and insights were further shaped by civic design courses at Brooklyn College and professional training at the Graduate School of Design, Harvard University. The latter included an independent project with landscape professor Hideo Sasaki and then a kind of hands-on apprenticeship in his office. Since then, forty years later, my own campus planning and design practice has yielded significant opportunities to foster campus landscape design as an essential feature in campus development. This book melds the accumulated ideas, ideals, and information into a reference book for all concerned about advancing the art.

Such is timely, I believe. Campuses will be centerpieces in our twenty-first-century culture, and greenery that serves and symbolizes colleges and universities a hallmark. The cachet *campus* will continue to be applied to other places that utilize the physical forms of institutions of higher education. There are no books known to the writer dealing extensively with the subject matter of campus landscape. Aspects of the topic have been treated in the author's previous publications: *Campus Planning, Campus Design,* and *Campus Architecture,* all in print as of fall 1999. The best overview on campus development remains Paul V. Turner's *Campus* (Cambridge, 1984). Ira Fink's bibliography published by the Society for College and University Planning (1999) includes significant material on facility planning and campus design, as does George Keller's compendium *The Best of Planning for Higher Education,* also available from the Society for College and University Planning. The bibliography *Contemporary Landscape Inquiry Project,* organized by the University of Toronto and available on the Web, is a good source for citations about landscape design history and modern trends and ideas, though little is yet indexed to campuses.

In preparing the text, I have used materials acquired in professional practice, lectures and conferences, and informal research. Quotations and graphics used in this book are credited directly to the source. For several decades, I have been fortunate to have access to the Francis Loeb Library,

Harvard University Graduate School of Design. There several generations of librarians have guided me through the use of their exceptional collections, and most recently helped refresh my memory of articles and documents read and recorded in ruminated browsing.

The photographs used in the book are reportorial, not artwork. They help illustrate the text and where noted are indicative of models worth considering in creating campus landscapes. Most of the photos are from the author's collection, gathered or taken in the field while on assignment or independent study. While color and professional photography might enhance the text and explain further the captions, the cost is prohibitive for a reference work of the kind now completed. For supplementary illustrations that were provided with goodwill and dispatch for this book, I am particularly grateful to Karen Berchtold, Roger du Toit, Perry Chapman (Sasaki), Keith A. Covey (Carleton College), Sandy D'Elia (EDAW), Patrick William Dober, Lawrence J. Dober, Garrett Eckbo, Lawrence H. Fauber, Michael Graves, Hoover and Desmond, Kate Hastings (Hastings + Chivetta), Trudis Heinecke (University of California, Merced), A. C. Martin, Clinton N. Hewitt (University of Minnesota), Stephen Holl, Frederick W. Mayer (University of Michigan), George Patton, Richard Rigternik (JJR), O. Robert Simha (Massachusetts Institute of Technology), Pam Stewart (University of Washington), John Ullberg (Cornell University), Michael Van Valkenburgh, Phil Williams (Stanford University), and Carol L. Wooten (Brown University). Photos on pages 133, 57, 30 and 118 were given to me with permission to publish several decades ago by the late Hugh Casson, Sir Basil Spence, and George Patton. Their landscape skills and friendship are much missed by the author.

At John Wiley and Sons, editor Margaret Cummins, editorial and imports program coordinator Jim Harper, and associate managing editor Eileen G. Chetti, and copy editor Sue Warga, gave me clear directions and help in all aspects of manuscript preparation. For their encouragement and logistical assistance I thank Laura Alves, Calvert W. Audrain, Dorothy Atwood, Mary Bush-Brown, Charles A. Craig, Claire B. Danaher, the Reverend William J. Danaher Jr., Patrick Lee Dober, Jean Dow, John Furlong, Charles W. Harris, Andy Gillespie, Nathaniel Gorham, Mary Ann Hill, Arvid Klein, Amy Lambert, Lorie Lawrence, Arthur Lidsky, George Mathey, Dori Mottola, and all those who participated in my workshops and presentations on campus design. Questions and comments from the last of these have sharpened my views and added substance to the current work. Errors and omissions are the author's responsibility, of course.

Special thanks to my brother Lawrence J. Dober, who served as driver and observer on two lengthy campus landscape study tours through the Southwest and mid-America, 1998–1999. My wife, Lee, did the same in the summer of 1999—visiting several dozen institutions in Texas and

Oklahoma, including a memorable week spent in the Panhandle with the daytime outside temperatures over 110 degrees. Her contribution, counsel, and support then and always have inspired the author to complete a work that at times seemed beyond accomplishment.

Richard P. Dober, AICP
Cambridge, Massachusetts

PREFACE

▶ "...Fundamental Signals From Fundamental Laws..." (Emily Dickinson, Poem 1295)

▶ Despite its continuity over the centuries, the American campus has experienced major changes in its form which reflect not only evolving notions of architectural planning but changing educational and social principles as well. (Paul V. Turner, *Campus* [Cambridge, 1984])

▶ The Norman campus of the University of Oklahoma has become a visitor destination point. New and restored facilities, fountains and statuary—and landscape to die for. Where once the attraction was largely for college-shoppers, now tourists and day-trippers swing off the interstate just to take in the sights. We are looking good and proud of it. (*Sooner* magazine, spring 1998)

This book provides information, ideas, and instruction about planning and designing the green environment that situates, serves, and symbolizes higher education.

Campus Landscape provides information, ideas, and instruction about planning and designing the green environment that situates, serves, and symbolizes higher education. The approach and coverage are comprehensive. The text and graphics encompass the extraordinary variety of colleges and universities here and abroad, with their distinctive purposes, sizes, locales, histories, and senses of place. As a preview of the coming discussions, the portfolio of images that follows suggests the variety and richness of an art form not well understood and seriously underestimated. The collection is also selected to introduce important themes, explicated and illustrated throughout the book. Thus the view of a traditional quad is counterpoised with a contemporary interior landscape—campus greenery in the twenty-first century should include both conservation of older masterworks and a significant increase in the presence of greenery inside new buildings. A contemporary collegiate plaza, designed as a visual reminder of the arid region in which it is located, is contrasted with a sparkling open space concept with water featured. A campus walk photographed on graduation day is a reminder that the routes of passage one takes both metaphorically and literally through the campus landscape can be arranged in recollection and reality as exceptional esthetic experiences. The photo of a parking deck with its sur-

TRADITIONAL QUAD / University of Chicago
Lawns, trees, and walks form the traditional exterior image of a campus as a landscape setting long associated
with colleges and universities.   *Photo:* Kaufmann and Fabry; courtesy University of Chicago.

rounding landscape epitomizes, and thus encourages through credible
citation, institutional commitments to high-quality campus design for
even a utilitarian structure.

TAXONOMY AND
DESIGN DETERMINANTS

Traditionally campus landscape is seen as a green carpet upon which
buildings are placed, or it is articulated as a device to extend a building
design concept into open space, with a garnish for an architectural feast.
Often and ephemerally, landscape materials will be selected, arranged,
and installed by a well-motivated physical plant staff at the approach of
graduation or for some other memorable campus event that deserves
nature's beauty. Uplifting indeed is a vernal version of Hollywood pho-
tographer George Hurrel's dictum: "Bring out the best, conceal the worst,
and leave something to the imagination." These are legitimate objectives
for campus landscape, often commanding but not exclusive.

INTERIOR LANDSCAPE / Illinois Wesleyan University, 1999
A comprehensive campus landscape plan will include clusters of interior spaces and greenery that provide attractive places for participation in all aspects of campus life.   *Photo:* Scott McDonald; courtesy of Hastings + Chivetta.

CAMPUS PLAZA / New Mexico State University
Not all campus landscapes are green. Here the designers use paving and geological specimens to create an eye-catching regional design as the entry area to an engineering complex.   *Photo:* R. P. Dober.

Our plea and exposition will take an expansive stance. As we will demonstrate, campus landscape requires a fresh look at issues and possibilities. More and better landscape is our clarion call, with expected tangible, valuable, and worthy results. Through amplitude and application a significant increase in campus landscape will strengthen the image and substance of higher education venues. Colleges and universities will then be in a better position to attract and retain faculty and students, advance educational and research programs, energize fund-raising appeals to alumni and friends, demonstrate environmental design concepts and ethics, enlarge the presence of art, and strengthen the campus as a community design asset.

In the course of our exposition we will describe the means and methods for multiplying the number and kind of campus landscapes and their visual effects. We will cite the lives and good works of landscape professionals whose contributions have been undervalued or neglected in most historical accounts of campus design and campus development. We will validate a purposeful vision: In service and symbol, today's campuses are the contemporary equivalent of cathedral precincts in medieval life, palaces and civic centers in the Renaissance, and railroad stations and central business districts in the age of commerce and urbanization. Recognized and evaluated in these terms, a campus with minimal landscape is incomplete, inchoate, and incapacitated.

How might the imperfect be corrected, the limited expanded, and the exceptional protected and enhanced? For planners and designers, col-

Through amplitude and application a significant increase in campus landscape will strengthen the image and substance of higher education venues.

WATERSCAPE / University of California, San Diego
The unconventional design includes a cascading water feature that slashes through the expected green lawn. Contrast equals a strong sense of place. *Photo: R. P. Dober.*

lege and university administrators and staff, their patrons, and all concerned about the quality of the campus environment, we offer a *taxonomy of opportunity,* that is, thirty specific forms of campus landscape. These are listed in the model Campus Landscape Matrix, page xxii. Arguably, each of the thirty items in the taxonomy will have perceptible characteristics that are the result and impact of *design determinants.* We identify

CAMPUS WALKS AND PATHS / Trinity College, Connecticut
The design of circulation systems will generate significant opportunities to devise memorable campus landscapes.   *Photo:* Trinity College, Hartford, Connecticut.

PARKING STRUCTURE AND ENVIRONS / University of Oklahoma
A utilitarian structure is treated as a prime site for demonstrating campus landscape values. *Photo:* R. P. Dober.

CAMPUS LANDSCAPE DESIGN DETERMINANTS

Climate: Macro and Micro
Vegetation
Environmental Suitability
Land Form Concepts
Terrain Modification
Subsurface Geotectonic
Site Size
Site Configuration
Environs
Style
Program
Visual Character
Technology
Funds
Factor X

CAMPUS LANDSCAPE DESIGN TAXONOMY

Surrounds
Perimeter
Boundary Markers
Gateways
Campus Roads
Walks
Bikeways
Threshold
Terminus
Parking
Heritage Spaces
Secondary Spaces
Tertiary Spaces
Wetscapes
Dryscapes
Botanical Gardens
Horticultural Gardens
Arboreta
Natural Preserves
Nature Walks and Trails
Gardens for Art
Amphitheaters
Special Theme Gardens
Site History
Play Fields and Recreation
Interior Spaces
Signs
Lighting
Site Furniture
Seating

IMPACT DIAGRAM / Design Determinants and Design Taxonomy
Components
The design determinants are itemized and the campus landscape components are
listed in the taxonomy. The diagram suggests the latter will be influenced by the
former, thus giving the forms and features unique characteristics evocative of the
specific location and situation.   *Graphic:* Dober, Lidsky, Craig and Associates, Inc.

thirteen of these factors and influences. They include the basic landscape trilogy of climate, topography, and land size and configuration as
well as style, programmatic direction, client budget, and the designer's
knowledge, experience, and creativity. As a result of this interaction,
functions give rise to forms, and forms are inflected by design determinants and made distinctive by physical features established through disciplined planning and design routines.

The taxonomy is pragmatic, not theoretical. The mix is intentional.
Obviously some elements overlap and reinforce others. For example,
campus gateways help mark campus boundaries; the latter serve as the
perimeter-defining landscape. Our objective is to tease out the individual
elements as design forms susceptible to functional and aesthetic articulation as well as to confirm their particular contribution to an overall campus landscape concepts.

	Existing Situation	Actions	Notes
Surrounds			
Perimeter			
Boundary Markers			
Gateways			
Campus Roads			
Walks			
Bikeways			
Threshold			
Terminus			
Parking			
Heritage,			
Secondary			
Tertiary			
Wetscapes			
Dryscapes			
Botanical Gardens			
Horticultural Gardens			
Arboreta			
Natural Preserves			
Nature Walks and Trails			
Gardens for Art			
Amphitheaters			
Special Theme Gardens			
Site History			
Play Fields and Recreation			
Interior Spaces			
Signs			
Lighting			
Site Furniture			
Seating			

Existing Situation:
+ = strong element
- = weak or missing
0 = satisfactory

Actions:
1 = Add
2= Extend
3= Enhance
4= Conserve
5 =Remove
6= Other

USING THE MATRIX / Paradigm College

The graphic shows one method for using the matrix when identifying and evaluating campus landscapes.

Column 1 is a list of the taxonomy elements as described in this book. In certain situations one might wish to vary the list or change the nomenclature to fit the circumstances at a specific institution so as to describe and communicate more fluently information, names, and characteristics of a local nature. For example, if the major campus space (which we define as a heritage space) is referred to and known as the Great Quad, then that name would serve better than "heritage space."

Column 2 summarizes the evaluations. Three judgments are shown (strong, weak or missing, and satisfactory). Presumably these are objective reckonings, and susceptible of being annotated with photos and references to models elsewhere. The ratings can be expanded to afford finer-grained opinions, and adjusted for numerical expression. For example, a 1 to 10 rating for each item—weighted for adjustments in the value and significance of each of the thirty items—would yield 300 as a utopian index for the total campus landscape. A lower number would suggest a campus landscape to some degree deficient. Opportunities for remedy would be revealed in the tabulation of the individual items.

As to actions (column 3) we note six: add, extend, enhance, conserve, remove, and other. The latter leaves room for special factors and considerations. Again, the matrix should be tailored to local circumstances and strategies for action.

Column 4, for notes, can be used to guide the reader to detailed documentation or to highlight some critical matter. *Graphic:* Dober, Lidsky, Craig and Associates, Inc.

In practice, the Campus Landscape Matrix can be used as a kind of ignition system for a focused design process. The taxonomy serves as a checklist of items to be considered in arranging, expanding, and improving the landscape elements in the built environment. One screens an existing campus to identify the presence of the taxonomy items, rate their quality and contribution to the overall design, and take action accordingly. For those designing new campuses or campus sectors, one would use the matrix as an index for locating, designing, and installing appropriate landscapes.

Buildings and grounds are integrated into a green precinct that is pleasant to see, well defined physically with a specific sense of place.

OTHER APPLICATIONS

We also note that the word *campus* is increasingly used to define and promote certain kinds of physical development that imply the use of a landscaped setting reminiscent of higher education. Buildings and grounds are integrated into a green precinct that is pleasant to see, well defined physically and with a specific sense of place, and productive in encouraging serendipitous and synergistic interaction among those sharing the site. Examples are research centers, medical centers, office and production complexes serving the computer and biotech industries, retirement communities, performing-arts centers, housing for the elderly and the retired, government complexes, and boarding schools. Thus, the typology below could be utilized in conceptualizing and designing any large area where the presumed values and physical forms of colleges and universities can be transformed and transferred through appropriate application. The resulting environment would be configured and embellished by a combination of structures and landscapes, human in scale and arranged and inflected with suitable greenery indoors and out, with the ensemble textured and colored by the changing seasons and nature's rhythms.

FORMAT

The book is divided into two sections: thirteen design determinants and the thirty-item taxonomy. The illustrations and commentary reflect the author's forty-plus years of experience as a campus planner and designer, discussions with colleagues, numerous site visits to see and experience firsthand significant examples of commendable campus landscape, and the residue of a fast-paced professional practice. The latter includes clippings, photos, articles, letters, field notes, drawings, and a representative sample of campus plans and design documents. The collection has been mined for quotations and graphics that help define campus landscape design determinants and the taxonomy components. The illustrations serve several purposes. Some are historical examples, credible reminders

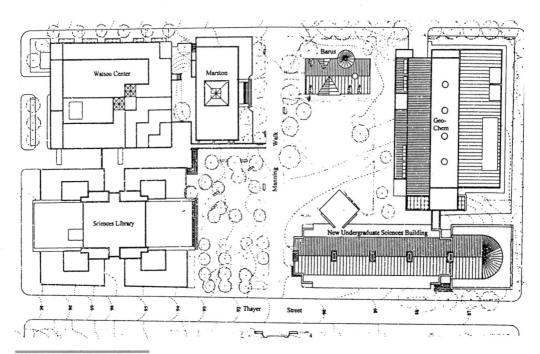

OPPORTUNITY LOST / Brown University

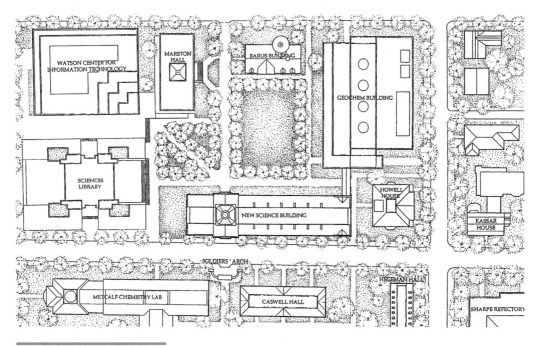

OPPORTUNITY GAINED / Brown University

Proposed landscape treatment (*bottom*) strengthens the design concept and promotes campus greenery as an admirable companion to the architecture and site composition.   *Graphics:* Author's collection.

of ideas and ideals that have raised campus landscape to an art form germane for our own time. Some help explain three-dimensionally the landscape function being defined. Others are diagnostic diagrams expressing deficiencies pictorially and the self-evident location of opportunities for improving the campus landscape.

RELATED MATTERS: PROJECT BUDGETS, RESTORATION, MAINTENANCE

As noted, the bulk of the book is devoted to design determinants and the taxonomy and evaluation matrix. A few words on related matters are added here for professionals and patrons needing encouragement and those acting as stewards and proselytizers of campus landscape. Page xxiv displays recent competition drawings for a new building at Brown University, both prepared by eminent architects. One ignored the opportunities for envisioning new campus landscapes; the other expressed ideas worth considering. In principle no new capital investment in campus architecture should be advanced without a parallel expenditure for campus landscape in the project area.

An instructive account of campus landscape must also deal with regeneration, restoration, and maintenance. There are many reasons to begin treating campus landscape as an endangered art form deserving care, conservation, and curatorial interpretation and assistance. Under the guise of economy, groundskeeping staff have been reduced. Mature landscapes have disappeared and funds for replacement have been eliminated. Campus designs that are nature's equivalent of a great painting have been allowed to decay and deteriorate. Accordingly, we advocate the articulation of a national list of notable examples of campus landscapes now in distress, especially those that are paradigms worth emulation. A century ago, Charles Eliot Norton presciently heralded these as "great works which answer the needs and give expression to the life of our immense and miscellaneous democracy." Design professionals working with colleges and universities should assume the obligation to help reverse any downward spiral of diffidence, indifference, and neglect. At the least, as one prepares campus plans or sector plans the location and condition of items in the taxonomy should be identified, with recommendations for remedy.

Comments and suggestions on improved grounds operations and maintenance are woven into our text. Actions of course will vary with the type of landscape. Most landscapes will remain viable with periodic mowing, edging, fertilizing, and pruning. Others, given heavy use, location, and design, will require more labor-intensive care. A statistical profile of the Columbia campus of the University of Missouri sheds light on both maintenance needs and an ideal response. The 296-acre central campus zone has 7 miles of landscaped roads and drives, 27.5 miles of sidewalks, and 5,082 trees. The latter had an estimated value in 1999 of $4.8 million. The collection included 264 species and cultivars, including an emblematic pin oak with a 50-inch diameter. Twenty-eight thousand flowers are planted annually. Turf maintenance requires planting 11,000 pounds of grass seed annually and applying 35 tons of fertilizer. The university's award-winning Landscape Services group includes arborists, horticulturists, landscape architects, and groundskeepers as well as managers and supervisors. As part of a budget strategy, they sponsor an Adopt-a-Tree association. Income from tax-deductible gifts of $250 per member is pooled to support a campus tree trail project, which includes labeling and maintaining 115 varieties of trees, and distributing a guidebook that helps promote the importance of campus landscape.

In sum, *Campus Landscape* is organized as a handbook for the practitioner. It is also a call for action and a demonstration of how and why an important art has universal appeal and relevance in our time and for our culture. It is a guide for planners, designers, and their clients wishing to develop and improve college and university buildings and grounds with various kinds of landscape. As indicated in the acknowledgments, I am most grateful to those who provided me with material to supplement my random harvest of citations and exemplars, as well as encouragement to complete a book on a subject that has kept me intellectually and professionally enthralled for half a century. One hopes that the book's utility is self-evident, that the judgments are reasoned, and that any omissions and errors are exculpated by the author's attempt to treat objectively and comprehensively a subject not yet well represented in the professional literature and reference works.

Richard P. Dober, AICP
Dober, Lidsky, Craig and Associates, Inc.

SECTION 1

CAMPUS LANDSCAPE DESIGN DETERMINANTS

▶ All landscape designs differ essentially according to three factors in their making: first, their physical environment,—the topography, country, climate, vegetation, materials of construction, and so on; second, the people who make them and for whom they are made,— their nationality, traditions, tastes, training, and other social conditions; and third, really the product of the first and second factors, their function, the purpose for which they are made. (Henry Vincent Hubbard and Theodora Kimball, *An Introduction to the Study of Landscape Design* [New York, 1917])

As a prelude to defining and illustrating the components in the campus landscape taxonomy, a general appreciation of the broader factors and considerations that inform the design process and outcomes is in order. The campus landscape design determinants are listed in the diagram on page xxi. They range from nature's endowment (climate and site) to human intervention (program, style and taste, and funds). Experience suggests that the convergence of the determinants will generate appropriate and distinctive landscape designs, each varying with the relevant weight given to the determinants and their impact on each other.

The idea of interacting cause and effect is as old as the profession of landscape architecture itself. No new theory is implied in our take on the subject. The commentary that follows will illustrate how commendable campus landscape designs came into being in response to the determinants and, via the examples, offer encouragement for emulation. Not all determinants are treated at equal length or discussed comprehensively. A knowledgeable summary of terrain analysis would itself take up several chapters; the relationship of soils, plant selection, and esthetics would fill a book; the philosophy and psychology of taste and style occupy a shelf of documents in several languages. Our selection is skewed toward paradigms seen, felt, enjoyed, and on occasion explicated on site in the company of their designers and their clients. Professional journals and papers, long forgotten, have been scanned to uncover and understand antecedents and precedents. Due respect will be given to place making (design invention) and place keeping (the conservation and enhancement of existing campus landscapes). Further, certain aspects of design determinants will be reviewed again in descriptions of the typology. Design is more a reiterative process than a linear one. Overlapping commentary will help reinforce certitude or isolate a potentially untenable opinion. Above all, respect (if not awe) will be given to what historian Hugh Hawkins calls "the alternatives and the imponderables and an awareness of the strange interlacings of persistence and change" as designs intermingle.

1.1 CLIMATE: MACRO AND MICRO

▶ Forward in the name of God, Graffe, set, plant and nourish up trees in every corner of your ground; the labor is small, the cost nothing, the commodity great... and God shall grace your good mindes and diligence. (John Gerard, *The Garden Book* [17th c.])

▶ Their Groves (whenever they planted any) were always regular, like unto orchards which is entirely wrong; for when we come to copy or imitate nature, we should trace her steps with the greatest Accuracy that can be. And therefore when we plant Groves or Forest or other trees, we have nothing more to regard than the outside lines be agreeable to the Grove, and that no three trees together range in a straight line; except now and then by chance to cause variety. (Batty Langley, *New Principles of Gardening* [London, 1728])

▶ Ere the planter undertakes his toil,
Let him examine well his clime and soil,
Patient explore what best with both will suit,
And, rich in leaves, luxuriantly shoot.
For trees, unless in vigorous health they rise,
Can ne'er be grateful objects to the eyes.
(R. P. Knight, *The Landscape* [London, 1795])

▶ Climatic factors are often thought to be of secondary importance.... But it will be shown that plants are the material of the design itself, second only in importance to the ground, and that both land and vegetation are subject to climatic influences.... [C]limatic factors must be recognized as being a fundamental influence on all landscape design. (Brenda Colvin, *Land and Landscape* [London, 1947])

▶ Students, asked whether they would be happier in going to school in California or in a colder climate, predicted they would be happier in California, both because of the climate and overall. In fact, students were equally happy in different parts of the country, despite the climate. ("Forecasting Their Emotions," *New York Times,* Feb. 16, 1999)

Climate here includes temperature, humidity, rainfall and snow, wind velocity and direction, and the length and intensity of sunlight. With their seasonal variations, these are the energies fueling nature's bio-dynamics, which in turn affect campus landscape matters such as the selection, vitality, and appearance of plant materials, the use of outdoor areas, and the siting of buildings and greenery to mitigate harsh climatic effects. At the macro scale, considerations of climate may inform the overcall campus plan and its constituent landscapes. Picture-postcard beauty in major spaces and minor precincts and the sense of place established and reinforced by plant materials are in the broadest sense climate-determined designs.

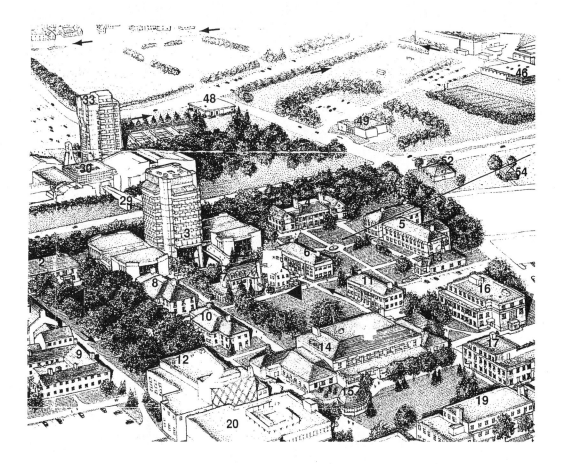

CAMPUS AS LANDSCAPE / Hofstra University
Competing for students and national recognition, Hofstra University markets its campus as an arboretum. In this high-quality environment something green and blossoming can be found year-round. The campus map and guidebook encourage students, faculty, and visitors to "[s]top and read those little plaques. Our outdoor learning center is sure to please." *Graphic:* Hofstra University.

CLIMATE BENIGN, TERRACE SUBLIME / University of California, Santa Barbara
Michael Graves' design for the Institute for Theoretical Physics provides a sophisticated landscape setting adjacent to the institute's commons. The location and design are planned to foster dialog, discussion of ideas, and sharing of information between faculty, graduate students, and guests. *Photo:* Peter Malinkowski/InSite; courtesy Michael Graves.

Extremes in climate may be a constraint but are not an impediment to comfortable landscape designs. The collection of praiseworthy courtyards and patios at the University of Arizona reflects a keen evaluation of summer sun and shadow and temperature differentials in January and July. At Hofstra University (New York), those responsible for the arboretum setting (purposely created to give the campus a singular sense of place) have included definitive and attractive winter landscapes. Michael Graves' outdoor terrace and lawns for teatime and intellectual discussions at the Institute for Theoretical Physics (University of California, Santa Barbara) epitomize benign climate as a design determinant. Microclimatic considerations do (or should) govern large-area campus landscape design concepts as well as the articulation of small-scale project areas. Building placement and vegetation patterns can induce beneficial thermal results, mitigate uncomfortable

PICTURE-POSTCARD BEAUTY / Wake Forest University
Campus landscape is seasonal. The clouds, trees, sun, and shadow that blend into traditional and contemporary site compositions are climate determined.   *Photo:* Gregg Studio; courtesy Wake Forest University.

winds and draw sedating breezes, and absorb radiation and increase evaporation to cool temperatures when and where desired. The cyclic changes in the direction and presence of warm and cold air, the day and night differences, can be tracked and applied with good advantage in designing outdoor patios, terraces, and courtyards. On a frigid day, how comforting a seating area facing the southwest sun and sheltered from the wind; how pleasant the cooling wind passing through the shaded area when nature has reversed the temperatures.

The cause-and-effect relationship between macroclimate and greenery having been noted, how stupid, then, to site a building or plant a landscape without reference to this knowledge, which can be charted from local weather bureaus or national meteorological services. If, as many professionals were taught, every map determining campus landscape needs a compass rose and scale, add to these a summary of climate data. Projected hours and days of use—programmatic information for landscape desiderata—can be correlated to variations in temperature, sunlight, and precipitation, and prevailing winds.

The subject of microclimate has a rich literature, from Vitruvius and his thoughts on how climate generates architectural styles to Victor Olgay's *Design with Climate* (Princeton, 1963). Pioneering research, too often overlooked, Olgay's work continues to offer good advice applicable to campus landscape design.

1.2 VEGETATION

Climate affects the choice and use of vegetation. Every plant has its own individual forms, profile, color, and textures, which the wise designer studies to match design intentions with the actual visual results. While there are many possibilities, choices are limited. Climate (particularly temperature and precipitation) affects habitat, the plant's natural environment. Choices that run counter to habitat are usually counterproductive. In the main, common sense prevails in applying climate-related horticultural principles in campus landscape designs. Thus designers are not likely to suggest palm trees to define the roadways at St. John's University, Minnesota, nor specify redwoods to mark the paths at Haverford College, Pennsylvania. The trees selected for controlling sun and shadow at the University of Alaska will be different from those planted at the University of Nevada.

Honored in collegiate songs and folklore, the iconic aspect of campus landscape should never be discounted. The campus shield will often display landscape-related institutional values. One will find a pine tree featured on the William Warren College crest. A single deciduous leaf appears in the Grinnell College and Vanderbilt University campus graphics. Grass and trees are visible in the Oberlin College medallion. A stylized nut evokes the Pima Community College environment, and two stately trees straddle Old Main on the University of Evansville's escutcheon. Here, then, are good clues for recognizing local campus landscape materials that are differentiated by climate.

Trees and lawns are a standard campus landscape. Observe a campus scene in clement weather, and note where people sit, alone and in a group. Are not trees salubrious in their contribution to people's sensing, perhaps atavistically, an ambiance safe and agreeable? Trees "lend charm [and] provide shade…[forming an environment] gently calling into play thoughts which have no outlet during working hours but which must have activity if a person is to come to a practical task each day with zest and enthusiasm." So proclaimed the tree expert F. A. Bartlett (*American Landscape Architect,* November 1930). Poets, planners, and physicians would endorse his view that trees are "instruments of physical betterment, mental relief, and spiritual in-

POMONA COLLEGE
From its inception in the late nineteenth century the Pomona campus was intended by the college founders to be a garden with buildings, with lawns that were reminiscent of the older New England institutions. During its first decades, the use of regional landscape materials suggested to some that Pomona was "the Oxford of the orange belt." *Photo:* R. P. Dober.

spiration." His thoughts are thus linked to Garrett Eckbo's plea for "landscape for living." For Eckbo, greenery that is therapeutic as health science and inspiring as art should get full play in campus landscape design. In a world shaped by the technology and demands of cyberspace, landscapes that attract and provide pleasant places for informal participation in campus life offer an anodyne for electronically induced anomie.

Trees and campus landscape are a treasured design duality, from the ancient Grecian groves of academe to twentieth-century American campuses. Single trees may be found occupying campus open space as green sculpture. Aligned in rows, trees reinforce and clarify the location and direction of paths, roads, and boundaries. When well selected they will make the routes through campus more pleasant. At the campus perimeter trees may be clumped and planted thickly as greenbelts, for visual screens, to reduce noise, and to raise air quality by acting as a filter for airborne particles.

THE REALITIES OF NEW ENGLAND CLIMATE / Harvard University Graduate School of Business
A winter climate constrains having lush greenery year-round, but the positioning of a landscaped enclave (courtyard, garden, or seating area) facing southwest can provide a pleasant scene and gathering area on many school days.   *Photo:* R. P. Dober.

SUN, SHADOW, REGIONAL LANDSCAPE / University of Arizona
Architects AR7 Hoover and Desmond collaborated with landscape architect Michael Van Valkenburgh to create a climate-sensitive courtyard design. The interface space between two wings of the Aerospace and Mechanical Engineering Building is planted with palm trees and greenery that reinforces the sense of place. *Photo:* R. P. Dober.

Trees can reinforce architectural compositions like a frame on a picture. Theories on mixing and matching can be found in classic and contemporary esthetic treatises. Humphry Repton (1794) ruled that Gothic architecture required round-headed trees, and Palladian structures looked best with pointed trees. Charles Z. Klauder and Herbert C. Wise (*College Architecture in America,* New York, 1929) applied utilitarian standards in tree selection. "The first demand of trees for the campus should be their strength to withstand storms without injury.... Species without character, such as the Norway maple, the Norway spruce, and the pin oak should be avoided. Plane trees (sycamores) and horse chestnuts make litter and increase the difficulty of keeping the lawns and walks in order."

Campus trees are major elements in a well-composed landscape, traditional or modern. In selecting trees, designers have considerable choices for achieving artistic results. John Edward Jefferies (*Landscape and Garden,* winter 1935) suggested that trees can be arranged by height, shape, texture, color, fruit and flowers, or compatibility with land con-

THE GROVES OF ACADEME, AMERICAN STYLE / Brown University
From Providence, Rhode Island (Brown University, *above*), to Claremont, California (Pomona College, page 9), trees and lawns form the revered image of the American campus. The scenes vary with the use of regional plant materials and are climate related. *Photo:* R. P. Dober.

tours; to celebrate seasonal changes; or for longevity and ease of maintenance. Reiterating an ecological imperative, he said all options should be compatible with soil conditions and climate. As to form, noting the ascent of modern architecture, with its lines "mainly horizontal and without ornament," he urged that such buildings would be best framed with "trees of fustigate and tortuous growth...most effective when planted near buildings of this description." C. A. Sargent (*Garden and Forest,* New York, 1888) cautions: "Of form it may furthermore be said that a tree is not well understood until is well understood in all the stages of its growth."

Too often, on too many campuses, we note that young trees are crowded together for immediate effect. When they age they nudge each other out of position, compete for sun and air, and in their deflection blur the symmetry sought in the original design. Worse, an unnatural density accelerates blight and disease, leaving gaps in the design concept that are then hard to fill with new material.

As there are heritage buildings existing and intended, so also trees can be utilized as emblems of institutional permanence. Properly

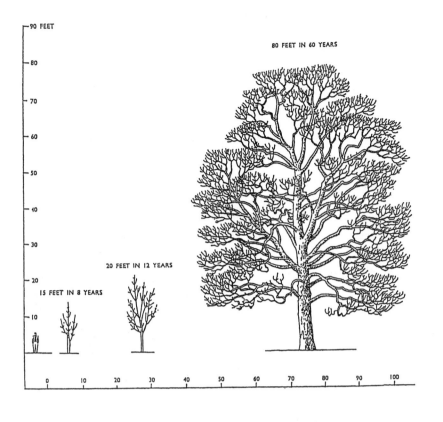

80 FEET IN 60 YEARS

20 FEET IN 12 YEARS

15 FEET IN 8 YEARS

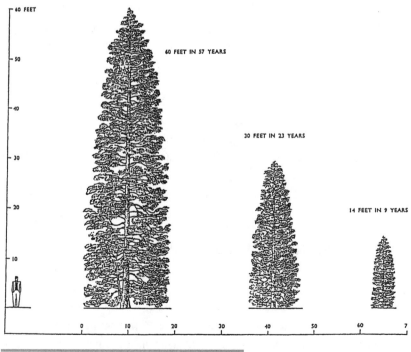

60 FEET IN 57 YEARS

30 FEET IN 23 YEARS

14 FEET IN 9 YEARS

THE VISUAL CONSEQUENCES OF AGE

Maturation effects for two trees, deciduous and evergreen. Nine years is the office span of a dean, twenty-three years the tenure of a senior faculty member, and sixty years the time remembered by the oldest alumni recalling the heritage first planted. *Graphic:* Author's collection; courtesy J. Tyrwitt.

selected and maintained, such landscapes can last for centuries. In these instances an immediate effect is not likely in the first planting. Heritage trees require an appropriate level of maintenance, which groundskeeping budgets should reflect. Occasionally an external opinion may be necessary to ensure proper care or to take such remedial work as conservation requires. A great campus landscape is a living work of art. Like paintings and sculpture, duplicates and replacements lack the conviction of the originals; thus keeping viable the heritage is the proper stance.

Brenda Colvin and Jacqueline Tyrwhitt encourage landscape architects to consider rates of maturation in selecting species (*Trees in Town and Country,* London, 1947). Though written for the United Kingdom, their approach to tree selection is a textbook example of applied esthetics. Their advice: Use trees to "form the masses and voids of the design... [take delight] in tree forms, and in all the texture in wood and foliage." To their exultation, Richard St. Barbe Baker might add his paraphrase of a fourth-century Chinese writer: Trees should be laid out to "combine cheerfulness of aspect, luxuriance of growth, shade, solitude and repose, in such a manner that the sense may be deluded by an imitation of rural nature." *Deluded* is a negative word; substitute *calmed* and one will find in Baker's gloss the value of campus dendrology as art. And, of course, not all will find simulations of the rural landscape soothing or deserving of imitation. Of the esthetic conflicts between the contrived pastoral and the calibrated orthographic, whose outcomes have significantly shaped extant campus landscapes, much will be noted shortly.

Teaching landscape composition at the University of Cincinnati (c. 1930), M. E. Bottomley praised the use of trees as visual countering devices for any building "too large for its surrounding, too tall for its width, too broad for its height, overdesigned and overdecorated, too plain and lacking interest." It is a rare campus that does not have one or two buildings that would benefit from this uncomplicated application of a design determinant.

1.3 ENVIRONMENTAL SUITABILITY

Environmental suitability should have as much weight as the desired image, and thus is a design determinant. For example, overreliance on a single tree species to achieve a spectacular, singular design statement (not uncommon in past decades) should always be questioned. In some instances the choices have proven to be unwise ecologically, expensive to mitigate, and visually distressing when some of the trees succumb to disease or fail to mature, leaving gaping holes in the campus scenery, an aspect of design we reiterate with good cause.

So too, one urges an ecological approach to lawns. Icons emblematic of higher education, prevalent at most North American campuses, definitional, lawns appear as strong images in the mental picture most people have of a typical campus. Whether the grassy greensward is appropriate in water-shy regions or suitable in terms of fertilizing practices or the energy consumed by mechanical mowers is neither a moot issue nor a minor decision these days.

On the other hand, when addressed, shortcomings can inspire some interesting solutions. There is a renewed interest in alternative ground covers such as wildflowers and grasses that do not require extensive cultivation and water. The United States Environmental Protection Agency, through an informative Web page, promotes native plants and ground covers: "beautiful, hardy, and once established [they] require less maintenance than a conventional lawn." EPA believes that plantings of this character, once in place, will not need "fertilizers, herbicides, pesticides or watering."

ECKBO AT ALBUQUERQUE / University of New Mexico
A paradigm of inventive regional campus landscape, Garrett Eckbo's design for the pond and grassy slopes and trees, extensively used and enjoyed, provides a splendid contrast to the nearby traditional designs. *Photo:* Garrett Eckbo.

Further signs of a brightening awareness: The avoidance of dependence on a single tree species has encouraged nurseries to find and enlarge their stock. Xeriscaping—the ancient art of landscape in dry places—has gained in prestige and honors. And where the icon is desired, a gesture may serve as a symbol in place of extensive lawns in arid climes. Two projects in New Mexico are interesting exemplars.

At the University of New Mexico (Albuquerque), the dry plazas and courtyards are beautifully balanced with an artificial lake designed by Garrett Eckbo. Contoured by a grassy slope that invites participation in campus life, the area seems out of place as a regional design on first encounter, but then rewarding and comforting as a subtle artwork and reminder of differing climes and cultures. More recently, in 1990 Santa Fe Community College sited its linear and connected buildings to embrace a patch of trees and green lawn that suggests continuity with traditional campus landscape design, a site composition in sharp distinction to the desert land in which the campus is situated. These and comparable designs in the American Southwest can be traced back conceptually to the Alhambra, where in response to aridity the fifteenth-century Moorish architects used the sound of water, limited greenery, decorative paving, and arcades that divided sun and shadow as place-marking design components.

Where lawns are the chosen design objective, the negative aspects of some installations can be mitigated by matching grass types and regional climate. For these purposes, the turf expert Fanny-Fern Davis divides the American continent into three climatic regions: dry, cool humid, and warm humid. Accordingly, "grasses which produce excellent turf in one section of the country may not even be able to survive in other sections." As to matching, there are over 1,100 species available in the United States, but "not more than 30" of them will produce satisfactory turf for "enhancing the architectural beauty of the school or college, in eliminating mud and dust, or in providing a good playing surface on recreation fields."

Color, texture, dormancy, and seasonal appearance will vary considerably with climate. A viable grassy lawn requires technical expertise in choosing what nature and climate will permit. Buffalo grass, for example, is drought resistant, and centipede grass "thrives on light, dry, sandy soils," Davis says. "[F]or cool, moist, shaded areas," *Trivialis* is best. And where lush growth may induce fungi, like acne scarring an otherwise beautiful face, "lower growing species and strains [will be] more desirable than the tall upright ones because they require less mowing."

1.4 LANDFORM CONCEPTS

▶ What we are seeking is an eligible site for the College, high, dry, open. (Thomas Jefferson, 1818)

▶ All designs should begin with an appreciation of the surface upon which they are situated...and there is nothing more useful than a topographic map. (Arthur A. Shurtleff, 1930)

▶ The smallest project may call for the greatest ingenuity. The more restricted a property in size and potentials, the more passionately and devotedly we must make an inventory of those potentials. (Richard Neutra, *Mysteries and Realities of the Site* [New York, 1951])

▶ [The] instinct has been to think: "Would the view be finer if the mountain were raised here and cut off there?"...That is what it means to be a landscape architect. Examining the land. Mentally dissecting it for better or worse. Planning possible changes and designing them in detail. After that just spade work until the transformation is complete. (Fletcher Steele, *Gardens and People* [Boston, 1964])

▶ The instinct to climb up some high place, from which you can look down and survey your world, seems to be a fundamental human instinct. (Christopher Alexander et al., *A Pattern Language* [New York, 1977])

Terrain—the earth's topographic surface—ranges from the larger geological landforms, such as a hill or slope that holds an entire campus, to the subtle geomorphic ripples of a smaller site. These are basic conditions that inform campus landscape concepts broadly and in detail.

The design history of many early American campuses documents well their founders' preference for an elevated site over flat land. Why? The views to and from campus were better, the ambient air was presumably healthier, and waste drainage was easier to engineer. A building or two on a commanding site had emblematic value. Like a cathedral, castle, or capitol, a campus occupying the highland would immediately convey purpose, presence, and possession. Thus Boston College would gain the cognomen "The Heights" and Kentucky State College the referential nickname "Hilltoppers," proud self-identifications that can be seen in the design of their first landscapes and site compositions.

In categorizing topographic influences as campus landscape determinants, it is useful to discuss first macro-scale concepts and then smaller-scale terrain modifications. The first are those masterworks whose magnitude and amplitude help inform and create panoramic scenery comparable to the Acropolis or a medieval castle crowning the heights with the townscape draped down the slopes. The second are more localized in their visibility and contribution to a sense of place. The comments that follow focus on dramatic landform concepts—which is not to say that flatland designs lack a visual interest that is topographically determined, for even the seemly horizontal plane has a wrinkle or two that can add esthetic interest to the landscape.

Wellesley College's development pattern is a noteworthy and accomplished matching of topography and terrain that has some features evident in many large-scale landform concepts. The overall design framework was established by Frederick Law Olmsted Jr., including a typology of landforms that Olmsted believed should determine the built-unbuilt campus design template. These included wet meadows, irregular plateaus above steep slopes, small rounded hills, and big hills. The lowlands would remain open in Olmsted's approach, with crests and higher land devoted to buildings. As site historian Elizabeth Meyer has summarized, "[F]ootprints of new buildings were to follow the shape of the hills, not some abstract geometric shape, and in doing so, create shaped courts or quadrangles, which framed vistas of the surrounds [*sic*] hill and meadows." Olmsted considered the glaciated topography as an "endowment [of] landscape beauty" whose sensitive use was a "peculiar obligation to posterity."

These objectives were attractively accomplished in such Wellesley precincts as the Tower Court Quad complex and its relationship to Severance Green and Rhododendron Dell to the east. In some areas—the Academic Quad, for example—the manner in which the buildings grip the landforms, and vice versa, has the strength and design conviction of a Mt. St. Michel.

The deficiencies in Olmsted's projections were not of his doing. The heavy automobile traffic along Route 135 has destroyed the usefulness of the gateway entrance to Hazard Quad, while the southward expanse from Alumni Hall is filled with ugly parking (ugly as in a strict dictionary definition: "offensive and unpleasing to any sense"). These and related issues are being addressed in landscape architect Michael Van Valkenburgh's 1998 Wellesley College campus landscape restoration plan.

Of comprehensive campus landscape landform concepts in which the larger campus design structure is essentially determined and informed by terrain, three basic approaches are evident: draping, flattening, and insetting. Of the first, the west side of Cass Gilbert's University of Minnesota plan, facing the Mississippi River, exempli-

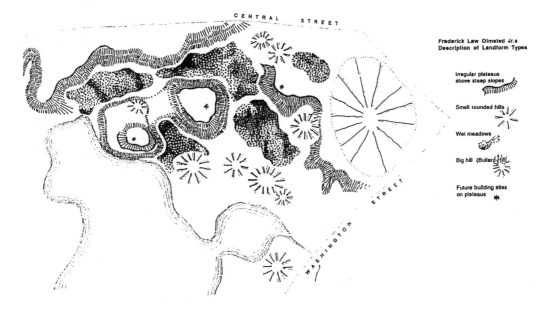

MACRO-SCALE CONCEPTS TO MICRO-SCALE PROJECT / Wellesley College

Above, Elizabeth Meyer's recapitulation of Frederick Law Olmsted Jr.'s terrain analysis. *Below*, the Academic Quad, a model interpretation of Olmsted's concept. Terrain modification was accomplished through skillful grading. *Graphics:* Courtesy of Michael Van Valkenburgh.

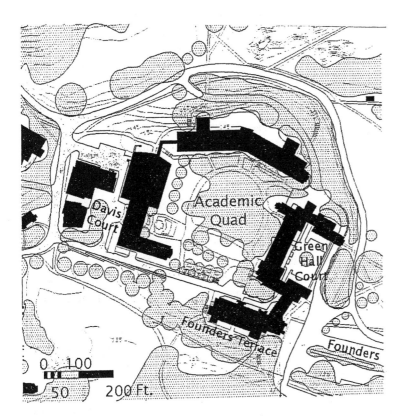

RIVERBANK TERRACE / University of Minnesota
Cass Gilbert's classical tiered terrace design includes an emphatic linear landscape with four vertical trees in the foreground, bringing the eye to the center of the composition. Arguably, such greenery might not grow to the uniform heights and widths suggested in Gilbert's rendering. On the other hand, periodic pollarding, pruning, and pleaching could impose a human geometric order on plant and tree forms and shapes where nature untamed would yield a looser planting profile. The technique is as old as the art of landscape design itself.   *Graphic:* Author's collection.

fies the Beaux Arts approach, with its cascading terraces that bring to mind the hanging gardens of some lost civilization. Where classical schemes will not conform to contours, the contours themselves may be changed—a questionable approach these days, but one evident when reviewing Duke University's campus design history. University benefactor James B. Duke flattened acres of hillside in Durham, North Carolina, to create his Collegiate Gothic West Campus. The textured walls, encrusted with faux medieval details, are a beautiful foil for hanging ivy. Ground planes and planting in the connected quadrangles are simply treated. The artificiality of the place becomes apparent, sometimes in a pleasant way, as one leaves the precinct and encounters the adjacent buildings and landscapes humbled into idiosyncratic compositions by Duke's imperial concept.

Denys Lasdun's University of East Anglia (UK) scheme (1965) is free from such artificial gestures, or is so intended as a reflection of modern architectural canons. The step-down student housing, for example, takes advantage of changes in elevation. The campus landscape thus embraced (i.e., a grass carpet with a few trees) recalls the Norfolk agricultural scenery. The progression upward from greenery to housing and to the connected megastructure beyond (containing academic and support spaces) is further dramatized by the absence of vehicular circulation and parking, which is kept to the north side of the upper-level linear buildings.

Conceived around the same time as East Anglia, Scarborough College (Ontario) is another place-marking blending of terrain and building. Both schemes were praised as examples of connected functional

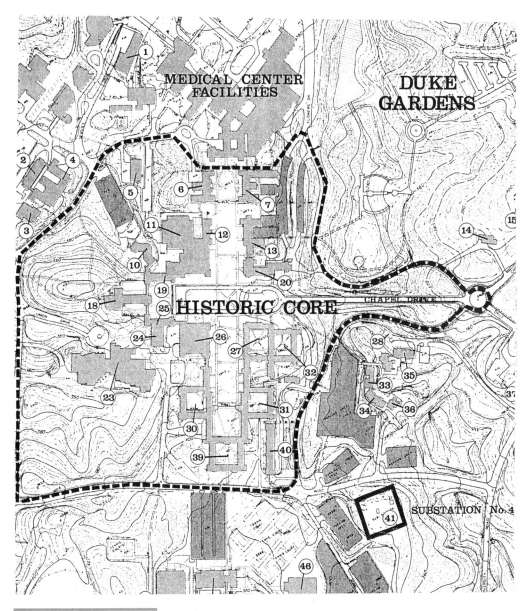

HISTORIC CORE DUKE / Duke University

So as to achieve a pancaked site design presumably complementary to Collegiate Gothic architecture, James B. Duke encouraged his designers to flatten the hills on his preferred location for a new university complex. The resulting awesome and audacious terrain modification is in sharp contrast with the nearby land, which was more or less left unmodified. Landscapes in the core being different from those adjacent, such as the Sarah B. Duke Gardens, the topographic contrast accentuates the uniqueness of the founder's design. *Graphic:* Dober, Lidsky, Craig and Associates, Inc.

spaces melded to the landforms, dramatic in scale, splendid to see in their surrounding greenery. The Ontario birthing was not easy. Stimulated by seemingly adverse circumstances (a steep slope and a conservation restriction limiting development to 50 acres in a 200-acre precinct), architect John Andrews and landscape architect Michael

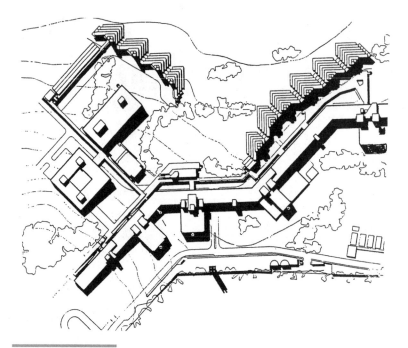

MEGACONCEPT / University of East Anglia

Denys Lasdun's 1964 megastructure follows the site contours to embrace a green field on the lower level and establish a skyline landmark architectural composition on the upper terrain. The unity of functions in one structure (teaching, research, and residential life), sandwiched between simple landscapes, was a refreshing alternative to separated buildings in quadrangular arrangements. Lasdun wanted to create a place where "activities merge and where the individual can sense his identity with the whole ... To derive full benefit the spread of the university must be limited; this also preserves the natural landscape. *Graphic:* Author's collection.

Hough created a linear scheme that, like East Anglia's, follows the site contours in layering the interiors. The Scarborough building drops down the slope at a dramatic angle, five floors to the open space and the forest land below. From that angle the complex has the visual magnitude of a large dam. Landscaped parking lots are situated on the upper level, with significant tree cover on either side in the conservation zone.

Among honored mid-twentieth-century large-scale designs with topographic significance, the Santa Cruz campus of the University of California and Simon Fraser University, in British Columbia, are polar examples of concepts determined in the main, though not exclusively, by response to terrain. The former is an acropolis scheme, crowning the topography. The latter is composed of a series of colleges spread carefully over the land. Each is a paradigm in its own particular manner; the contrasting concepts (single site versus dispersion) informed and helped shape the smaller-scale landscape designs within the specific campus boundaries.

Simon Fraser instructed the architects engaged in a design competition to devise a campus that would seem complete at any one time, growing like a tree from its nucleus. Indoor spaces would be joined so that student and faculty would avoid the nuisances of traversing the campus during the region's incessant rain. The functional spaces were to be arranged as a seamless design supporting interdisciplinary work, in contrast to individual departments having separate sites. The winning scheme merged mountain and buildings into a megastructure, dramatic in its horizontal composition, with a series of terraces linked to an academic quadrangle, seemingly timeless in the simple use of water, grass, and sculpture, and a logical termination to the vertical and horizontal circulation network. The ensemble is held together by the clever, terrain-responsive positioning of stairs and paths. The conceptual differences between the first- and second-place submissions are instructive. The Arthur Erickson and Raymond Massey plan uses the highland for linear building sites, with play fields and parking stepped into the slopes. The runner-up concept, by William R. Rhone and W. Randle Iredale, keeps the hilltop open, interspersing buildings with play fields and the remnants of the site's original forest land. The first scheme assumed a unitary academic program for eighteen thousand students. The second divided the campus population into nine separate colleges.

> **What nature cannot provide, occasionally designers can invent.**

Seeking an image of place to be seen along a major highway—reminiscent of the desire of early American colleges to find their place physically and symbolically on the skyline—the James Madison University College of Science and Technology captures and reinterprets aspects of both Scarborough and Simon Fraser. The upper ridge of the JMU site is developed as a compact, linear academic zone. Housing is draped down the hill. A generous distribution of contrasting landscapes, a sparkling mix of formal and informal designs, melds both precincts to the adjacent parking areas and commons building.

Down the Pacific coastline, in California, astute scattering of human habitation over the sloping terrain informs the design of the University of California, Santa Cruz. The limitations and potential of the site were noted early in the planning. Conveying the development concept work to the university president, Clark Kerr, the local chancellor, Dean E. McHenry, wrote: "Although the site is one of extraordinary beauty, it presents some difficulties that are unique or unusual [including] rough topography [which] means fewer good sites for buildings and roads, and added expense for fills and bridges [and] longer utility runs."

Envisioned was a series of small residential colleges, sharing some common facilities, all set out in the abundant natural and agricultural greenery. The impact the original designs had on subsequent

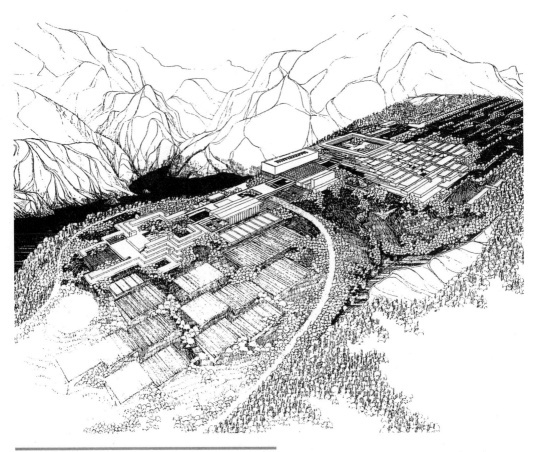

SAME SITE, CONTRASTING TREATMENT (*above & right*) / Simon Fraser University
Competition Drawings

The Board of Assessors report on the Simon Fraser competition (November 1963) noted, "The problem of almost overwhelming magnitude facing each [designer] ... [is to bring] together in some form of harmony the dramatic and romantic site on Burnaby Mountain; then resolving both [program and site] in terms of architecture."

The winning scheme (*above*) uses the upper terrain for a series of connected buildings and landscapes that serves a unitary educational system. Play fields and parking are situated on either side of the linear core and fitted to the terrain. "The landscaping has been accepted in natural state, with little modification, except that necessary for the fulfillment of function," wrote the design jury.

growth of Santa Cruz's academic programs and the institution's collegiate culture merits some additional comments as an example of the constructive transformation of educational mission into a campus design heavily accented by campus landscapes.

The Santa Cruz site composition, inspired by the university's first landscape architect, Thomas Church, gives each of the constituent residential colleges a landscape setting and architectural expression uniquely its own, while preserving large acres of redwood forest and meadow surrounding each college site. Where Simon Fraser and Scarborough are impressive in their compactness, Santa Cruz is notable for

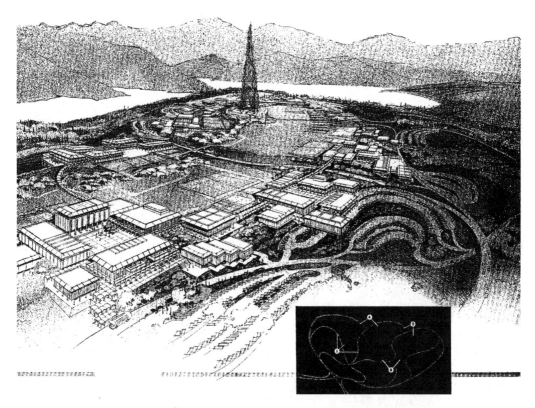

The second-place concept (*above*) envisioned nine separate colleges embracing a sequence of play fields and open spaces and landscapes along the high points of the contours. This is, commented jury members, "a pattern analogous to the Athenian Acropolis...human in scale...simple and logical." *Graphics:* Author's collection.

its bountiful bucolic ambiance. The blending of long-range views and vistas from the upper terrain to Carmel across Monterey Bay, the blankets of tree cover that embrace some of the college precincts, the mix of large and small open spaces, meadow and farm—all this is highly photogenic. No surprise, then, that Ansel Adams was involved in the early planning. In support of Church's approach Adams wrote: "[T]here are few places on earth where such a phenomenon might occur." Further appreciating the undulating topography, ravines and ridges, in counterpoint with groves and pasture, he said, "[A]ny manicuring of this area will produce a commonplace effect."

Today of the 2,000 acres, a fifth has been set aside as a campus natural reserve. Significant acreage is devoted to an arboretum and an agroecology demonstration farm, with the remaining land not assigned to the educational and residential buildings carefully managed as conservation zones. In creative gestures to site history, the old limestone quarry has been converted into a landscaped amphitheater, and several structures dating back to the days of cattle ranching have been preserved, adapted, and landscaped for university purposes. Santa Cruz's renowned doctoral program in ecology stands high on the list of those involved with environmental ethics. Nonetheless, the reality

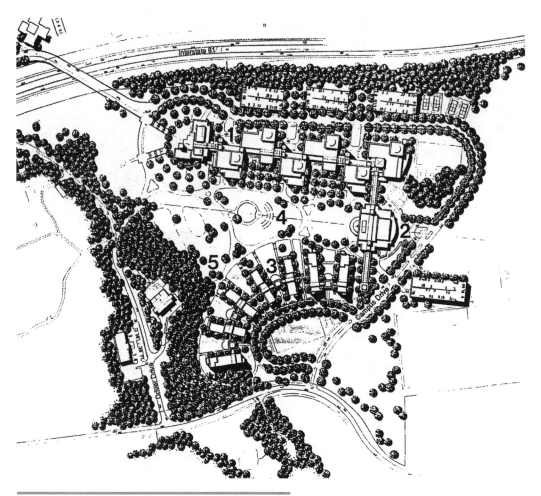

COLLEGE OF SCIENCE AND TECHNOLOGY / James Madison University
Programmatic objectives (a unitary educational mission with landmark high visibility from an adjacent interstate highway) and site realities (a prominent hilltop terrain) were combined to establish a dramatic terrain-influenced campus design and landscape concept. *Drawing*: Charles A. Craig; courtesy Dober, Lidsky, Craig and Associates, Inc.

TERRAIN IMPACT ON SITE DETAILS (*right*)
In place making, landscape details can be designed to reinforce the basic landform concepts. Two instructive examples: the rustic bridge through the woods at the University of California, Santa Cruz (*top*), and the urbane pedestrian bridge (*bottom*) at the University of California, Irvine, by A. C. Martin Partners. Each bridge—in theme, scale, and materials—complements and enhances the broader environmental context in which it is situated; further, the bridges communicate local values and institutional objectives. Irvine seeks a "leading-edge" image. Santa Cruz is secure with its pastoral sense of place. *Photos*: R. P. Dober.

The University of California, Santa Cruz

The University of California, Irvine

of operating a major university has required some adjustment in site design to accommodate connections between the cluster colleges and the shared buildings. Fortunately these adaptations are informed by the continuing high regard for the founders' conservation principles. Empathy is found in the details, the designer's choice. Contrast the Santa Cruz bridge with a comparable crossover at the University of California, Irvine. Both are commendable designs, in comfortable climates, similar in function and scale; one evokes studied urbanity with decorative paving, while the other is appropriately casual, rural, and rustic.

What nature cannot provide, occasionally designers can invent. The University of Zurich at Irchel transformed a 20-acre site into a multipurpose collegiate sports ground, integrated with play areas for children and passive recreation. The eccentric design required moving about 400,000 cubic meters of rubble and earth to shape the fields, create an artificial lake, and build a mound to muffle traffic noise from the adjacent highway. The ensemble serves as an interface area between campus and community. Plant materials were selected and installed around the lake as natural, regional biotopes, in contrast to traditional decorative horticultural designs. The intentional disjunction of site appearance from expected reality was then heightened by boulders, paving stones, granite setts, and wooden decking that are placed in a heavily textured and scattered pattern overlaid on the topography. Here again, one can appreciate the range of inventive solutions that can be achieved when using terrain as a design determinant. At the broadest scale of the mediated outcome are masterworks, as fundamentally different as site-integrated Simon Fraser and Scarborough, site-fabricated Duke, dispersed Santa Cruz, multifaceted Wellesley, and idiosyncratic Irchel.

1.5 TERRAIN MODIFICATIONS

Left as is or *reshaped*—those are the main branches in the decision tree affecting campus topography. One encounters few sites that are ready-made for the ultimate landscape expression. Topographic modification is accomplished through grading—the primer coat for subsequent landscape beauty. Difficult topography can yield inspired designs through large-scale site engineering (Academic Quad, Wellesley College, page 19) or minor grading (Memorial Garden, Temple University, page 30).

A particular site may be altered slightly or dramatically for one or more reasons:

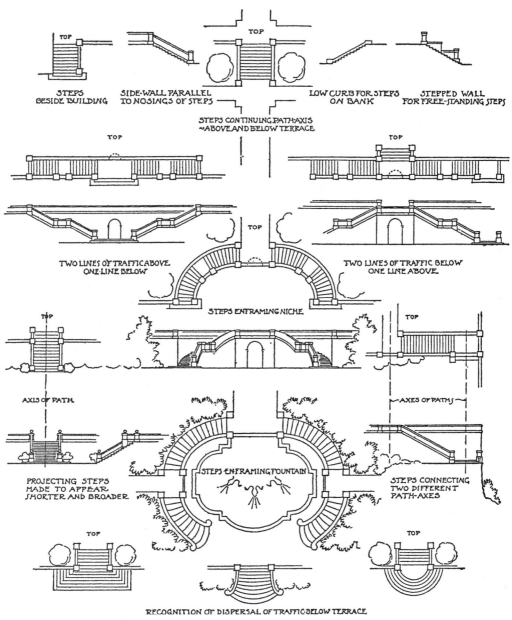

SOME TYPICAL FORMS OF STEPS

STEPS BESIDE BUILDING

SIDE-WALL PARALLEL TO NOSINGS OF STEPS

STEPS CONTINUING PATH-AXIS ~ABOVE AND BELOW TERRACE

LOW CURB FOR STEPS ON BANK

STEPPED WALL FOR FREE-STANDING STEPS

TWO LINES OF TRAFFIC ABOVE ONE LINE BELOW

TWO LINES OF TRAFFIC BELOW ONE LINE ABOVE

STEPS ENFRAMING NICHE

AXIS OF PATH

AXES OF PATHS

PROJECTING STEPS MADE TO APPEAR SHORTER AND BROADER

STEPS ENFRAMING FOUNTAIN

STEPS CONNECTING TWO DIFFERENT PATH-AXES

RECOGNITION OF DISPERSAL OF TRAFFIC BELOW TERRACE

CHANGES IN GRADE: THE CLASSIC VOCABULARY

Those manipulating topography in the Arcadian style in the late twentieth century seem to be more successful than those imposing formal designs on a rolling and undulating terrain. Landscape designers trained in the classical mode had a substantial design vocabulary for the transition from one grade to another. One notes with regret that many contemporary versions seem to lack the geometric grace and design skill of their antecedents. This is a campus landscape opportunity deserving of attention. *Graphic:* Author's collection.

PATTON'S GENTLE SLOPES / Temple University

A slight change in grade provides an attractive topographic setting for a memorial garden. A skillful eye and a good topographic map can yield some admirable designs in what seem to be the most unlikely locations. Particularly important is the juncture of the building walls and the ground plane. Time-saving designers will casually treat these visually prominent junctures as sites for bushes and other greenery, to cover up their indifference to terrain modification. *Photo:* Courtesy George E. Patton.

- To merge and meld building and site in a topographically pleasing manner
- To provide better and cheaper drainage
- To capture good views or screen out poor vistas
- To level land for athletic and sports fields
- To mitigate erosion in steep areas
- To contain water as a visual element or impound excessive runoff
- To help define road alignments visually and accentuate their direction
- To create certain kinds of artworks that involve sculpting the land surface

The alert designer searches for such opportunities to modify topography through a disciplined study of existing conditions and an eye to what is possible functionally and visually. Ironically, contemporary design has yet to articulate the vocabulary of forms seen in classical concepts, where changes in grade are treated as major components in the landscape (see page 29). Worse still are raw and rough designs that use topography for functional reasons (inserting a parking deck to gain entrances and exits at two levels) but ignore the potential for an attractive surrounding landscape.

If professional papers are a window to understanding how honored practitioners approach topography, A. R. Nichols' 1923 description of the designer at work is informative. The experienced eye, he wrote, seeks "the best use of things that exist in a picture originally [so as to make] buildings and their surroundings seem to look as though he had never worked on them and that the scenery just happened to be beautiful in itself." In the Nichols formula structures are situated "in an orderly, logical relationship." The resulting scene is "fascinating." Buildings appear "to have been dropped into a lovely setting of massive forests and distant hills with broad lawns on which apparently no work

TOPOGRAPHY UTILIZED, LANDSCAPE IGNORED / University of California, Berkeley
A clever solution in an urban area, but also an opportunity lost to develop an attractive surrounding landscape. Comparable examples elsewhere, unfortunately, would suggest the benefits of having a campus design ombudsman to review and evaluate landscape projects in terms of their visual impact and then suggest (better yet, impose) landscape mediation. *Photo:* R. P. Dober.

HILLTOP RECOLLECTED / Yale University
With landscape architect Dan Kiley, Eero Saarinen uses a slight change in elevation to suggest the spatial sequence evocative of an Italian hill town. *Photo:* R. P. Dober.

has been done, and yet the effect is subtly attractive." He acknowledged that such a design, despite a "natural appearance, is decidedly artificial in development," thus the importance of a detailed topographic survey and intimate knowledge of site conditions to achieve such ends.

Parenthetically, such designs also required, thought Nichols, the "warmth and interest [of] luxurious planting." Advised Prentiss French, decades later: "[O]ver-planting is costly at the start, occupies space otherwise useable, may shut out light and air, is expensive to maintain, and creates inferior visual effect.... An extremely simple design neatly maintained is much preferred to an over-ambitious one of shabby appearance." He praised a "prominent" designer who "lays down a concrete strip four to five feet wide all around" the buildings for "the very purpose of preventing injudicious" plantings. This kind of design by interdiction should be cautiously applied as a design determinant.

Three examples now follow of smaller-scale landscape designs, terrain-related modifications at Yale University, Columbia University, and York University. Thematically we have an interesting mix of the

STAIRCASE AS CROSSROADS / Columbia University
McKim, Mead & White's classical stairs and urban landscape treatment evolved into a beloved crossroads meeting place for students and faculty.   *Photo:* R. P. Dober.

faux, the urban, and the picturesque. The Yale citation may be also categorized as a Factor X campus landscape design determinant (see page 76)—the unexpected work of genius, assisted by landscape architect Dan Kiley. The Columbia scheme is influenced by Beaux Arts classicism, a version of temple architecture, with its dramatic cascading design inserted into the slopes. The York project mediates a harsh physical environmental setting and helps carry through some earlier landscape objectives discovered in the site analysis that impacted the university's first campus plan.

Morse and Stiles Colleges at Yale University are seemingly perdurable in appearance, site design, and visual impact. As a gesture to continuity and connection to older Yale buildings in texture, color, and profile—as harbinger of a national mood for design in context and as an antidote to sterilized modernity—Saarinen's scheme stands

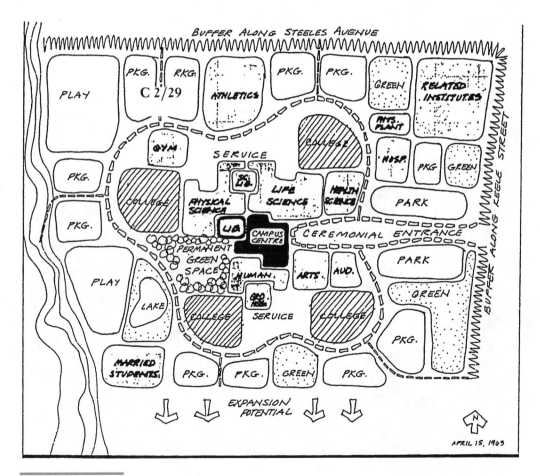

DAWSON'S LAKE / York University, Canada

Stuart Dawson's initial site and topographic analysis identified some immediate and long-range landscape themes. *Graphic:* Author's collection.

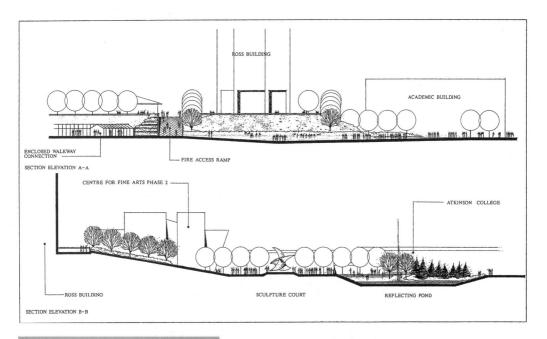

SECTION ELEVATION A–A

ROSS BUILDING

ACADEMIC BUILDING

ENCLOSED WALKWAY CONNECTION

FIRE ACCESS RAMP

CENTRE FOR FINE ARTS PHASE 2

ATKINSON COLLEGE

ROSS BUILDING

SCULPTURE COURT

REFLECTING POND

SECTION ELEVATION B–B

THE LAKE CONCEPT REALIZED / York University
Decades later the university landscape architects refined the earlier concepts to help mediate a harsh physical environmental setting and to implement some of the earlier terrain-determined landscape objectives.   *Graphic:* Courtesy York University.

alone in the hierarchy of great mid-twentieth-century contemporary collegiate architectural compositions. Seeing slight changes in the New Haven topography, Saarinen was reported to have observed: "San Gimignano, I think we can do something here in the way of a little Italian village." The suggestion of being in a hilltop Tuscany complex comes from the design of stairs and paths that pierce the center of the Yale site, and the angled walls and paving. Missing from Saarinen's Italian equation, of course, are the flat-top pines, the begirding olive groves, and the distant views of other hilltops. Campus landscape as an opera set? Let's do *Parsifal* and *Don Giovanni,* campus woods and gardens.

As a landscaped stage for campus life, the ensemble of steps, benches, and plaza on the south side of Low Library at Columbia University is a successful formula easily replicated in intention, if not form and architectural style. The sloping terrain of upper Manhattan is implied but not exposed in McKim, Mead & White's 1895 classical composition. The design's functionality and image of place was recognized when the university successfully closed the adjacent street and was thus able to expand the design and increase its utility by removing intrusive vehicular traffic. Later in the taxonomy, we will

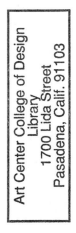

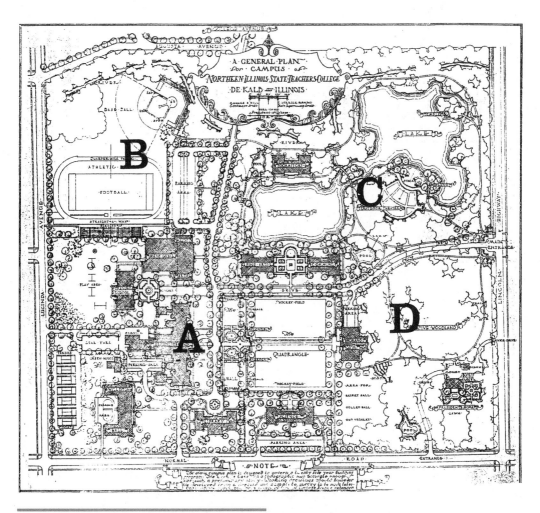

INTERTWINING CAMPUS LANDSCAPES / Northern Illinois State College
A classic drawing, concepts well conceived, never built as intended, but with an instructive mix of terrain related landscapes: (A) flatland quads; (B) sports fields; (C) the sloping outdoor theater and lakes; (D) a wooded lot with a slightly rippled surface. *Graphic:* Author's collection.

cite additional landscape designs that recognize and thus support the instinctive gathering of students, faculty, and staff at the building threshold, and why and how such should be identified and expressed as a palpable campus landscape component.

Good ideas, however, have long lives, particularly on campuses where some creative concepts cannot be implemented early. At York University Stuart Dawson's first views of the campus topography (1963) targeted the sloping land and shallow lake as an existing site condition worth acknowledging as a special campus landscape opportunity for functions not then describable. The 1987 plan for the area strengthened the views to and from the lake, dimensioned and constructed new play fields, furthered the idea of an arboretum around

1920 AIR VIEW / Bates College
Photo: Courtesy Special Collections, Bates College, Lewiston, Maine.

the lake, and clarified locations for new buildings inserted into the undulating landforms. Architecturally, much of York University is an extreme version of mid-twentieth-century modernism—extreme as defined in the campus's first vocabulary of hard-edged buildings and the paving and the monumentality of the central area. Splendid in sunny spring and summer, the site is a grim and dismal place in the cold, gray winter months. Some relief is expected from the thickening landscapes being installed in the late 1990s near the Dawson area.

Historically interesting are plans that attempted to meld several topographically inflected landscape concepts into one grand scheme. The 1920s plan for Northern Illinois State Teachers College is exemplary for its ambitions and ideas, though it was not built as planned because of the advent of the Depression. The southeast sector is a superb rendition of a flattened, calibrated formal campus landscape, with play fields serving as the green lawn in the open quads. The back precinct is arranged as an idyllic composition of informal gardens, lakes, and outdoor theater with the implied rippling landforms in

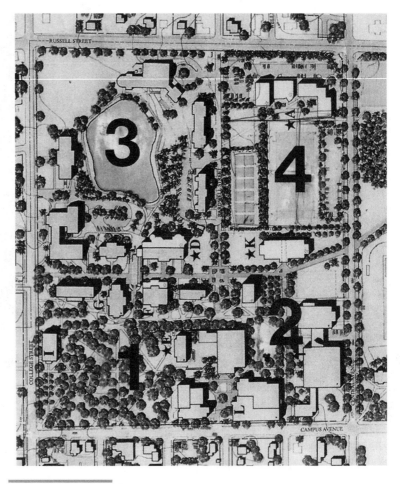

CURRENT PLAN / Bates College

Patience, funding, and viable ideas—landscapes with varying topographic consequences continue to guide the campus development. The traditional quads (1) and new quads (2) are enhanced; the impoundment area is completed (3); (4) a new quad is started at the edges of recreation fields. *Graphic:* Dober, Lidsky, Craig and Associates, Inc.

splendid contrast with the leveled terrain. Interestingly, the formal entry and landscaped drive leads to the laboratory school, where on many campuses the library or chapel would terminate the long vista.

The Bates College development pattern is a recent case example of some early ideas coming into fruition, with topography informing campus landscape design themes at a scale smaller than a mountain-top and larger than a courtyard. The 1920 air view shows four land development areas, existing and nascent. The 1993 campus plan illustrates their evolution and confirmation as specific broad-scale campus landscape design zones. The parklike sloping terrain is conserved and enhanced as a traditional nineteenth-century New England campus, that is, an open quad with lawns and trees. The shallow water-impounding area in the northeast is deepened and contoured to serve as a setting for surrounding buildings, with the sloping terrain buttressed by a stone wall that is designed as an amphitheater. The graded play fields are extended and enhanced into a recreational greensward adjacent to new housing. Further, the configuration of John Nolen's 1914 Beaux Arts flatland quadrangle is reinforced spatially with a proposed campus center facility. Each zone is then treated with landscape improvements appropriate to the setting and use; for instance, a tree-replacement program for the nineteenth-century campus sector, a new site-enhancing landscape treatment at one end of the lake in conjunction with a new academic building, and landscaped walks.

1.6 SUBSURFACE GEOTECTONIC

During recent decades, the acceleration of urbanization, the demands on agriculture, national energy requirements, the impact of large populations seeking outdoor recreation, and military postures and preparedness have stimulated a science, a profession, and a technology with important outcomes for campus landscape philosophically and in practice.

The attitudinal call includes Ian McHarg's *Design with Nature* (New York, 1969), the scientific discoveries of W. D. Thornbury's *Principles of Geomorphology* (New York, 1954), the applied professionalism of Collin W. Mitchell's *Terrain Evaluation* (London, 1972). Accordingly, graduates of landscape architecture schools, such as Harvard University under Carl Steinitz, are acquiring insights and skills that raise the quality of analytical approaches to land design. Their tools include ground-piercing radar, remote sensors, infrared scanners, computerized mapping, and three-dimensional modeling. Arguably, the new technology may blur certain perceptions that were once gained by on-site mapping and crude sketches of existing conditions by the designer who walked the land and felt its presence. However, one suspects that intuitive ideation is not lost in cybertechnology. For our purpose, Douglas S. Way states the desired cause-and-effect relationships of subsurface conditions succinctly: Any campus site development and its landscape expression "must be compatible with both the possibilities and the limitations of our natural environment and its resources" (*Terrain Analysis,* Stroudsburg, 1973).

Nature's endowment as it may affect campus landscape includes topography, landforms, vegetation, rock type, soils, ground and surface water, and minerals. The upper-surface physiography has been outlined (climate, vegetation, terrain). Some challenging subsurface geotectonic features are now noted. The latter include gumbotil, high water tables, karst, marsh, outcrop and ledge, and vernal springs. Their presence may help mark build/no-build zones, define broader landscape concepts (linear scheme versus rectangular), rationalize road and play field locations, and, like climate and terrain, affect planting choices and their disposition. When discovered, the impediments, after being carefully examined and evaluated, can be rectified by blasting, grading, excavating, filling, stabilizing, and tilling the land. Large-scale site changes can have dramatic results, as seen in site development for the universities straddling the Charles River, Massachusetts. Significant acreage at Boston University, Harvard University, and the Massachusetts Institute of Technology now occupy filled land. Northwestern University's lakeside extension is another example of expansion through landfill. What the masterful moves begin, less dramatic actions will continue. Limited by land and river boundaries, MIT has progressively increased the density of occupation along the Charles River, a development pattern that has been enhanced by new campus landscapes. Boston University's linear landscape, of recent vintage, strengthens the school's sense of place for those passing the site at highway speeds. After a frustrating century of accommodating athletics on soggy Soldier's Field, in 1999 Harvard is engineering some of its land area so as to keep it dry for play year round.

Pockets of the *unbuildable* draw the landscape designer like iron filings to a magnet. Oxford University is a three-dimensional encyclopedia for seemingly poor conditions transformed into epitomes of campus landscape. Addison's Walk, following the banks of the Cherwell River, was begun around 1630, was completed in the nineteenth century, and now is being replanted with trees more favorable to the soils in terms of appearance and survival. The rocks at St. John's College inspired H. J. Bidder (1890) to create a horticultural setting that melded topography and soils and plant types into a prototypical design whose publicity launched a fad and fashion worldwide. Worcester College's lake (1830) is reclaimed swampland, configured to express Alexander Pope's formula for a campus landscape paradigm: "contrasts, the management of surprises, and the concealment of bounds." For Ralph Cornell at Pomona College (1928), there was no such thing as "bad land." Some of the college's scruffy, original terrain was kept "natural" to serve as a design foil for a manicured lawn and stylish courtyards and quad.

At the micro scale, we claim that in principle there should be no campus land with difficult subsurface conditions that cannot be beautified with an appropriate landscape treatment. For example, the softening of the edge of the parking deck at Central Connecticut State University (a dramatic juncture of outcrop, topography, and manmade structure) is achieved by channeling groundwater, moving rocks, and adding trees and benches into a linear landscape. The automobile drop-off at St. Regis College accepts the presence of ledge, and with grass, trees, and lighting creates a simulation of a traditional New England landscape at the front door of the arts center. Brandeis University is visually interesting because geotechnical obstacles (glacial rocks and ledge) have been left in situ and integrated into the campus landscape as distinctive elements. Of marsh and swamp transformed into campus landscapes, see the typology component "Wetscapes," page 197. In some instances the difficult conditions that seem unalterable might be identified as site history components, and with placards and descriptive designs they may serve educational purposes or commemorate the founders' will and the designers' skill for overcoming obstacles and impediments. See page 234, "Site History."

1.7 SITE SIZE, SITE CONFIGURATION, ENVIRONS

Campus landscape is not an abstraction but a reflection of dimensioned reality, of which site size, configuration, and situation and the character of the environs are formative determinants. For a new public campus in California (Irvine, 1963) about 1,000 acres were acquired. Historic Brown University exists on 148 acres (as of 1998). Assuming a ten-minute walk from the periphery, the time typically scheduled for a change in classes, 125 acres would be sufficient for a campus core area for up to five thousand students with reasonable open space and no recourses to high-rise structures. A site this size in a dense urban area may be unrealizable; at the metropolitan edge it would be considered minimal acreage.

Noting the probability of many exceptions, nonetheless arithmetical formulas can be devised to rationalize site size. The formula would include projected building space, parking, athletic fields, requirements for service yards—calculations based on anticipated population multiplied by acceptable space standards for the type of institution being quantified. The projected space would then be translated into acreage via desired ground and floor coverage ratios, with set-asides for growth and an additional allowance (generous, one hopes) for amenity. The projection would then be adjusted to geographic, fiscal, and political realities.

Town Center

The Town Center will be the focal point of the University Community's activity and identity. It will be located immediately adjacent to the core of the campus, providing a place where University students, faculty, and staff can come together with local residents for shopping, dining, entertainment, cultural activity, recreation, civic functions, and socialization. A variety of uses will be accommodated including retail, offices, services, restaurants, entertainment, overnight lodging, and cultural facilities. Housing will be integrated with the commercial and cultural uses to establish a 24-hour, mixed use environment. It will complement those activities located in downtown Merced and other commercial centers.

"Develop a strong sense of place with a focus on public and open spaces as much as building design."
(Urban Form Panel)

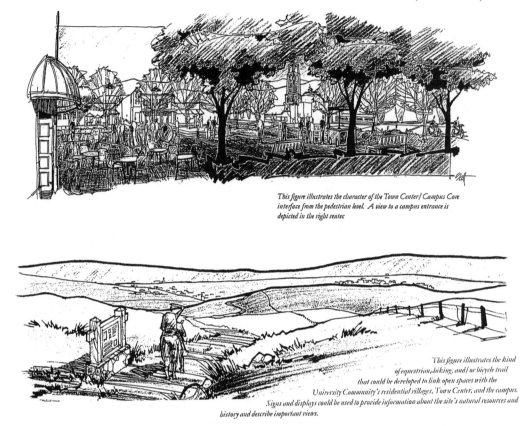

This figure illustrates the character of the Town Center/Campus Core interface from the pedestrian level. A view to a campus entrance is depicted in the right center.

This figure illustrates the kind of equestrian, hiking, and/or bicycle trail that could be developed to link open spaces with the University Community's residential villages, Town Center, and the campus. Signs and displays could be used to provide information about the site's natural resources and history and describe important views.

SIZE AND VARYING CAMPUS LANDSCAPES, 1999 / University of California, Merced

Those following positive trends in campus landscape are tracking the progress of the new University of California, Merced, campus. The project may serve as the paradigm for other regions worldwide seeking to optimize higher education's presence as a form-giving factor in urban design. At Merced significant undeveloped acreage and constructive town-gown dialog are drawing the best ideas from other campuses. The campus landscape ideas include a vibrant town center/campus core concept and campus and community recreation trails threaded throughout the university land. *Graphic:* Courtesy University of California, Merced; illustration by Richard Scott, Troller-Mayer Associates, University Community Concept Report, May 1999.

Having settled size, what about configuration and situation? Judgments: Rectangular sites are more flexible in use than linear ones. A single land holding is more advantageous than land fractured and broken by intervening streets and properties belonging to other owners. Compatible *active* land uses provide a better situation than inactive ones. Thus a shopping street with inexpensive restaurants, bookstores, cafes, bicycle rentals, and a travel agency is a better neighbor than a cemetery or food-processing plant. Contemporary research parks are more compatible a neighbor than extractive industries. A mass transit station will make the campus more accessible than large parking lots.

From these truisms one can derive an essential observation: Scale and surrounds as well as acreage and configuration are significant campus landscape determinants, but polar differences are not impediments to quality. Sandwiched by woodlands and agricultural plots on one side of the campus and a town on the other, Cornell University displays an extraordinary and commendable range of landscape expressions. In dense New York City, the Fashion Institute of Technology tailors its landscape expression to its self-evident reality of limited acreage, a configuration set by city blocks, and a vibrant but noisy surrounding situation. Lake views in Ithaca, streetscape and courtyard in Manhattan: Each landscape reflects a sense of place.

> **Campus landscape is not an abstraction but a reflection of dimensioned reality, of which site size, configuration, and situation and the character of the environs are formative determinants.**

1.8 STYLE

▶ Nature's alphabet consists of only four letters, wood, water, rock and ground; and yet, with those four letters, she forms such varied compositions and such infinite combinations, as no language with an alphabet of twenty-four letters can describe. (Adolph Strauch, *The Spring Grove Cemetery,* [Springfield, 1869])

▶ To some the idea of a landscape plan for a campus suggests nothing more than a planting plan for growing things.... [A] master plan... considers primarily and directly efficiency, good organization of elements, basically sound design for use. Beauty will come readily if the campus is well organized; it is usually is impossible to bring anything but superficial adornment to a campus that lacks a well articulated skeleton. (Arthur H. Carhart, "Convenience and Beauty in the Grouping of Buildings on a College" [*Landscape Architect,* 1925])

▶ We architects work with dead material. You landscape architects work with living things. You have thus a privilege and an opportunity that in a sense is almost greater than ours. To make our buildings vital, to give them the greatest power of expression, you are bound to work in the closest harmony with us poor architects who have only dead stocks and stones to deal with. We cannot get along without you and you cannot get along with us. This will be increasingly true in the future. (Ralph Adams Cram, "The Unity of the Arts," [*Landscape Architecture,* April 1933])

▶ The landscape architect must consider the relationships between a building and its surroundings, the topography, orientation, walks, roads and planting. He must be aware of the influence exerted by climate, and the relationships of earth, plants, water and building materials to create an architectural landscape integrated with the natural and man-made environment. (A. E. Bye, *Art into Landscape, Landscape into Art* [New York, 1988])

Selection of a style is a design determinant, campuswide or in sectors. While landscape elements (trees, shrubs, ground cover, paving materials) seem universal, in style one finds shuffling diversity in their use and arrangement. In taste, fads, and fashions, in the main, landscape follows and supplements architecture like Tonto serving the Lone Ranger—steady, secure, and faithful. The first crop of designers professionally trained as landscape architects (circa the mid-nineteenth century) were divided as to what was an appropriate style for American clients. In their journals and books style as a design determinant seems to begin and end with opinions about two distinctive and contrasting landscapes on either side of the English Channel: the French and the English, exemplified visually in the work of LeNotre (formal) and Capability Brown (informal). The varying viewpoints continue in today's trade magazine and dialogs at professional conferences: the orthogonal in contrast to the less calibrated, simplicity versus complexity. It is also evident that, theoretically, the division (formal and informal) today does not suit some leading modern landscape historians and scholars. They find that comparative methods in anthropology, social geography, and ethnography offer the most meaningful entries and exits for transforming the minutiae and arcane aspects of landscape design history into a significant account of stylistic cause, effect, and meaning, and their transfer and application for quotidian professional practice.

For our gloss simplified polarity is acceptable. Stylistics—the scholarly certitude of description and definition—is too vast an undertaking to be compressed into a few sentences. Suffice it to say that campus landscape architecture as an *art of styles* has yet to find its Bannister Fletcher, Bernard Berenson, or Sigfried Gideon. Their kind of explanatory approach to architecture does not yet exist for landscape design, and certainly not for campuses where the documents and materials for rich exposition are available. Wanted is a comprehensive description and critique of those contributing to paradigm campus landscape styles, including the inventors and innovators, patrons and presidents, communicators and advocates, peers and emulators, taste makers and fashion followers. An instructive history would trace their interaction and the outcomes, including clock-stopping and clock-starting styles. The former are those special moments when the college or university recognizes that it has in place a historic landscape that should be respected and conserved. The latter is the realization that a new expression is timely and desirable, not as a substitute for the existing treasures but as an addition. Instructive are those campuses where several styles exist side by side and can be seen and appreciated as three-dimensional cultural history, such as Union College. In splendid adjacency is the formal design of Joseph-Jacques Ramée (1812) and the picturesque gardens developed by Isaac Jackson (1831 to 1877); tucked between the two is a slice of contemporary campus landscape. (See also page 180.)

Back to our overview on style. The French model was marked with geometric ordering of spaces and plantings. Hedges and masonry walls edged ground planes that were patterned and regulated like a chessboard. Trees and plants are clipped, made uniform, set in rows like soldiers displayed for their monarch. The disciplined designs, it could be said, announced emblematically that nature was not to be feared but an artistic medium that could be controlled and contained. Ironically, some of the impressive formal gardens such as Versailles also had nearby faux naturalistic refuges for the rulers. Queen Antoinette could play shepherdess in a setting that Disney's managers and designers might envy for its safe and accessible simulation of rustic life.

Formality as design conviction carried weight in France through the birth of modernism. At the first meeting of the International Congress of Garden Architects, a leading French designer explained, "The aim of the modern garden is explicit in the provision of regularity and order, by means of formal arrangement, as an antidote to the shifting sands of political change." Discounted, though recognized, were exploratory extant designs echoing in garden design the Cubist and Art Deco movements. Such was inspiring to Christopher Tunnard when reporting back to his British colleagues in "What Other Countries Are Doing" (*Landscape and Garden*, summer 1937). Tunnard was moved by what he saw as the end of an infatuation with conventional canons, formal or informal. Designers in the future, he thought, "will not be concerned with outworn formulae or man-made theories useful for other times and no longer applicable for our own. They will demand the freedom to draw on any art in any age for inspiration, adapting it for use in accordance with individual needs for expression."

Brown's work is also an invention, spectacular in its simplicity. Bucolic in spirit, draped over a rolling existing topography or on landforms shaped artificially for similar effect, Brown's casual and comfortable scenery aims at contentment with nature, spreading to horizons seemingly not contained by contrived and constructed inter-

Stylistically few campuses are of one piece; a mosaic is more typical, with segments and sectors different in landscape expression. This multiplicity may have educational value. The campus landscape can be perceived as layered history. Our formula: Respect the past, and welcome the new as another volume in the library of styles.

ventions. Where the French would mass their trees in geometric phalanx, the British would feature in the Brownian designs an informal cluster, or occasionally use as a punctuation mark in the picturesque essay a single splendid specimen. Like trophies from war and conquest, exotic trees were imported by some eighteenth-century patrons to fill that scene; thus Asian and North American species enriched the local design vocabulary. The collecting instinct had its benefits, early in scientific gardens created in the Renaissance universities, and later in America.

As noted, landscape style traditionally has been expressed in opposites: formal versus informal, pastoral versus urban, classical versus modern, picturesque rambling versus geometrically controlled. As with painting and sculpture, each turn of the wheel called style will have historic antecedents and precedents, in sequence discovered and rediscovered. Changing tastes in American campus landscape are cyclical: regulated Jeffersonian, Olmstedian arcadia, irregular but enclosed Collegiate Gothic, Beaux Arts linearity, campus as a rambling park, Miesean formality, and the countering of hard-edge modernism with softer configurations. These days, it seems, one can attach the prefix *neo-* or *post-* to any esthetic from the past and find fresh interpretations and energetic proponents.

Stylistically, few campuses are of one piece; a mosaic is more typical, with segments and sectors different in landscape expression. In this regard multiplicity may have educational value. The campus landscape can be perceived as layered history. Our formula: Respect the past, and welcome the new as another volume in the library of styles.

And why new? New here will mean novel, unexpected, modern—essentially that which is original. In a troubled world with natural resources disappearing at a continental rate, with the psyche overloaded with the anxiety of artificial cyberspace, why not sustain, strengthen, and expand *alma mater*'s greenery with comforting and familiar campus designs? Arguably, for institutions committed to continuity and change, the new is emblematic. Further, institutions should promote and foster the arts. The creation of new landscape is an art-nurturing action. Novelty is also a possible anodyne for cultural bias or indifference. A seemingly unexpected campus landscape might give energy for an upward-tending curve among students who arrive set in their ways. And always welcomed are *parega* (the word is Italian), landscapes that have no other reason for being but to delight the eye and refresh the spirit.

Vernacular American (VA) would be a good label for such *parega* on many American campuses. Pervasive and photogenic, VA landscapes

STYLE: AMERICAN VERNACULAR / Harvard University
The informal arrangement of trees and grass in Harvard Yard is arguably the oldest campus landscape design theme in the United States—respected, imitated, emulated nationwide. In recent times the pattern has been analyzed by professional landscape designers so as to reveal the cues and clues it offers those responsible for landscape continuity, replacement, and maintenance. *Photo:* R. P. Dober.

come into being as groundskeepers and nursery staff add trees, grass, and plants to fill a vacant space near a campus building or to cut off an unbecoming view or to direct pedestrians to a safer route. Informal, the landscapes mature and take on a permanency and beauty that blur their origins as expeditious and intuitive landscape designs. Comforting, safe, valuable, they offer no challenge intellectually or esthetically.

What will the deliberately new look like, and where will it appear? The answers might be found in different campus landscape realms: the broader geographic context surrounding the campus, the campus as a design entity, sectors of the campus, project areas, and embellishments.

The first realm would seem utopian, every designer's dream of being able to fix campus *and* community into some kind of static design framework. This is highly unlikely after the first construction unless the campus is frozen in time, unaltered by changing program requirements, tastes, and technology. Witness the quadrangular mod-

VERNACULAR AMERICAN: REGIONAL VARIATION / New Mexico State University
Here a self-evident opportunity for visually improving the area is met with a regional variation of Vernacular American, with trees and ground cover intuitively arranged. *Photo:* R. P. Dober.

els of Oxford adapted at the turn of the twentieth century for guiding development at Washington University (St. Louis) and the University of Chicago. These were strong concepts mandated by purposeful patrons in the founding years. These ideas have subsequently been diluted in parts of the campus with some unconvincing additions and modifications to the original schemes.

Here again is a challenge peculiar, we think, to landscapes at colleges and universities. How does one balance the stewardship of conserving an existing art form—landscape at its best—with the encouragement of and advocacy and action for the new? And what is really new? With its bizarre ordering of trees by forms and plants by Latin name, faux machicolation, and arcades, the sixteenth-century garden at the University of Montpellier is comparable to many of today's eccentric, eye-catching concepts. For simplicity, classic seventeenth-century Christ Church, Oxford, has few peers.

At first glance, mid-twentieth-century new campuses seem to have distinctive landscapes, such the United States Air Force Academy, Odense University (Denmark), and Southeastern Massachusetts

University. In these and other examples of peer-honored modern architectural enterprises, however, the new appears to be the old reinterpreted. Landscape is a vegetal blanket, architectural buffer, besprinkled planting arranged to satisfy an expected gesture to human craving for nature's presence. The threads of traditional design can be seen in many landscape fabrics: linearity, simplicity, leveled ground, predictable spatial sequences, combinations of grass and paved areas. Of the pastoral type, Foothills Community College, highly honored for melding topography and planned layout, has less formal geometry and more textured expressions in its courtyards and connected greenery—a fine adaptation of conventional designs but not a leap forward into the radically novel. There was, of course, no expectation that any of these designs should be that special. Indeed, at the Air Force Academy the congressional committee charged with funding the new school and concerned about the proposed modern architectural styles were assuaged in their opposition by descriptions of traditional landscapes with Rocky Mountain themes.

Sector areas as they are developed (in contrast to an entire campus) might offer the chance to implant a totally new campus landscape expression as a counterpoint to the broader and conventional design images. New would be equated with unexpected. The palette for innovative landscape designs would thus include variegated combinations and arrangements of trees, shrubs, ground cover, paving materials, rocks, sculpted objects, outdoor furniture, fountains, walls, and gates. The ground plane might be undulating or sharply inclined.

Computerized lighting could be adjusted to diurnal changes, and dynamic pieces of the landscape could occasionally emerge from the landscape for visual effects, like stage scenery for a special occasion. All such would be recognizably different from— (let imagination and experience complete the sentence).

The sector design methods outlined above probably can also be applied to site-specific building projects; that is, new architectural concepts would have a complementary campus landscape. Laurin Olin's designs at the Wexner Center for the Arts (Ohio State University) points the way. A dimensioned theme garden (for example, a memorial to a person or event) would also be a potential project area for determining and implanting styles truly new, as would a site-specific landscape-as-art project.

For some institutions any departure from the norm will be cultural genocide. The search for stability in designs, methods, and results may give rise once again to esthetics as class warfare. John Miller's *Egotopia: Narcissism and the New Landscape* (Tuscaloosa, 1997) is an early-warning signal that among some critics the democratiza-

University of Montpellier

tion of art has led to "private passions" that taint and diminish long-respected canons of taste and fashion. Other related agendas? Some say design schools must be tuned in to "an increased interest in critical practices which theorize and construct those sites and artifacts that interpret the diverse identities in our society" (conference overview, 1997 meeting of the Association of Collegiate Schools of Architecture). The outcome would be "new models" which will "negotiate the spatialities of race, gender, ethnicity, sexuality by proposing an architecture whose artifacts reflect difference rather than commonality." Will campus landscape again follow the lead of architecture? Better, can it serve multiple objectives, diversity and commonality?

Conjecture about landscape design beyond the horizon must inevitably address signature designs. These are concepts that have a distinguishing mark, such as the pronounced X in a Stuart Davis painting, the lacy webbing of a late Jackson Pollock, a Louise Nevelson assemblage, or a Calder mobile. Each stylistically differs from the others in form and substance, and each is readily recognized for its uniqueness. All are modern nonpictorial art, and in a broad view are categorized as such. Campus landscape has not yet had an equivalent, that is, a three-dimensional representation of a designer's ideas that with repetition but variation gains and holds attention as a signature piece, though some current practitioners are ready and able to create such masterworks. Two such, with work relevant to this book, are George

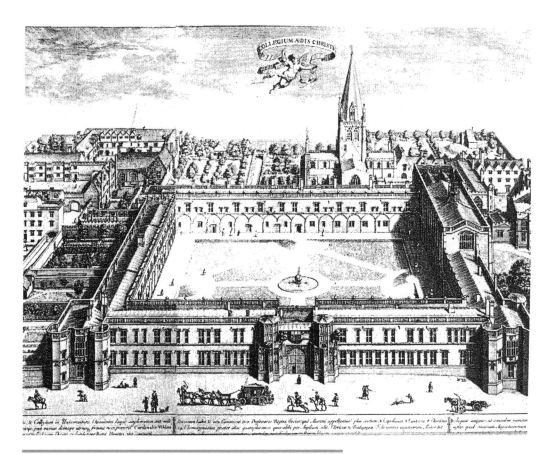

RENAISSANCE ANTECEDENTS AND PRECEDENTS / Christ Church College, Oxford
Campus landscape styles oscillate between simplicity (*above*) and intricacy (*left*), each era seeking and finding an esthetic interpretation uniquely its own.   *Graphics:* Author's Collection.

Hargreaves and Peter Walker. For the Library Square, University of Cincinnati, Hargreaves substituted a grid of elongated neon cones, green like trees, and decorative paving for grass. The square is the upper level of a parking garage, which could not be constructed at reasonable cost to carry the weight of traditional plant materials. Further, the design was loaded with emblematic overtones. The paving materials spiral like a Fibonacci form, suggesting a connection between nature's perfection and a humanistic pursuit of knowledge. Walker's Taubman Fountain at Harvard (an informal circle of seaside boulders and water spray) is a tour de force as four-season campus landscape. The misty spray is cooling in the summer, the winter ice is a transitory sculptural effect, the ensemble a narrative recall of some abstracted regional symbols.

Efforts such as those cited are likely to agitate people who are comforted by traditional preconceptions of landscape as art. Uniqueness will strain judgments as to a landscape's appropriateness on cam-

University of Cincinnati

pus; its maintenance will be challenged; as art its value will be debated. In time some new approaches will fit Matthew Arnold's "class of the truly excellent." Others will fade as transitory novelty, championed in the beginning as a style that will endure, but discovered later in fashion's dustbin. Particularly troublesome will be the works of campus teachers, beloved as professors of the arts, occasionally marginal artists if known at all beyond their region. What obligation is there to leave their efforts decorating lawns and courtyards when their time has passed and their work has become stale and dated as imitative of other and better work?

Some additional thoughts on a subject never easily settled, new styles as campus landscape design determinants: Introducing a collection of thoughtful essays entitled *Modern Landscape Architecture* (Cambridge, 1993), Marc Treib sees ideas in architecture following "about 15 years after those in the fine arts, and landscape architecture about 15 years further behind." The sweeping statement needs clarification. It would suggest that all the plastic arts have a connection. So to Treib's conjecture we add a caveat from the author's former teacher and acclaimed artist, Ad Reinhardt. There are kinds of fine art that are complete unto themselves, Reinhardt's late paintings being one.

STYLE SIMPLE AND STYLE COMPLEX / Kansas State University
Oscillations in contemporary styles: The courtyard at the University of Cincinnati is purged of traditional
landscape elements for a convention-shattering image of a particular place. The Kansas State University concept
fills the space with benches, planters, and fountains with equal place-making bravura. *Photos:* R. P. Dober.

He would declare that his kind of easel painting was "pure, abstract,
non-objective, timeless, changeless, relationless, disinterested." At the
extreme end of campus landscape design spectrum there would be
designs that *are* because they *are*. Whether such should fill the campus
vistas is arguable, for some are, in landscape critic Brenda Brown's
words, not only "coolly intelligent, witty, insightful, [and] beautiful"
but also "harsh [and] distorting." It is the latter, we think, that probably impedes installation of new styles extensively on campus, where
landscapes, in the main, should provide more physical comfort than
intellectual conflict.

It might follow, then, that five kinds of campus landscape styles
could be realized depending on the situation, the site, and the esthetic
inclination of those promoting campus landscape and those charged
with design and implementation. The five are:

- Landscape designs that serve and support function, such as an
  outdoor sitting area or visual barrier around a loading dock

- Designs that are informed by the local ecology, such as an arboretum or a massing of plant material associated with the local climate and terrain
- Designs that emulate and interpret older existing styles, such as landscape in an adjacent new quadrangle or continuation of a landscaped walk
- Designs that reflect campus site history, such as a memorial plaza or alumni campanile and garden
- Designs that are individualistic expressions of contemporary art, the campus landscape equivalent of a Reinhardt painting

Some of the approaches could overlap and be interconnected, thus strengthening the value and acceptability of continuing a style or encouraging departure, and perhaps on occasion give cause to help conserve, restore, enhance, and save an existing campus landscape because it has become recognizably special.

1.9 PROGRAM

▶ A detailed description of the proposals for buildings to be constructed in the near future to meet present needs of the college cannot be given... but the program briefly is as follows.... Obviously the requirements of the student body, the teaching staff and the operation of the entire composition, as an integral part of the intellectual life of the college, have been chief considerations. The belief prevails that if these ideals and needs are carefully fostered, the new Mount Holyoke College will retain all the loveliness of the old Mount Holyoke, but will gain greater beauty with its greater usefulness. (Arthur A. Shurtleff, "Program for Campus Development of Mount Holyoke College" [*American Landscape Architect*, January 1930])

▶ Warmth without sacrifice of dignity, richness without cloying quaintness, vitality without the jitters, order without sterility, humanity without immaturity, regional quality without eclecticism. (James Fessenden, "Foothill College—Environment for Learning" [Office of Ernest J. Krump and Associates, 1961])

▶ A program is a communicable statement of intent, a formal communication between designer and client in order to determine that the client's needs and values are clearly stated and understood... an operating procedure for systematizing the design process... a set of conditions for review by those affected by its implementation.

(Henry Sanoff, *Methods of Architectural Programming* [Stroudsburg, 1977])

▶ Programming is intended to facilitate communication among designers and providers of the built environment...[a process] that elicits and systematically translates the mission and objectives of an organization, group or individual...resulting in an efficient, functional building or facility. (Wolfgang F. E. Preiser, *Programming the Built Environment* [New York, 1985])

▶ The facility program becomes the management tool for reviewing designs and documents at each step of the design and construction cycle, so as to ascertain that the program requirements, designs, and costs are in balance with each other. If they are not, the facility program becomes the basis on which to act decisively and intelligently, so as to make the project feasible. (Arthur J. Lidsky, *Making Projects Feasible* [Belmont, Mass., 1992])

Diagrams are often the designer's programmatic lingua franca, useful when teasing out of luminous imagination the larger landscape concepts. Gabriel Epstein's first sketch for the University of Lancaster's new campus (1964) states graphically and succinctly project goals and objectives. The megastructure design dominates the topography. High and low buildings are configured for courtyards, paved or planted. The slopes are designated for grass or play fields. Woods, "partly existing, partly planted," serve as a greenbelt on the eastern side of the site, muffling highway noise and obscuring motion. On the western side the woods provide a definitive edge to the main entrance road and give visual relief and interest to the open spaces.

A singular site impression, simply stated, may turn out to be programmatically the key to a splendid landscape design. Seeing the array of beech trees on the raw site selected for the University of Sussex (1962), Sir Basil Spence is said to have declared that "these will scale and inform the university plan and no building will be taller than the trees." A gratifying photo of the site under construction reinforces pictorially the designer's intentions.

Arthur Shurtleff in 1930 gives one early credible citation for the use of the word *program,* which in his essay becomes more reportorial than an objective and detailed reckoning of design desiderata. Here, and in the years that followed, Creative Writing 101 seems to animate numerous program statements. Whether or not designers can meet the poetic expectations of prescriptive language such as the Foothill College quote may be questioned. In this instance talent prevailed. From opening day there was enough landscape "to provide places

There would appear to be no formula for a stylistic design determinant that holds for all time and place.

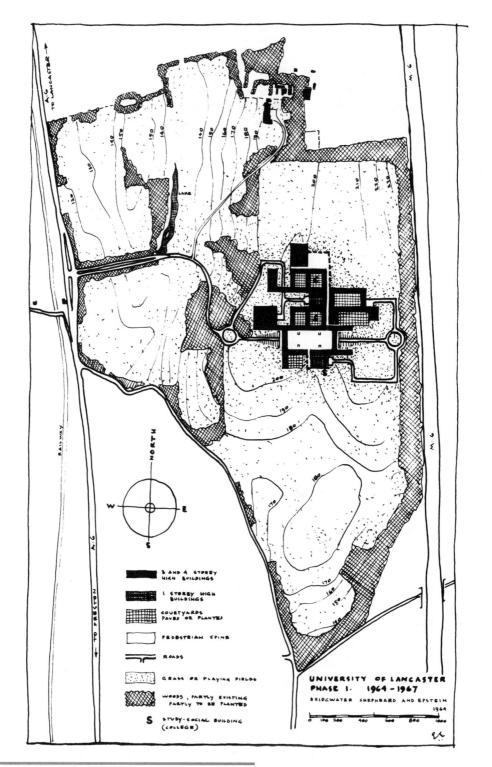

Labels within diagram legend:
- 3 AND 4 STOREY HIGH BUILDINGS
- 1 STOREY HIGH BUILDINGS
- COURTYARDS PAVED OR PLANTED
- PEDESTRIAN SPINE
- ROADS
- GRASS OR PLAYING FIELDS
- WOODS, PARTLY EXISTING PARTLY TO BE PLANTED
- S STUDY-SOCIAL BUILDING (COLLEGE)

UNIVERSITY OF LANCASTER
PHASE 1. 1964 - 1967
BRIDGWATER SHEPHEARD AND EPSTEIN
1964

SITE DIAGRAM AS PROGRAM DEFINITION / University of Lancaster

Campus landscape programmatic goals and objectives are succinctly diagrammed in a simple graphic that structures the overall Shepheard and Epstein design. See also York University, page 34, for a comparable programmatic diagram. *Graphic:* Author's collection

56

inviting natural informal gathering, intimately related to the instructional areas—so that the academic aura prevails amongst the students the livelong day." It was a green concept, free, truly modern, whose maturation marks well one of the twentieth century's model community college landscapes.

In the 1970s and onward, the research and work of David Cantor, Gerald Davies, Wolfgang F. E. Preiser, and Henry Sanoff, among other environmental design specialists, have blossomed into a general acceptance of programming as an architectural design determinant. In the main, however, landscape architecture has not yet had an equal effect in structuring programming theories and devising methods of application, particularly at the project level.

Programming landscape designs as an activity should be particularly attractive to institutions that prize collective enterprises, and

THE OBSERVING EYE / University of Sussex
First impressions can yield some conclusive ideas for shaping campus landscapes programmatically. Seeing the existing beech trees on the proposed university site, Sir Basil Spence declared that no building would be taller than their crowns and the heritage landscape would be used as a welcoming icon for the new campus. The view of the site under construction confirms the judgment of an observing eye and its contribution to the subsequent landscape concepts. *Photo:* Henk Snoek; courtesy Sir Basil Spence.

DRAWING D

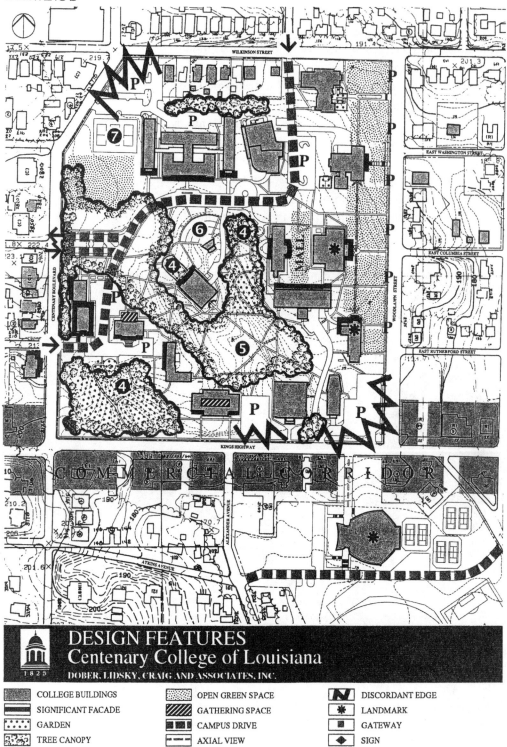

DESIGN FEATURES
Centenary College of Louisiana
DOBER, LIDSKY, CRAIG AND ASSOCIATES, INC.

COLLEGE BUILDINGS		OPEN GREEN SPACE		DISCORDANT EDGE	
SIGNIFICANT FACADE		GATHERING SPACE		LANDMARK	
GARDEN		CAMPUS DRIVE		GATEWAY	
TREE CANOPY		AXIAL VIEW		SIGN	

58

where shared information and decision making are typical and expected routines. Having those affected by the design outcomes involved in the description of project goals, objectives, and desiderata is a meaningful distribution of responsibility. For a campus with multiple missions, many purposes, an activity mix, and local culture and rituals, programming as a process and product would seem efficacious and generative. At the least it would be a barrier to solutions that are dysfunctional, uneconomic, culturally antiseptic, unsound, an insult to common sense—design conceits that are inappropriate, inexpedient, and inexplicable. Examples: injudiciously selected plant materials that do not survive their climate and situation; decorative paving that becomes warped and cracked because of an inadequate subgrade; courtyards that are open to uncomfortable prevailing winds; seating that is mired in puddles of mud; intersections that are too narrow to carry the volume of traffic passing between classes; and attractive views, subtle and manifest, that are blocked by poorly located greenery. Each deficiency could have been avoided with programmatic guidance.

In this optimistic view of the future, where programming will be seen as a productive design determinant, two cautions need mention. The first is attitudinal. The inexperienced or egotistic designer may dismiss programming as an abrogation of professional duties or an impingement on creative thought. Deep-rooted is the fear, perhaps, of the ultimate design program, so complete that it would lead to but one design solution. That possibility is as unlikely, however, as counting with certainty the exact number of grains of sand along the continental shelf.

The second is to confuse two kinds of design research as input to the programming process. As a practical matter, there are relatively few design commissions that provide the time and money to support a patient, systematic study and investigation of the fundamental facts and principles that serve as input for quotidian programming chores—such as the work of the Land Use and Built Form Studies Group, University of Cambridge, or the Center for Research and Development, School of Architecture and Planning, University of New Mexico. On the other hand, the working professional, by definition *professional*, has the obligation to acquire and build a body of knowledge germane to his or her undertakings. Such can be gained from continuing educa-

IDENTIFYING DESIGN OPPORTUNITIES (*left*) / Centenary College of Louisiana
A comprehensive site analysis can reveal programmatically landscapes to be preserved and landscapes to be developed. The latter, in this instance, are visually blemishing discordant edges. Solution: Landscape the parking lots. *Graphic:* Dober, Lidsky, Craig and Associates, Inc.

tion, discussions with colleagues, books and journals, participation in professional associations and workshops, advice from experts, cues and clues from articulate clients, postproject evaluations, insights and ideas afforded by site visits, and an objective assessment and application of one's expanding experience. That too is research.

Paradoxically, a studied statement of intended use and desired visual effects—a design program—may inform the campus landscape design more significantly than prescriptions for style, for, arguably,

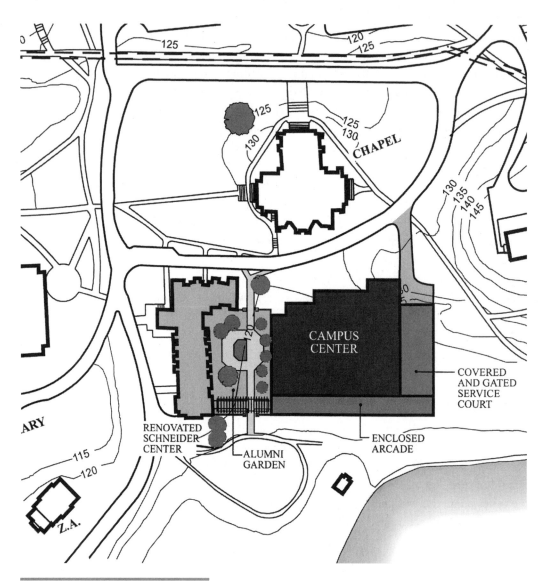

CAMPUS CENTER STUDY, 1999 / Wellesley College

Just as a building can be programmed as a prelude to design, so too can a site. In this instance a new landscape element (Alumni Garden) is proposed as an interface element between new and renovated space. *Graphic:* Dober, Lidsky, Craig and Associates, Inc.

different styles could satisfy any one specified function and situation. Five centuries of collegiate landscapes at Oxford University provide a reasonable test case of this assumption. In purpose and functional components (bedrooms, dining hall, commons, library, chapel, tutor's offices, and porter's lodge, all arranged in a quad) many of the Oxford colleges are alike. But there would appear to be no formula for a stylistic design determinant that holds for all time and place. In building and landscape at Oxford one can find excellent examples of textured expressions preferred over the bland, the monotone over the colorful, the startling over the expected. Commonality in the programmatic necessities has not compromised design differentiation.

Programming helps the search for design distinction. For American campuses, with their varied use patterns, a student residential precinct is likely to have a different landscape treatment than the campus core. Such distinctions and design directions can be stated programmatically. The core will require landscape forms and features that serve heavy use, as well as the emblematic role of being the central place. The residential precinct, on the other hand, might benefit from degrees of tranquility, security, a sense of being in a defined community. Play fields and recreation areas can be dimensioned in accordance with rules that govern play and competition. Parking requirements can be identified in terms of code requirements and other statements that separate the mandatory and necessary from the convenient. Major roads in the circulation network can be differentiated from minor paths through programmatic landscape design statements. Desired visual effects and spatial sequences can also be programmed, as well as the design experiences to be engendered as one moves through the campus. Landscape as elucidated choreography is a reasonable and achievable objective, as instructively described in Philip Theil's landmark notational system *People, Paths, Purposes* (Seattle, 1997). Mentioned earlier were the potential symbolic and emblematic uses of plant materials. Choosing and planting a species associated with local history and culture, and making such known as an element of site history—this too is an example of a programmatic campus landscape design determinant.

Campus landscape programs may be stated as generalized principles, presented as design criteria, or incorporated in project specifications. For existing campuses, the generalized principles are likely to reflect an analysis of prevailing conditions. A combination of the typology evaluation approach and visual character mapping outlined later is a productive starting point. Take, for example, addressing the *ragged edge syndrome.* Perceived and recorded gaps in the boundary planting and other visual deficiencies along the campus border can be translated into a programmatic principle and a subsequent action: creation of an attractive and definitive perimeter.

For new campuses, the programmatic principles may be couched in a descriptive narration that informs, anticipates, and gives direction to the designs that follow, as in this excerpt from a program for Paradigm College.

▶ Paradigm College buildings and landscapes will be designed and grouped so as to establish a strong and distinctive sense of place; a collegiate precinct immediately perceptible by the overall campus design composition, architectural features, and generous landscapes.

The Paradigm College buildings will be human in scale, no taller than the crowns of mature trees, minimizing vertical circulation, optimizing horizontal circulation.

The arrangement of buildings, landscapes, and circulation systems will take into account the seasonal differences in temperature, moisture, wind patterns, microclimate, and sun and shadow effects.

Within the precinct, emphasis in site design will be given to creating a landscaped zone that provides comfortable and easy pedestrian circulation between Paradigm College buildings and outdoor areas.

Vehicular traffic will approach the Paradigm College precinct via an entrance from the main highway and proceed as expeditiously as possible to the Paradigm College parking areas. Through traffic will be discouraged. Buildings and sites will be accessible to emergency and service vehicles.

The Paradigm College precinct walks, roads, other paved areas, outdoor furniture, lighting and signs will be located, selected and/or designed so as to reinforce the sense of place—giving visual clues that one is approaching the Paradigm College grounds or has arrived inside the precinct.

The boundary areas between Paradigm College property and neighboring residences will be marked by a greenbelt, whose design will be responsive to local concerns about visual intrusion. (Dober, Lidsky, Craig and Associates, Inc., *Landscape Principles Informing and Configuring The Paradigm College Campus Plan,* 1998)

As another example of a general programmatic statement leading to a specific, model document, consider the University of California, Berkeley's *Long Range Development Plan 1990–2000.* It establishes and illustrates the programmatic, cultural, and historical framework for detailed campus landscape proposals. These are folded into the plan's general policy statements with some site-specific and ecologically sensitive actions, such as the restoration of Wellman Courtyard and the enhancement of Central Glade (a historic landscape) in conjunction with an underground extension of Doe and Moffitt Libraries. The plan also confirms earlier decisions to preserve and enhance three central campus natural areas, labeled Ecological Study Areas (ESAs). Programmatic interdiction by prescription, the Berkeley language makes clear what should be done and what should be avoided.

Another example is Cornell University, where guru William J. Rewark wants institutions to be places where "standards are exacted—standards in literature, standards in the quality of scholarship, standards in the artistic expression of its own physical components." In response the Cornell programmatic guidelines provide design determinants that are exacting because they consider such impacts as climate, institutional size, resources, past experience, and culture. Thus, Cornell University provides its designers with a smart set of instructions identifying five ways that trees should be seen as contributing to Cornell's sense of place and thus be applicable in future campus landscape projects. The "contributing design concepts" are specimen planting (tree as sculpture), allée (flanking circulation elements and directing line of sight), massing (plantings with collective visual impact), ceiling and canopy planting (ground view control and/or umbrella effects), and barrier (view and circulation containment).

As designs move from broad concepts to project specificity, value engineering can become a programmatic factor, that is, information that helps rationalize programmatic conclusions. Robert Groot says value engineering is the "art of getting a problem solved with the least ecological and social impact and minimal costs" (*Landscape Architectural Review*, September/October 1986). His multivariable methodology includes materials, methods of construction, maintenance, quality performance, economic life, environmental costs, economic costs, and social acceptance. His formulation is sufficiently loose to enable each of those words to be interpreted and stated as narrative or quantified, or combined to fit the occasion. "Economics, ecology, social impact, and aesthetics... will give a sound basis for making well-founded decisions," notes Groot. He also is realistic. Not every client, he hints, has the "fortitude or resources of NASA or an Olympic Committee" for applied design research. Not all aspects of a landscape project can be subject to intensive quantitative analysis. Where fees and time do not permit, a general discussion of the undertaking will nonetheless be useful. Intended to encourage application at all scales, one of Groot's value engineering examples is particularly germane to campuses: seating. If nothing else, a campus is a landscaped venue for seeing, learning, socializing while sitting in a pleasant place. What follows is an interpretation of Groot's screed, germane to our discussion on programmatic deter-

Not every client has unlimited resources for applied design research, and not all aspects of a landscape project can be subject to intensive quantitative analysis. Where fees and time do not permit, a general discussion of the undertaking will nonetheless be useful.

minants. In this approach, one would begin the programming process with a checklist of possible seating purposes and functions: resting, reflecting, reading, viewing, watching, talking, eating, and waiting, alone and in groups. Answers would lead to alternatives and decisions: quantity, type, and location of seating, and site consequences, such as handling trash, lighting, security, intensity of use, design suitability, and maintenance requirements. Targets and limits would be set for project costs, a weighty variable in seat purchase and construction, since there could be a 750 percent difference between the simplest factory-produced designs and high-style solutions or custom seating designs fabricated on site.

To reiterate: In the main, the programmatic embraces all information leading to, describing, and directing the desired outcome. Illustrations of programmatic goals ("Pragmatism" in Michael Van Valkenburgh's 1998 campus landscape master plan for the Illinois Institute of Technology) help clients understand problems and solutions. Occasionally the programmatic imperative could take a three-dimensional form that then becomes part of project specifications; this approach is exemplified in Gilmore D. Clarke's essay "Notes on Texture in Stone Masonry" (*Landscape Architecture*, April 1931).

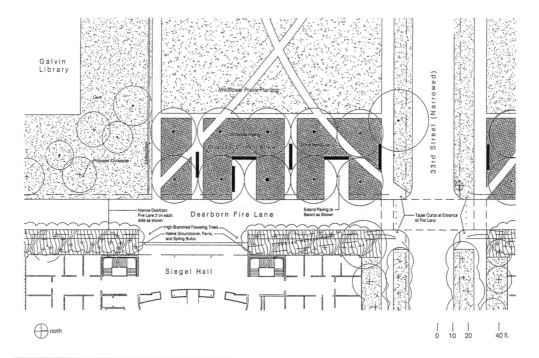

PROGRAMMATIC ILLUSTRATIONS / Illinois Institute of Technology
Realistic diagrams of problems and opportunities help clients see and understand project design goals and requirements. *Graphic:* Courtesy Michael Van Valkenburgh.

Clarke's problem: the choice of facing stone to bring the bridge "structure into closer harmony with its surroundings…leaving the impression that it is an integral part of the earth it is built upon. This does mean that any two structures should ever be alike, since no two sites are exactly alike." Clarke envisioned two kinds of harmony in stonework: the refined, cut to size and shape, or the rugged, which by intention seems less crafted. Materials may come from the site, near the site, or distant quarries, or may be blended. Clarke's solution: Drawings for the contractor should be supplemented by the landscape architect's on-site sample of the imagined concept, a three-dimensional program-

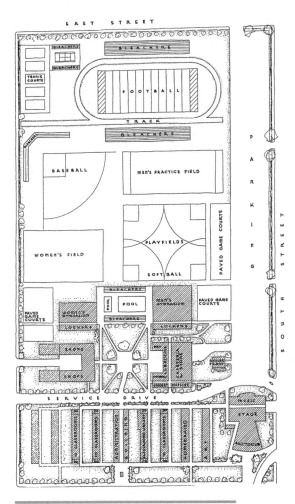

DIAGRAMMING INTENTIONS, 1946 / State Department of Education, California
Useful for suggesting broad functional relationships, some generalized diagrams can be misleading when setting landscape programmatic desiderata for specific sites, hence the value of site-specific analytical studies, including visual character. *Graphic:* Author's collection.

matic statement. He advocates using the finished texture in the sample as a benchmark in guiding and judging the work, and as a reference point for settling contractor disputes.

As noted, programming the landscape components for campus plans or projects has not yet reached the stage of sophistication as architecture. Simplicity may lead to a nontenable abstraction. Elaboration may be flawed by unrealistic expectations as to ease in interpretation and application. A well-intentioned site development diagram prepared as a template for California community colleges (circa 1946) is an illuminating example of the struggle to identify and illustrate graphically certain universal principles and criteria. In this instance the diagram aimed to illustrate site size, building configuration, and landscape relationships—presumably an archetypal function-based design concept. Not being site-specific, and with minimal gestures to campus landscape, the drawing was too diagrammatic to guide designers dealing with nonconforming venues or to judge the efficacy of their proposals.

Text and drawings in the 1973 campus development plan for the University of Kbangsaan (Malaysia) provide a better model of site-specific programmatic information. As an overview for guiding designs, three kinds of landscape are highlighted. The *rural* is the natural-state vegetation, which with selective clearing of the heavy undergrowth permits specimen trees to be featured visually. *Semirural* adjusts the rural by adding "soft-textured landscape" to give shade and contrast to the building groups. *Urban* is the landscape in spaces formed by and between the structures. These areas require paving and hard surfaces, which can be mediated with plant material that is in scale with the adjacent spaces and the pools and lakes that handle the runoff from heavy wet weather. The prescription for the use of water as a design theme is accompanied by a proscription against addressing local conditions, such as preventive measures for controlling mosquito breeding and silting in the pools and water channels: "Unless particular attention is given to the design and detailing the results could be disastrous."

Responding to local culture and climate, the Kbangsaan planning team highlighted other desired landscape design themes—for example, *relaxation areas,* "spaces where people can sit under trees...for meetings, studying, or simply relaxing." Here they would experience "pleasant views, attractive planting, and the use of pools or lakes to give the feeling of coolness." Outdoor eating facilities would be situated along the major pedestrian routes, situated in landscaped groves, with the sitting areas protected from the rain by lightly constructed space frames.

A design program for a campus landscape project is thus a document that in words and graphics will inform and guide the design team.

In another cautionary note, applicable to campus landscape universally, the design team stated:

▶ Particular attention must be given to the scale and extent of landscaping and planting in spaces of differing size and quality. The planting of isolated bushes or shrubs in large open areas is nearly always unsuccessful; the use of pretentious detail and half-hearted planting will always result in an unsatisfactory environment. If grass is used it should be well maintained and contained by paving or kerbs in built-up areas.

Documents of this character and content are also educational opportunities, alerting the client team and others affected by the design outcomes as to what is required to accomplish high-level landscape design in a specific situation. M. Robert Fenton's technical report for the future landscape development of the University of Pittsburgh (1968) is a second good example of goals and objectives translated into a programmatic design vocabulary that a larger audience can understand, appreciate, and use. The information helps articulate design goals and objectives and the review and evaluation of subsequent proposals.

As the planning team's landscape architect, Fenton aimed for the "landscape effect," that is, "the total emotional reaction to the form, size, quality and character of the greenery in this urban campus setting." Fenton's programmatic design determinants included four spatial types: *entry spaces,* where one encounters the campus for the first time; *district spaces,* which in combination create the image of a *major open space;* and *architectural spaces,* which are contained by the confining buildings. In mapping these various areas, he was able to demonstrate that for an urban campus such as Pittsburgh the sense of openness as a landscape quality was a university asset worth preserving. Further, the incomplete linkage of these areas functionally and visually was a fundamental flaw in the existing environment that new campus landscapes could address and mediate.

Fenton's analysis—the prelude to programmatic design—also included a detailed mapping of the tree cover. For convenience in finding the broader patterns, he divided the trees into two size categories, large and small, with a 4-inch tree diameter being the dividing line. He then noted that there were "no areas where there is a presently a concentration of trees within the campus...no differentiation is apparent in the tree planting from campus to non-campus areas." Accordingly, additional planting and variety, including evergreens for the winter scene, were emphasized as necessary.

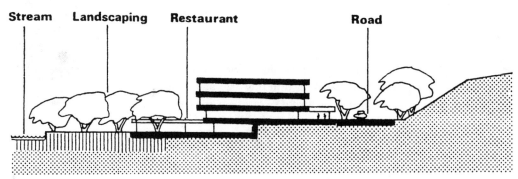

a. faculty club

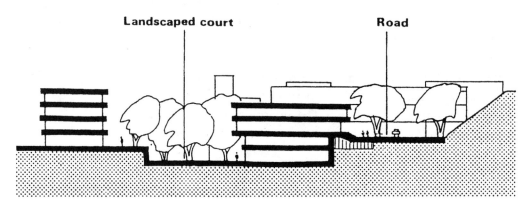

b. health centre

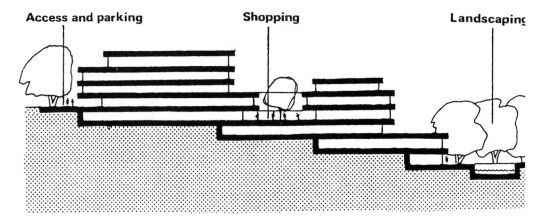

c. student union

DIAGRAMMING LANDSCAPE SITE REALITIES / University of Kbangsaan, Malaysia
Culture and climate impacts are defined and landscape design outcomes expressed in the programmatic diagrams outlined in the 1973 University of Kbangsaan, Malaysia, campus plan, a model effort. *Graphic:* Author's collection.

Fenton's recommendations were illustrated with programmatic design diagrams. Three sets are reproduced here, a kind of elementary but instructive textbook for establishing a design direction programmatically. One set explains choices in massing, rhythm, and composition. Another outlines the desired landscape treatment of large, intermediate, and small areas. The third deals with site topography, the surface wrinkles that give this part of Pittsburgh a natural image. For the latter, Fenton offers two design treatments: leave as nature-given or change the site character to increase its use and insert walks for accessibility.

A design program for a campus landscape project is thus a document that in words and graphics will inform and guide the design team. The program should include general goals and objectives, specific requirements and expectations, design criteria, site location, site history, an account of opportunities to sustain and support local values and traditions (or to strike off in another direction should that be the client's desire), and the project budget targets. The narration would also include a description of the project's contribution to the campus master plan and make reference to and cite where possible specific guidelines. Such a *brief* (the British word for a program) can also be used in design competitions.

This kind of programming has precedent, including landscape architect Warren H. Manning's 1898 critique of the design competition for the International Competition for the Phoebe Hearst Architectural Plan for the University of California, Berkeley. While his comments are directed to the competition, his views merit attention as a rationale for programming and as a spirited case for the involvement of the landscape architect in its formulation and utilization.

The Hearst competition architects were expected to conjure a design so ideal that it would "fix the plan and a consistent policy regarding it so firmly that that their successors would not depart from it." Not likely, editorialized Manning. In his critique, a valuable historical document for those tracking cultural attitudes about campus design and implementation, Manning described how vulnerable such plans were in his own lifetime. He decried the shortsighted who under "temporary financial embarrassment" sold land needed for plan completion, and he castigated weak administrators who ignored "the established plan of grounds" and the mandated "style of buildings." The blunders happened, Manning observed, because of "purely local or personal considerations, such as the presence of a temporary building, a group of unimportant trees, an established

A PATTERNS OF MASS

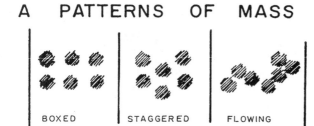

BOXED · STAGGERED · FLOWING

1. Best located in major open spaces and steep slopes.
2. Texture (species type) shall be consistent within masses.

B RHYTHMS

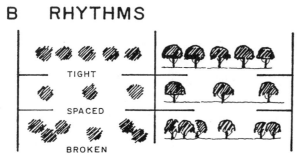

TIGHT

SPACED

BROKEN

1. The number of rhythmic patterns shall be minimal.
2. Rhythms will develop along vehicular and pedestrian corridors.

C FEATURES

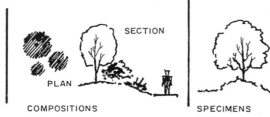

SECTION

PLAN

COMPOSITIONS · SPECIMENS

1. Compositions can accent building entrances.
2. Specimen give scale and depth to an open space.

A NATURAL ECOLOGY

Where maintenance is a problem, natural ecology is best.

B REFINED SLOPES

1. Slopes can be important linkages visually as well as physically.
2. They can provide vistas, backdrops and passive recreation areas.

C LARGE AREAS

1. Shaping large spaces is best accomplished with mass planting, buildings, earth forms, and walls.
2. Open quality is enforced by depressing areas.

D INTERMEDIATE AREA

1. 3 to 4 foot mounds foreshorten distances.
2. These will screen pavement and other low elements.

E SMALL AREA

1. Reinforce with flowering trees and textural evergreen shrubs.
2. Should be strongly defined with walls, curbs, and shrubs.

FENTON AT PITTSBURGH, 1968 / University of Pittsburgh

With simple diagrams, landscape architect M. Robert Fenton provides the client with an instructive analysis of the area's landscape potential, thus reinforcing the programmatic descriptions with a rudimentary but educational design manual. *Graphic:* Author's collection.

path, or an individual's desire to design or have designed a building markedly different from the established type and to locate it in a position where its individuality would be conspicuously evident."

Manning thought the Berkley competition instructions were too vague and made it appear that "there was no intention on the part of the framers of the Programme to invite landscape-architects to take part in the competition." Having visited the site, he outlined the reasons why the eventual designs would be flawed—such as the amount of land available, the potential for "mutilation" of trees, ill-proportioned distances between buildings, and structures crowded on "rugged and irregular land," which at the time of his critique was unappreciated or not acknowledged by the designers. For Manning the landscape challenges were "so unusually intricate that the advice of a skilled landscape designer would have been of much assistance." He would have added to the program (thus establishing a design determinant) an assessment of the site size and its suitability for the projected buildings and "means of communication [circulation], and their association with existing and proposed plantations." Manning concluded that a useful design program would have included an accurate topographic map, a description of the site character and views, and a more precise notation of specimen trees. The latter would give "material assistance to the designer [for some] are very tall with high trunks, and others very broad-spreading with branches almost touching the ground."

Then as today, programming is an opportunity to introduce and integrate expert advice from members of a campus population that may be qualified to address technical issues, spotlight and explain comparable work elsewhere, or deal with the quotidian issues of maintenance and site suitability. As a document used in the design process, the coverage may be more useful than the volume of information. If all the important matters are indexed, then greater detail can be gathered and noted as the work proceeds. As suggested, the program document can also become a reference work for client evaluation of the specific designs and for alternatives that interpret the program in ways unexpected at the start of the work. Realistically, one admits there may occasionally be campus landscape concepts that will be difficult to program in the sense that too fine a definition will impede artistic license and interpretation. The benefits and difficulties associated with these "over-the-horizon" designs were discussed earlier (see "Style," page 43). In these instances general statements about desired outcomes are better than specific programmatic instructions.

Concepts and proposals best begin with an appreciation of the significant existing physical circumstances and conditions that appear to give a site its perceptible distinctions and the relationships of those elements to one another, including the environs.

1.10 Visual Character

▶ To secure an adequate campus plan it is not necessary or wise to discard all of the ideas of those who founded the institution. There are always portions of the college plan which, like a city plan, should be preserved. There may be others which should be rearranged to enable the greatest possible use to be made of the site.... It is here that the landscape architect with his intimate knowledge of the larger aspects... can bring to the scheme an originality and breadth of view not always possible when but one building is to be built and all interest concentrated upon that need. (F. A. Cushing Smith, editor, *The American Landscape Architect*, 1930)

▶ Standards of any form must however be regarded critically when speaking in visual and functional site planning terms as no one site is the same as another; it follows that if all sites were the same, no individuality or originality in the visual and functional message would occur. (Christ College [New Zealand] Development Plan, Landscape Architecture section, 1973)

All aspects of campus landscape development, from the first design impulses to the definitive programmatic statements, will benefit from an analysis of the site's visual character. Physically each campus is different in its wholeness and in detail. Concepts and proposals best begin with an appreciation of the significant existing physical circumstances and conditions that appear to give a site its perceptible distinctions and the relationships of those elements to one another, including the environs. Surveys may reveal complex or simple conditions, and not necessarily ones related to institutional size or acreage.

A new campus, of course, poses different opportunities than does an established institution. In 1999 the author dealt with two extreme variations in visual character. In Egypt, the American University in Cairo was planning to relocate to a new large, unencumbered property on the edge of the expanding metropolis. Stark, sparse desert land, awesome in its rawness, the site was a *tabula vacus*, the proverbial slate unwritten, with unlimited potential for multiple campus landscapes. In New England, the site for the F. W. Olin College of Engineering was marked by a rolling topography, extensive tree cover, wetlands and vernal springs, the rights-of-way for a metropolitan aqueduct and a regional gas transmission line, the remnants of stone walls from early settlement, and some play fields that belonged to a neighboring institution and were too expensive to relocate. These

A visual character analysis will reveal opportunities for some early action, a landscape proposal that would self-evidently help remedy a deficiency that didn't require a total plan.

were tangible site features, giving each place a particular visual character. Landscape concepts had to reflect and fit site realities and constraints.

Aspiring work at the proposed new campus for the University of California, Merced (1999), exemplifies the search for the specific visual character of a region and the impact it can have as an eventual campus landscape determinant. Geologically the 15-square-mile development area is a transition zone between foothills and the adjacent flatland farms, with slopes and ridges forming bowls. The visual character, notes the planners, "to many is the image of California . . . that has been represented in Hollywood's movies from its earliest days." Envisioned are opportunities to orchestrate "a progression of views" starting inside the bowls to sight-line corridors that "open

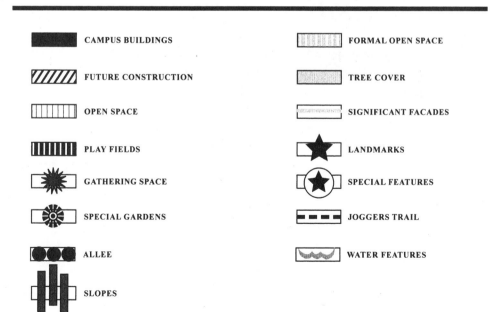

VISUAL CHARACTER

FURMAN
UNIVERSITY
CAMPUS PLANNING STUDIES 1997

DOBER, LIDSKY, CRAIG AND ASSOCIATES, INC.
Campus and Facility Planning Consultants

CAMPUS BUILDINGS		FORMAL OPEN SPACE	
FUTURE CONSTRUCTION		TREE COVER	
OPEN SPACE		SIGNIFICANT FACADES	
PLAY FIELDS		LANDMARKS	
GATHERING SPACE		SPECIAL FEATURES	
SPECIAL GARDENS		JOGGERS TRAIL	
ALLEE		WATER FEATURES	
SLOPES			

VISUAL CHARACTER / Furman University
Each campus has its own particular visual character, which, identified and expressed, serves as an index for landscapes to be preserved, enhanced, extended, and added.   *Graphic:* Dober, Lidsky, Craig and Associates.

into wide panoramas." Overlaid with the colors and texture of grasslands, farms, and campus landscapes, the bountiful beauty will blend into a place that aims "to be more than just another campus or community, a place that one can uniquely identify with and value." Affecting 10,000 acres, the projected overall development will house a community with 11,800 households, farms, and a university with about 5,000 students in its first phase and perhaps 20,000 on completion. (See page 42. Quotes are from *University Community Concept Report,* [Merced, 1999].)

At existing campuses a customized account of the visual character will help illustrate and communicate the pluses and minuses of the existing campus landscape and thus set the agenda for improvement and extension. As each campus is different, so too is the descriptive vocabulary. The information can be displayed in map form, supplemented by photographs and narration. Typical coverage would include the campus edges, entrances, exits, boundaries, open spaces and their functional variations, architectural landmarks, specimen landscapes, circulation networks and the manner in which they give structure to the overall campus design, views and vistas, and a depiction of the good, the bland, and the ugly. Obviously the descriptions are best customized to tell the tale of the site as a special place. The Campus Landscape Matrix, page xxii, is a good place to start.

Parenthetically, we have discovered that a professional presentation of this material during decision-making processes, to which all campus landscape designs are eventually subjected, raises the level of confidence in the proposals. Further, quotable excerpts and enticing photos of the "before" and the "expected after" find their way into fund-raising brochures and related documents.

Occasionally visual character analysis will reveal opportunities for some early action, a landscape proposal that would self-evidently help remedy a deficiency that didn't require a total plan. Early actions can also help gain support for the process and product, being a kind of reward for participation in the planning process.

1.11 TECHNOLOGY

Absent in current literature, we think, is a comprehensive history of the impact of technology on campus landscape concepts. Earth-shaping machines, the mechanical mower, irrigation systems, lighting, the nylon grass and weed whip, and the computerized operations of traffic control gates—each in its own way has enabled certain landscape ideas to come into being and to be maintained economically. Through late-twentieth-century cloning techniques it is now possible to obtain an exact replica of a treasured tree or shrub. The technology for moving and replanting trees has advanced considerably. One tree-transplanting company advertises, "Why wait for nature to catch up with your ideas...we produce a finished landscape with mature planting that makes developments distinctive!" Technology as a design determinant in the future? Imagine genetic engineering to extend seasonal color, to avoid herbicides, to increase drought resistance.

1.12 FUNDS

Axiomatic: Funds available are a campus design determinant, both for the original installation and for the upkeep. Or no funds, as remembered in the early history of St. Hugh's College, Oxford (c. 1916). The first head, Annie Rogers, had little money for gardens, and so she visited "the men's colleges armed with an umbrella into which she popped cuttings of the planting she most fancied." St. Hugh's today has nine gardens, including a great lawn with sundial, rock gardens, and dell, plus bits and pieces of special horticultural collections—not a consistent and connected campus landscape design concept, just beauty in all seasons.

The Rogers approach is not likely at most campuses. More typical and challenging are the budget-setting sessions where landscape designs are confirmed in principle but not with realistic implementation prices. Overlooked are the significant differences in the costs of various landscape elements and their resulting visual effects. There are large variations in cost per square yard for paving and in the price of different types and sizes of lighting fixtures, benches, and trees. For high-quality landscape, there are few equivalents of an economy car. And, too often in building projects, the landscape allocation is usually targeted for the first budget reduction when there are building cost overruns, with the resulting scene on opening day becoming a baneful reminder of a shortsighted decision. As to maintenance, too many American campus landscapes are endangered by inadequate and declining operating budgets. There is a cost-cutting mood at the opening of the new millenium that is following the track of architecture, that is, where the reduction of landscape maintenance and replacement funding is considered an appropriate budget-balancing measure—a trend that is reversible, one hopes. It doesn't work for facilities, and it won't work for campus landscape.

Significant differences in the costs of landscape elements and their resulting visual effects are often overlooked in budget-setting sessions. There are significant price variations in cost per square yard for paving and in the different types and sizes of lighting fixtures, benches, and trees.

1.13 FACTOR X

▶ Landscape Architecture is a new art. It must have many tricks which have not been tried, many systems of organization which are unused. I think we should busy ourselves about finding them.... For myself I am convinced that there should be more art and less nature in our work,—more thought of design and less about fancy bushes. (Charles Downing Lay, "Some Opinions About Landscape Architecture" [*Landscape Architecture,* fall 1921])

▶ [E]cology is a comparatively new science.... It needs, therefore, to be translated into a form that will make it available, in nomenclature and substance, to all those who are doing work in which landscape and the vegetation which forms so vital a part of it come into consideration. (Elsa Rehmann, "An Ecological Approach" [*Landscape Architecture,* July 1933])

▶ The belief that sound landscape planning should be founded on an ecological basis will need cross-examination. Some of the sophisticated techniques of landscape evaluation should be reviewed and questioned in respect of their real accuracy and usefulness for planning purposes. (A. E. Weddle, "Landscape Planning—Aims and Scope of a New Journal" [*Landscape Planning,* 1974])

▶ [T]here is no such thing as the design of space or spaces. *Behavior,* not space, is enclosed by architecture. No dwelling, building, or city is planned to be empty. In order for the planner or architect to know the purpose of his design, he must know thoroughly the behavior he will enclose. (Robert B. Bechtel, *Enclosing Behavior* [Stroudsburg, 1977])

Factor X is one person's account of where emerging and new knowledge and knowledge recalled—such as the perceptual aspects of environmental design—are likely to become campus landscape design determinants. Pioneering efforts in basic design research (attitudes, methods, and application) from the 1960s and 1970s have moved numerous topics from the realm of speculative thought to application. Kevin Lynch's *Image of the City* (Cambridge, 1960) examined how we perceive the environment and in turn are shaped by those perceptions. Like a vineyard with many grafts, Lynch's work has produced volumes of related research applicable to campus landscape. For example, for designers concerned with arranging campus views and vistas, viscerally and symbolically, see any of E. H. Zube's research, all a reliable elaboration of Lynch's ideas.

Design and behavior studies such as Randolph T. Hester Jr.'s *Planning Neighborhood Space with People* (New York, 1975) have become standard bibliographic works in training professionals. Hester's design paradigm for a comfortable place to sit, for example, would be (and is) germane when evaluating campus proposals. The elements in the paradigm include convenience, safety, psychological and physical comfort, and esthetic appeal. Ditto work such as Wolfgang F. E. Preiser's *Evaluation of Outdoor Space Use: the University of New Mexico* (1982). His study team yielded pages of ideas that could animate and improve campus landscape designs anywhere. These pioneering efforts have in subsequent years inspired additional studies of the design-psychology-behavior triad, much of it available in publications distributed by the Environmental Design Research Association. Knowledge of this research will help one digest the candied canons of fad and fashion or gauge and counter the unsubstantiated, though often interesting and provocative, claims of pseudo-estheticians with their gloss on landscape design philosophy and intentions.

Ecological principles and environmental ethics have not yet peaked as potential campus landscape determinants. A journal such as *Landscape Ecology*, founded in 1987, is sufficient evidence that those concerned about the beneficial integration of the natural and built environments will continue to serve up cues and clues that can shape the campus beneficially. Journals, and their Web page equivalents, indicate where the profession is heading. *Landscape History*, published about the same time as *Landscape Ecology*, provides a meeting ground for many disciplines concerned with "the material evaluation of man's use of the land surface … [for] a more secure and penetrating comprehension of the processes at work together with an overall narrative account of landscape prehistory and history." Believing that the *memory of place* has significance for all campuses, we will outline later the case for a specific and universal campus landscape component: site history. Thus we will bring the typology into the twenty-first century with some Factor X considerations.

SECTION 2

CAMPUS LANDSCAPE DESIGN TAXONOMY

> ► [T]he first rule governing the creation of a landscape is that no matter where within the enclosure the observer may stand, he may not be permitted to see an objectionable thing from an artistic point of view. (Wilbur C. Peterson, "The University of Nebraska Campus Plan" [*Landscape Architecture,* January 1927])

> ► While our standards of building design have in many instances improved immeasurably, our standards of outdoor design have dropped to a very low ebb. (Elisabeth Beazley, *Design and Detail of the Space Between Buildings* [London, 1960])

> ► Preserving this landscape character is important not only for environmental reasons, but also for the University's intellectual future: the "Stanford ambience" is often cited by both students and faculty as a reason for choosing Stanford and as a significant factor in their satisfaction with the experience here. (Stanford University, Landscape Design Guidelines, 1989)

CREATING A DISTINCTIVE PLACE

The designer's slogan "Each campus is a distinctive place" is a faultless observation, like noting that the day begins at dawn and ends at dusk. Distinction comes as pieces of the landscape typology, function driven, are formed with features developed, stylized, detailed, located, and constructed in response to design determinants. In this section we identify and discuss the thirty items (components) that make up our campus landscape typology. For self-evident reasons, not all items are treated at equal length. Our objective is simple: to encourage the maintenance and conservation of the best existing landscapes, to promote their enhancement and extension as quotidian goals, and to urge the design and installation of additional landscapes using our typology as a checklist of opportunities. The utopian situation, of course, is to have all of the thirty components linked into some overall campus landscape concept that is functionally useful, esthetically pleasing, and recognizably appropriate for the local culture and natural conditions. Believing that the deficient explicated may be as instructional as a paradigm worth emulating, both kinds of examples are used in the typology and commentary below.

FIRST ENCOUNTERS

In application, there are several ways to perceive the campus as a landscaped environment amenable to design and redesign. For this segment of the typology we will describe campus landscape as a system of encountered experiences, individual landscape components that one might experience along the journey from the environs to a campus destination. Accordingly, one passes through the landscaped surrounds, arrives at the perimeter, enters the campus gateways, traverses campus roads to automobile parking or bike racks, and starts walking to the precinct and building thresholds along landscaped paths. (Alternatively one might arrive by transit, taxi, or car pool.) This would be a reasonable concept of connected landscapes. Some new campuses have successfully developed such designs. More often than not, however, the sequential visual experience on many campuses is disjointed, arbitrary, a melding of high-quality thoughtful designs and the indifferent and inexplicable, with any overall design concept in discernable disarray.

2.1 SURROUNDS

The arithmetic of possibilities is stunning. We generalize: In North America four thousand campuses are surrounded on four sides by land uses that may or may not be compatible with the institution's presence, and vice versa. The sixteen thousand combinations would include mixes of city, town, and rural development. Ideally it would be desirable to have the landscapes in those surrounds give some visual clues and cues of the campuses' presence, and/or to mediate any physical deficiencies or incongruent development, and/or to share and promote some common interests. Some examples of the latter: a cultural center, recreation fields, or a commercial area. Each such project could generate a landscape setting beneficial at the campus-community

DESIGN IN THE SURROUNDS AND EDGE, 1999 / Southeastern Louisiana State University
Led by the Foresite design team, town and gown collaborate on a unified landscape design. *Above,* the new university
gateway concept; *below,* the proposed visually compatible street scene.   *Graphic:* Foresite and Michael Morrissey.

interface. One perceives nationally (late 1999) significant efforts to
heal town-gown conflicts. Both sides of the campus boundary are real-
izing the economic and social benefits of joint efforts. We cite Southern Louisiana State University's initiative as indicative of what lies on
the horizon.

2.2 PERIMETER

Perimeter, periphery, edges—this is where the campus is presumed to begin physically, and thus it may require demarcation. Typically the perimeter is defined by the boundaries of the land holdings. Three property patterns can be discerned: self-contained and unified, fragmented, and scattered. The last two reflect land divided by streets and intervening property, or land and buildings on the fringe of the central campus obtained and held through gifts or purchases, and staked out for protection, possible growth, income, and land use compatibility.

How should the edge of the campus be landscaped? Our focus now is the self-contained campus or a land parcel large enough to form a campus precinct or zone and thus susceptible to unified design treatment. The introductory historical design images of Antioch College and Trinity College (below and page 85) are pictographs of two basic approaches: the informal and transparent, and the formal and opaque. In the first the campus is seen from the periphery, picturesque, welcoming, and readily accessible. The second defines its borders with buildings and landscapes that limit views and access, a

VIEW OF ANTIOCH COLLEGE,
AT YELLOW SPRINGS, OHIO.

Antioch College: Informal

CONTRASTING LANDSCAPE CONCEPTS / Trinity College: Formal
From the beginning of landscape architecture as a profession oscillations between formal and informal
landscape concepts have generated significant place-making designs.   *Graphics:* Author's collection.

EDGES: FRACTURE AND DISSOLVE / Virginia Polytechnic Institute and State University
The challenge: curing autosprawl so as to give campus edges a defined and visually unifying landscape
treatment.   *Photo:* Courtesy Virginia Polytechnic Institute and State University.

scene not necessarily unfriendly when seen through campus gateways or fences if scale and detail are not monumental. Some resulting contrasts: In the Antiochian concept the buildings are situated in a landscape setting textured like a Humphry Repton vision of pastoral tranquility; in the Trinity model buildings are in a calibrated alignment so as to configure the landscape with geometric quads.

Antioch and Trinity were essentially walk-in campuses, with landscape concepts still valid, that is, degrees and mixes of formal and informal

PERIMETER REINFORCEMENT / Central Connecticut State University
Banners and directional signs are used to reinforce the perimeter design and to assist visitors in finding campus entry points, building locations, and parking. The consistent use of the university logo is a positive graphic device; the change in typeface is questionable.   *Photos:* R. P. Dober.

Central Connecticut State University

greenery. Prototypes, seminal and sparkling ideas, never fully built as illustrated, the pictographs are statements of design intentions and possibilities prior to invention of the internal-combustion engine. Instructive, then, is the air view of Virginia Polytechnic Institute and State University circa 1960. The story line here is the fracture and dissolve of the borders of older campuses in an attempt to accommodate vehicular traffic and parking. Wavelike, this impact affected the landscape treatment of VPI's historic lawn and connecting open spaces and the formation of an overall sense of place at the periphery. Solutions to these kinds of design challenges have occupied generations of landscape architects since the growth of higher education and automobile use in the mid-twentieth century.

SOFT EDGE TREATMENT / University of Utah
A pleasant composition of earth mounds, lawn, trees, and entry sign give this perimeter a welcoming sense of place.   *Photo:* R. P. Dober.

Following World War II at dozens of campuses, large parking lots too often became the image-controlling campus design element at the perimeter. Preparing for extensive growth, the University of Guelph campus plan (1963) addressed the issue of *autosprawl* (the negative side of parking dominating the campus scene) by applying new civic design principles to campus development. In these instances the perimeter is marked with permeable or solid boundaries, with varying combinations of greenery, fences, and walls; landscaped walks and roads may serve as both boundary definers and peripheral circulation. Earth mounding, trees, lighting, and signs are used to enhance the edges and to divide the extensive parking along the edge into a landscape more pleasant than a second-rate shopping mall or drive-in movie theater. See also "Campus Roads," page 106.

Most new campuses, acquiring sufficient land of an appropriate size and configuration, have been able to give their perimeter a visually attractive edge treatment. The 1962 plan for the new community college at San Mateo, California (page 109), anticipated the demeaning impacts seen at VPI. Landscape architect Michel Painter thus wrapped the San Mateo periphery in a soft blanket of trees and grass, green play fields and landscaped parking lots. On arrival one walks into a pleasant landscaped pedestrian precinct. The San Mateo model is particularly applicable to community colleges outside the core cities, where heavy volumes of commuting students, car dependent, are moving in and out of campus throughout the day.

Development along the periphery of the Radcliffe Quad (Cambridge, Massachusetts) is a good index to typical edge treatments. Three perimeter design concepts are evident along the boundaries of

AIR VIEW, CONTAINED PERIMETER / Radcliffe College
From the air and on the ground one of the best American urban campus quads, worth experiencing as a total design and as an index to perimeter treatments. One flaw: a small parking lot that deserves a more emphatic landscape screening. *Photo:* R. P. Dober.

PERIMETER CONCEPT A / Buildings, Planting Strip, Sidewalk

PERIMETER CONCEPT B / Closed Edge: Walls and Fences

Photos: R. P. Dober.

a self-contained campus area. These are (1) sidewalk, planting strip, and buildings, (2) trees and lawns, that is, an open perimeter design, and (3) walls and fences, that is, a closed perimeter design.

The same kinds of landscape design treatment along the edge can be applied to the perimeters of campus subsectors. Here, land uses and buildings that have a functional affinity will benefit from having an image-enhancing landscape perimeter treatment. A successful design formula for the precinct edge would include landscaped paths bounding the site, area-defining hedges, (or shrubs and vines), and an

A DELIGHTFUL EDGE / Trinity College, Connecticut
Perimeter designs along the edge of the campus precinct can help define the area's function, indicate its geographic position and entry point, and together create a landscape masterwork. *Photo:* Courtesy of Trinity College, Hartford, Connecticut.

MR. JEFFERSON'S PARADIGM / University of Virginia

The form is structurally significant, the resulting landscape a well-honored paradigm boundary marker. *Photo:* Library of Congress.

articulated and landscaped entry point. The grouping of buildings and landscapes can be arranged as a picturesque ensemble that can be seen or sensed as one approaches the area, as in the paradigm Trinity College residential enclave. Among modern examples, the Sasaki, Walker courtyard enclaves at Foothills Community College have this quality of ensemble design. Of single-stroke boundary markers, Thomas Jefferson's serpentine wall at Charlottesville is the honored paradigm.

2.3 BOUNDARY MARKERS

▶ A grand wall is a precious thing in a garden, and many are the ways of treating it. (Gertrude Jekyll, *Wall and Water Gardens* [London, 1934])

Like an herb or spice raising the flavor of an ordinary dish into a memorable meal, boundary markers help raise the quality of the perimeter design. Markers of this quality include elements such as special lighting along a bounding boulevard, soft elements such as banners, and hard elements such as walls and fences. The last get further attention here as an example of a component in our taxonomy long associated with higher education.

Walls are traditional campus boundary markers, not only for the larger perimeter treatments, but also at many places inside the campus where a physical, visual, or symbolic demarcation is desired. Walls are rich with social and cultural implications for campus design. The monastic tradition called for enclosure of contemplative enclaves; thus walls separated the secular and the sacred. Later in the Renais-

COLLEGIATE GOTHIC: PEEKABOO / Yale University
Silliman College gate—a secure boundary in the Collegiate Gothic style—provides a view into an attractive interior landscaped courtyard. *Photo:* R. P. Dober.

FENCE AS ICONIC BOUNDARY MARKER / Harvard University
Honored as a symbol, the fences and walls bounding Harvard Yard were extensively renewed through a $2.5 million historic restoration project.   *Photo:* R. P. Dober.

sance years, as town-gown conflicts approximated civil war, the walls fortified the university precinct against unwanted intrusion. Subsequently, the walls became barriers for preventing students from leaving their quarters after hours, illicit dispersion into urban dissipation. Such regulations are now in history's dustbin. Ironically, at Cambridge University and Oxford the walls are considered valuable protection from today's pesky tourists who wish to see and photograph the college landscapes and in their pursuit of a good photo op upset collegiate routines.

When the European monastic model informed late-nineteenth-century American campus design, walls again appeared as defining elements in the campus landscape—what one critic has skewered as "a choice bit of the sort of modern medieval that is accompanied by architectural artificiality." For some the faux was a worthwhile price to pay for highly textured and intricate architecture. In honored examples at Yale University's colleges, walls continue to be useful for all the traditional reasons: as a component of the building and landscape ensemble, as place markers, as armatures for greenery and memorials, and for security.

In the United States a second historical influence in campus landscapes can be seen in the attempts to reflect the Iberian tradition. Here walls are part of a domestic archetype in which there is a clear dividing line between public and private space. Occasionally this design impulse is translated into collegiate versions of the barrios, with walls that enclose a courtyard in an architectural style of white plaster and tile, with Baroque decorations, that signals tribute to its Hispanic origins.

The symbolic character of the perimeter boundary marker as a campus design element should not be neglected or underrated. For Harvard University (1993), the $2.5 million restoration of the hundred-year-old walls and fences around Harvard Yard was deemed as necessary as any building renewal. An icon in campus design, the composition of brick, wrought iron, limestone, and granite, straight and recessed, plain and decorated, was world renowned. A visible manifestation of custom and prestige, the restoration, with its challenging replication of fragments that had disappeared, required the fencing to be treated like a historical artifact.

These kinds of physical forms are heavy with emblematic import. Stillman College, in Tuscaloosa, Alabama, a historically black in-

Fashion Institute of Technology (FIT)

stitution, defined and proclaimed its perimeter with an inspiring Georgian-like wall and gateway (1998). It was a first step toward a "quest to become better" with a "well-ordered aesthetically pleasing campus." The campus and community reaction to this visible and significant landscape project had a positive effect on a fund-raising campaign for scholarships and educational programs. For similar reasons, the University of Minnesota launched a comparable campuswide edge landscape program "to project a positive image, and to invite public access to its programs and facilities." The work restored and completed some historic fencing and reinforced the boundary landscape with shrubs, trees, signs, and lighting. Without this marking, noted the university designers, "the collegiate environment spills unceremoniously into adjacent land masses, becomes fragmented, and presents itself to the public in a way that invites confusion, frustration and disorientation."

In the main, the idea of walls as protection from the unwanted seems antithetical to the spirit of American higher education, which gives high value to openness, transparency, and mobility. If we accept this posture, walls of an appropriate size and configuration can none-

WALLS: STRENGTHENING CAMPUS LIFE / Oklahoma State University (OSU)
Two boundary markers contributing to campus life. At FIT (*page 95*) a serpentine wall marks the edge of the building complex along a busy Manhattan street. At OSU the wall separates the library plaza from the adjacent lawn. In both instances the walls serve as informal outdoor seating areas. *Photos:* R. P. Dober.

WALL AS AMPHITHEATER / Bates College
A clever design by the Halvorson Group transforms the wall function (a change in grade defining the Olin Arts Center) into an outdoor amphitheater.   *Photo:* R. P. Dober.

theless be used beneficially as boundary markers, especially when designed as a gentle device for separating territory without fortifying it. At the Fashion Institute of Technology (New York City) the strip of greenery that divides the sidewalk from the building complex is enclosed by a serpentine wall. At Oklahoma State University, a wall separates the library plaza from the green lawn beyond. In both instances the walls serve as a comfortable and convenient sitting area, contributing to campus life. Walls of course serve other functions in the landscape; they can be an opaque curtain hiding an unwanted view (parking or a service dock), a windbreak, a garden enclosure, or a backdrop for greenery and sculpture. At Bates College the wall between the arts center and the lake is designed as an amphitheater.

2.4 GATEWAYS

Gateways are significant institutional symbols and physical statements of hello and goodbye. Given several thousand campuses in North America, averaging 100 acres, their total periphery would easily stretch

Christ Church College, Oxford

from Washington, D.C., to Detroit, Michigan. And if so arrayed, the entrance and exit points along that line could be cataloged as an instructive three-dimensional manual of landscape attitudes and fashions, a fascinating mix covering three centuries of purposeful and simple, dramatic as well as vapid landscape designs. Gateways provide access, obviously, but they also can physically and emblematically link land use areas, form view corridors into and out of campus, and serve ritual purposes. The visual progression of ceremonial front gate, walk, and prominent building in the distance has in some regions become an honored landscape design sequence.

Faux and monumental gateways, loaded with overtones and undertones of local cultural reference, can provide esthetic as well as mnemonic satisfaction. Brown University, for example, opens certain gates for the freshmen when they arrive in the autumn and other gates for the senior class on graduation day. At Bucknell University the remnants of a campus gate, the old sector boundary now blurred, stand out like megaliths, here honoring the deeds of athletic heroes since departed. Street closures enabled McPherson College (Kansas) to consolidate its land holdings. The resulting vehicle-free sector be-

GATEWAYS CLASSIC AND CONTEMPORARY / Santa Fe New Mexico Community College
The Oxford gate (Christopher Wren, 1681) and the New Mexico gateway, with their hints of greenery just beyond, communicate well differences in objectives (selective entrance versus welcome for all), time, taste, and technology. *Photos:* R. P. Dober.

CENTENARY GATEWAY / McPherson College
Land consolidation led to development of a landscaped central campus, which led to the construction of a celebratory campus gateway. Lesson: Large budgets are not needed for these kinds of place-making designs. *Graphic:* Author's collection.

came a landscaped precinct, entered via a college gate, that commemorated the college's one hundredth anniversary, in 1987. The University of Oklahoma centenary was similarly celebrated with a landscape design. Twin faux gates for the years 1890 and 1990 were situated on either side of a stone stele describing local events and personalities. The detailing of the gates evokes, but does not imitate, aspects of the university's first buildings.

Similarly, the symbolic gates at Indiana University (heaviest traffic enters elsewhere) are detailed to suggest associations and connections

University of Oklahoma

GATEWAYS AS PLACE MARKERS / Indiana University

Both examples use materials and detailing that recall the physical character of their historic first buildings; both give access to significant adjacent campus landscapes—for Oklahoma a series of cultivated gardens, for Indiana, a dense forested area. Limited automobile access is provided through roadways situated on both sides of the areas shown. *Photos:* R. P. Dober.

and affinities among early and current generations. For example, the Indiana gateway uses limestone, which carries the same implication as brick does in Harvard Yard. Both the Oklahoma and Indiana gates are connected to significant campus landscapes. The former gives entry to a splendid series of place-marking cultivated gardens. The latter abuts a dense collection of trees filling the university's front oval. Well con-

Pedestrians and Emergency Vehicles

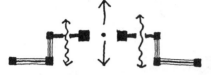

Pedestrians with Single Opening for Vehicles

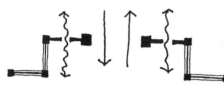

Pedestrians with Split Entry/Exit Opening for Vehicals

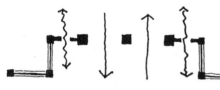

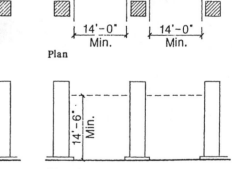

GATE TYPES

Typical gate types as defined by Moshe Safdie and Associates, Inc. (1989), in peripheral fence and gate study for the Harvard Business School. Actual designs can vary considerably in price. Variations include a mix of brick and granite for piers and side walls; type of metal gate, simple bar to decorative wrought iron; and barrier systems. *Graphic:* Author's collection.

102 Campus Landscape

SIMPLICITY / Oklahoma Panhandle State University

Five elements composing a utilitarian gateway, loaded with pride of place: the name of the institution, its values, and its mission; a sculpture celebrating local history, capping a stone wall large enough to be seen through an automobile windshield; wall materials suggesting the color and texture of regional vernacular architecture. *Photo:* R. P. Dober.

ceived and with emblematic significance, the first is a reminder of the university's transition from a raw and rugged pioneer college to a world-renowned research institution. The second is a visible reminder of the landscape as it was when Indiana University was founded. In these examples it is obvious (as Gertrude Stein might write) that a gateway is more than a gateway. Gateway design requires solving technical issues as well as ascertaining appropriate stylistic and cultural expression. Gate design will vary in type, width, and location in response to the functional mix of pedestrians and/or vehicles.

Related design issues include the size of the right of way; selection of computerized or manually operated barriers, if any; sign size, typography, and positioning; lighting; surface treatment of the gateway paved area and gradient; and the mix of trees and shrubs and planters that is to be included in the area design. Gates may be free-standing or connected to the abutting fencing, wall, or greenery. Some entry areas may have an information kiosk with a campus telephone system, and incorporate bus shelters. Boston College's main entrance, designed by Sasaki Associates, is a model example of this kind of mul-

MONUMENTALITY / Stanford University
A bold gateway, destroyed by an earthquake, then and now in memory an extraordinary campus landscape design element. *Photo:* Library of Congress.

INTERIOR EMBLEMATIC GATEWAYS / University of Arizona
These sculptural interior gateways (*above* and *right*) suggest points of entry to a campus sector. Excellent place markers and attention-gaining art, such designs are within the economic reach of most institutions. *Photos:* R. P. Dober.

University of Pennsylvania

tifunction gate. The materials and detailing echo the nearby Collegiate Gothic buildings. The security and information booth is immediately visible on entry but does not intrude into the neighboring boulevard.

Gates can include plaques and sculpture for memorial or commemorative purposes. At Oklahoma Panhandle State University, the main entry sign is capped with a statue of a farmer, a honorific gesture to the territory's first settlers. Of this type, the old gate at Stanford University in size and grandeur had (and has) few equals. Crumbled by the early-twentieth-century San Francisco earthquake, the sculpted three-dimensional eulogy to the university's founders combined the sentimentality of London's Albert Memorial with an archway of imperial Roman proportions. Less ponderous and most delightful are the sculptural place-marking gateways at the University of Pennsylvania and the University of Arizona. At New Mexico State University a symbolic "gateway to learning" on the library plaza signals with its shapes and plantings (palm trees) a visceral acknowledgment of the region's physical setting. These kinds of place markers are to be encouraged, particularly on large campuses, as they bring into public view artworks that enliven the campus scene. They also help generate among young people (one would hope) the kind of reaction and curiosity that higher education is supposed to generate—why this form, these plants, in this place? Of gateways devoted to moving automobiles in and out of campus with dispatch and safety, our comments on campus roads now follow.

2.5 CAMPUS ROADS

▶ A return to fundamentals would show us that garden design is the organization of space through which human beings are going to move. Rigidity, static formality, and blind obeisance to rules would then give way to fresh manipulation of materials. For instance, as a preliminary step one might follow a natural course over the ground, taking movies in order to record what movement over the ground suggests. The design of the garden might thus be as organic as the plants or the [site]. (Ray Faulkner, "An Approach to the Design of Landscapes" [*Landscape Architecture*, January 1936])

▶ [T]hought-provoking charts of pedestrian and automobile flow, pretty sketches of beautiful vistas, and well-done plans that achieve delicate balance between what is needed and what can be afforded mean nothing—absolutely nothing unless these plans have the proper follow through. (William Caudill, 1961)

▶ Circulation is an integral component of the Wellesley [College] campus landscape in terms of beauty, function, safety, clarity and wayfinding. (Michael Van Valkenberg Associates, Inc., *Wellesley College 1998 Campus Master Plan*)

———————

Campus roads are primary components in structuring the campus plan. Critical in any campus design pattern, yes; commanding and ruling, no. Roads should serve, not dominate, the campus scene. When carefully located, well designed, unrolling in a sequence that is visually interesting and informative, campus roads will be perceived as positive campus landscape elements. When they are treated as the shortest and cheapest route from place to place, obscure in their layout and frustrating in their cues as to direction, intersecting too often with pedestrian progress, they become safety hazards, obstacles to convenient movement, and a visual blight.

Functionally, campus roads carry vehicular traffic to and from the campus entry and exit points to various campus destinations. Heaviest volume is usually seen by parking areas, secondarily by building delivery docks or equivalent portals and pedestrian drop-off and pickup stations. Campus roads provide access for service and emergency vehicles, and some are arterial routes for campus and public transportation systems. As to forms and features, campus roads are overlays of campus planning, traffic engineering, and landscape architecture decisions. The dividing line as to responsibility may be blurred depending on the level and complexity of the design being articulated.

Four overriding principles seem evident at campuses where one would immediately recognize higher-quality campus landscape. Conventionally, pedestrian traffic is separated from vehicular traffic. A hierarchy of roads is utilized to structure and inform the broader campus land use patterns and the campus design image. Right-of-way design provides orderly cues and signs for channeling and controlling the traffic movement, especially where travel lanes are shared and direction may be uncertain for the visitor or absentminded. And all the physical components that generate the road experience are carefully detailed so that the pieces in the ensemble have some perceptible degree of visual affinity and consistency.

As a skeleton shapes the body, campus roads can be used to structure campus design. Landscape is added to flesh out the form, and in variety can engender becoming features that reinforce the objective of establishing a sense of place. Three honored examples illustrate the range of possibilities. The first is from the center of high-tech automobile manufacturing and high-speed travel, the second from a state that in popular literature has long been associated with the "car culture," and the third from a region that has traditionally sought a balanced view of the built environment. All three date from the early 1960s, a time when it became apparent that campus vehicular traffic and parking could no longer be treated as secondary components in campus design. Ad hoc solutions were deficient and damaging to functional and visual coherence in the built environment.

Bochum University (Germany) represents the compact, rationalized solution. Automobile traffic is carried directly from the adjacent autobahns to parking areas stacked beneath tiers of high-density buildings. The integrated complex is sandwiched between botanical

Campus roads are primary components in structuring the campus plan. Critical in any campus design pattern, yes; commanding and ruling, no. Roads should serve, not dominate, the campus scene.

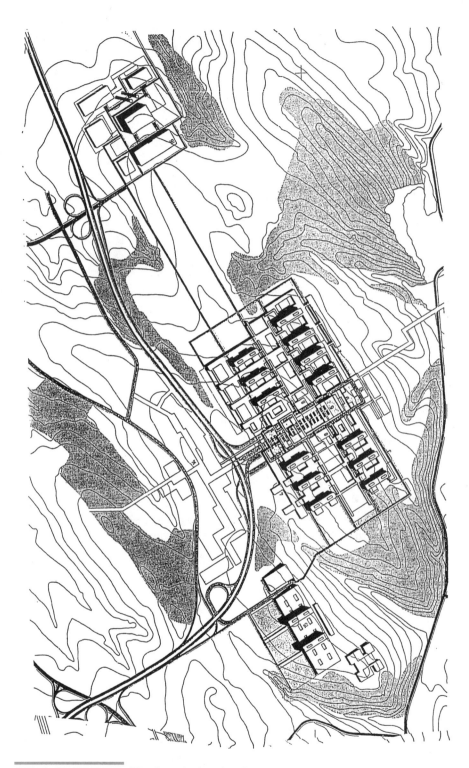

AUTO ORIENTED / Bochum University, Germany
Situated in an automobile-manufacturing region, intended to be a model campus, the total design was a marvel of rationalized engineering. The main megastructure is fitted into a landscape of gardens and forests, the roads and parking zones compact and efficient.   *Graphic:* Author's collection.

gardens and green spaces, with attractive views from the terraces to farms, forests, and hamlets nearby and on the far horizon. Much praised on its opening day as a model of methodical space planning and industrialized ferroconcrete building techniques, the executed concept now seems severely flawed by the bulky, repetitive building forms and the gray, monotone exterior facades.

The College of San Mateo is a representative sample of California's contribution to campus road design. As at Bochum, the buildings are grouped to form a vehicle-free precinct, in the San Mateo instance a linear pedestrian mall. The entrance roads feed the large parking lots and loop around the perimeter of the mall, like in a shopping center, with a major ceremonial drop-off area with guest parking and secondary service points. Where the Bochum campus landscape involves broad green

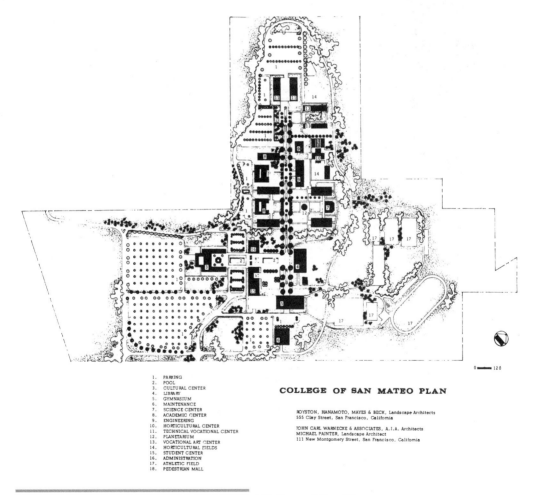

1. PARKING
2. POOL
3. CULTURAL CENTER
4. LIBRARY
5. GYMNASIUM
6. MAINTENANCE
7. SCIENCE CENTER
8. ACADEMIC CENTER
9. ENGINEERING
10. HORTICULTURAL CENTER
11. TECHNICAL VOCATIONAL CENTER
12. PLANETARIUM
13. VOCATIONAL ART CENTER
14. HORTICULTURAL FIELDS
15. STUDENT CENTER
16. ADMINISTRATION
17. ATHLETIC FIELD
18. PEDESTRIAN MALL

COLLEGE OF SAN MATEO PLAN

ROYSTON, HANAMOTO, MAYES & BECK, Landscape Architects
555 Clay Street, San Francisco, California

JOHN CARL WARNECKE & ASSOCIATES, A.I.A. Architects
MICHAEL PAINTER, Landscape Architect
111 New Montgomery Street, San Francisco, California

MIDCENTURY CALIFORNIA CLASSIC / College of San Mateo
A fine example of campus roads surrounding and framing the pedestrian-oriented campus core with landscaped parking lots and recreation fields on the perimeter. *Graphic:* Author's collection.

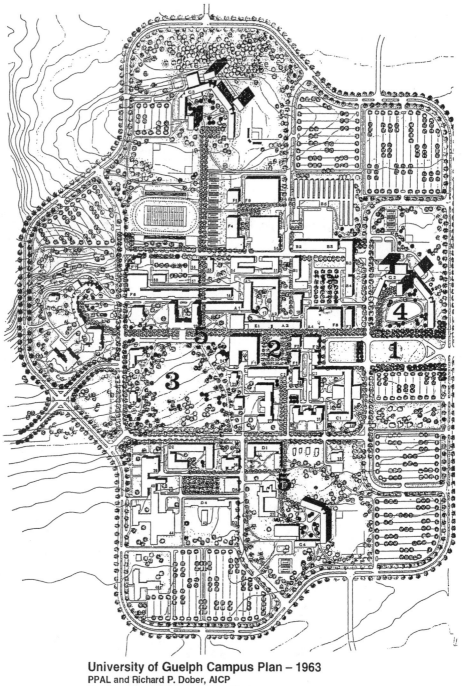

University of Guelph Campus Plan – 1963
PPAL and Richard P. Dober, AICP
Sert, Jackson and Gourley, Consultants

A HIERARCHICAL CAMPUS ROAD SYSTEM / University of Guelph, Canada
Applying a hierarchical road system: Major landscaped roads outline the campus perimeter, from which a formal entry (1) is designated. Secondary roads give access to campus precincts. Major campus pedestrian walks (5) capable of carrying service and emergency vehicles serve the central campus and connect it to other areas. A variety of special landscapes can be seen from the peripheral road and internal circulation elements, such as the old quad (3) and new landscapes (2 and 4).   *Graphic:* Author's collection.

brush strokes, the California concepts typically have a fine-grained land-scape pattern of interior courtyards and gardens surrounded by large playing fields and generously landscaped roads and paths.

The University of Guelph (Canada) utilizes aspects of the Ger-man and California circulation concepts to structure development zones at a campus that was tripling in size. Concurrently it was seeking to symbolize in its campus design, through landscape, the unity of three previously independent colleges that would be sharing the same site and common services. A circular road defines the perimeter, giving ready access to large parking lots. There is a primary, formal ceremonial road and gateway and several secondary entries. A nascent spine was strengthened with landscape to carry pedestrian and controlled vehicu-lar traffic (service and emergency) east and west through the central campus. The route is tied into two additional pedestrian spines to the north and south, capable of carrying service and emergency vehicles. Secondary curving roads, an intentionally contrasting departure from the linear, are used to place-mark several residential zones where the topography and building functions so dictate.

Hierarchy is a design classification system in which the road forms (number of lanes and layout) reflect differences in campus population, acreage, and mix of residents and commuters, and in turn vehicular volume, speed, and road location. In principle campus road capacity is higher at the periphery and lower at the core, reflecting the desire to develop vehicle-limited pedestrian zones in central campus. On cam-puses with extensive acreage, segments of the road system may resem-ble parkways and boulevards leading to the central campus. Close in to the central campus the cross section may be limited to two lanes, or a one-way loop road may be utilized. On smaller campuses the vehicular rights-of-way may have to be shared with pedestrians, thus roads and walks are designed as a functional unit. As to features, that is, detailing the campus road system, the campus landscape design choices include paving, curbing, curb cuts and cross paths, cutouts for emergency park-ing, signs, lighting, trees, traffic signals, banners, and sometimes park-ing meters. Here Caudill's caveat on "follow through" becomes an imperative for good design, especially if melded with Faulkner's plea for circulation design as motion realized as a kinetic art with landscape inflections.

Campus road design requires good signage. Objective: a graphic program that begins to instruct the traveler at the periphery as to where to enter campus and how to find one's way inside the perimeter. The program would include entry identifiers, a campus map, direc-tional signs that help sort out primary, secondary, and service routes, parking instructions, and banners and placards that announce the location of temporary events and how to get there. Designs for some signs, including speed limit, stop, yield, and pedestrian crossing signs, are configured by legal regulations and accepted practices. Others can be customized with the institutional colors, logo, and other signifiers; these constitute an art form when visually unified and arrayed along the roads or paths.

2.6 CAMPUS WALKS

▶ When the landscape architect comes to apply to the actual problems which he handles professionally the knowledge with which his experience has provided him, he tries to meet the demands of each problem with a design which, though most necessarily sacrificing some factors which are theoretically desirable, combines on the whole the maximum of esthetic and economic excellence possible for him to create under the particular circumstances. (Henry Vincent Hubbard and Theodora Kimball, *An Introduction to the Study of Landscape Architecture* [New York, 1917])

▶ Adequate wayfinding is not synonymous with simplicity and simpleness; environmental complexity stimulates interest, curiosity and exploration. Wayfinding is a dynamic affair. It involves movement through space and a continuous involvement in reading, interpreting, and representing space.... Wayfinding is closely linked with experiencing space in a physical mental and emotional sense. It is no doubt an essential ingredient in architectural appreciation. (Romedi Passini, *Wayfinding in Architecture* [New York, 1984])

Because of differences in purpose and assignment, some campus architecture is not entered or experienced daily. Everyone uses the campus walk system, however. People who move through the landscape as many as a dozen times a day deserve to have a functional, convenient, safe, beautiful, and uplifting design experience as they journey from place to place on campus walks, casually or on a schedule. In the central campus the routes should be direct, linked, continuous, free of conflicts with vehicles. Outside the central campus, meandering paths may be acceptable for esthetic and recreational reasons. Thus required are campus walk designs that capture and communicate a sense of place, respond to the realities of contemporary life, and, with skill and élan, meld the broader requisites of site location and topography with the minutiae of exquisite detailing.

The campus walk system is a significant *campus design determinant.* In principle, a well-designed pedestrian-oriented campus will have

People who move through the campus as many as a dozen times a day deserve to have a functional, convenient, safe, beautiful, and uplifting design experience as they journey from place to place on campus walks, casually or on a schedule.

PATH LOCATION AND DESIGN / Bates College
Campus paths are the arteries of campus life. Well located and landscaped, they make major contributions to campus design. Variations in plant materials, reflections of climate and region, will strengthen the sense of place. *Photo:* Courtesy of Bates College.

most of its buildings, landscapes, and walks situated within a (largely) vehicle-free zone whose diameter can be traversed on foot in about ten minutes. Obviously, the land holdings and topography will shape the configuration, so a circle is not the necessary form; the principle is the approximate distance. Assuming walking speeds of from 3.5 to 4.0 miles per hour and gradients of less than 4 percent, the space thus defined will be in the 100- to 125-acre range. Land this size would be an appropriate central campus area for most institutions. Additional acreage would be necessary for large universities, and beneficial for smaller institutions. The additional acreage can be designated as campus subsectors or precincts that are devoted to clustering compatible and synergetic land use functions, for example, residential facilities, professional schools, research centers, fields for outdoor recreation and athletics, satellite parking, gardens, arboreta, buffers from surrounding land uses, and amenities. In these instances, the central campus walk systems would be linked to the precinct walks.

University of Arizona
Photo: R. P. Dober.

Iowa State University
Graphic: Courtesy of Johnson, Johnson, Roy.

Campus walks will vary in size, length, cross section, and surface treatment. Physical forms include open walks across the lawns, tree-lined walks, walks through groves and arbors, walks that are along arcades or under building overhangs, walks built as breezeways, walks that become bridges or tunnels, and walks that enter or leave a building as part of a continuous pedestrian network. The landscape designer's varying interpretation of each of these can offer significant visual and visceral pleasure. Path systems can be also organized so as to set and reinforce the physical framework that defines the perimeters and boundaries of the campus and its precincts and subsectors. The absence of suitable landscape is dramatized in the early air view of Lamar University, a distressing scene that has since been well remedied with subsequent plantings. The delights of good design are evident in the segment of the University of Pennsylvania's Locust Walk on page 118 and in the walk at Cornell University on page vii.

CROSSOVERS / Berkshire Community College
Campus walks can pass through buildings, over roads, and traverse steep topography, and the surrounding campus landscape can be arranged accordingly. The University of Arizona bridge building (*page 114*) offers views and vistas below and to the horizon. The Iowa State University pedestrian bridge (*page 115*) connects at both ends with place-marking landscape. The bridgehead at Berkshire Community College is a gem, with its bell tower and ivy-covered walls suggesting a contemporary affinity to collegiate New England. *Photo* (Berkshire): R. P. Dober.

LANDSCAPE: THE MISSING ELEMENT / Lamar University
The missing element: the absence of landscape, particularly along the campus paths, is a self-evident design deficiency, remedied in subsequent years.   *Photo:* Courtesy Lamar University Press.

As a design experience, travel along campus walks inevitably, consciously or otherwise, will affect one's sense of being in a mediocre or high-quality landscape environment. Highly prized are network systems that separate pedestrian traffic from vehicular, this being a campus landscape objective that should be given highest priority in campus development. As to their features, path systems afford singular opportunities to install landscape design concepts that resonate with symbolic and physical imagery and appeal to many aspects of the sensorium.

How? Sight, of course, is one way. The immediate view of surrounds, the glimpses of views and vistas along the way, the appreciation of spatial sequence in moving from area to area, special night lighting to indicate the safest way to traverse campus—these are the by-products of attentive campus landscape design. As to sound, how pleasant to hear the buzz of a lively crowd as classes change and people move along an attractive route amidst landscaping that muffles noise from nearby automobiles. For the visually impaired or absent-mined, a change in paving texture can announce an intersection or road crossing. Temperature differences from landscape-induced sun and shadow effects can be recognized along the route, sometimes in

University of Pennsylvania
Locust Walk
*George Patton
Landscape Architect*

LOCUST WALK / University of Pennsylvania
A model treatment by landscape architect George Patton, with paving, ground cover, lighting, and trees intelligently detailed and selected for easy maintenance. *Photo:* Courtesy of George Patton.

concert with landscape materials or earth mounds that mediate the inclement winds. Tactility can be perceived underfoot in the selection of materials—soft, as with tan bark and crushed rock, to hard, as with combinations of concrete, tile, and brick. In some regions the crunch of autumn leaves is associated with campus life. These choices may also be affected by the ambiance desired (urban versus bucolic), as well as use and maintenance requirements and compatibility with the adjacent landscape. Noteworthy are chromatic epiphanies where the forms and texture of varying plant and tree forms lining and embracing the walks, with their modulated shades and tints of green, raise the campus landscape along the pedestrian routes to an artwork non-pareil.

Topographic changes can be sensed. Many attractive paths are those circuits where landscape architects have intentionally and carefully fitted the design of the walks to the contours so that the change in elevation is as comfortable as it is becoming. Straight lines and right-angled intersections reinforce formal designs. Looping and curving paths are found in the picturesque schemes. In these instances paths and trees have a design affinity. Trees along the paths can be selected to obscure or reveal the nearby landscape, to carry the eye through a tunnel effect, or to blend in with the hard-edged or soft-edged abutting spaces.

By manipulating and orchestrating the hierarchy of paths and their location, designers can create clues and cues for regulating the direction of movement. Path width and surface treatment help inform the hierarchy. Width and gradient are also technical issues that if casually treated and inadequately funded will diminish if not cancel out good intentions. Slopes up to 3 percent are preferred, but up to 5 percent seem permissible; steeper inclines may be best treated as a ramp. The width of campus walks can be calculated through manuals devoted to the subject. In the main, space for six people abreast, or a 15-foot-wide path, would be a major walk on most campuses. Paths narrower than 6 feet should be avoided. These rules of thumb are adjustable to local site conditions and climate. The needs of the handicapped are also well known and regulated, though not always recognized sufficiently in path design.

Along the walks, trees can be disposed cosmetically. The nuisance and cost of cleaning up fruits, nuts, or samaras from shedding trees may be counterbalanced by the color and texture they offer. Tree sizes, estimated at maturity, can be arrayed to mediate and temper scale changes from the human to the institutional to the monumental. In some instances large shrubs can be substituted for trees, and some interesting designs now under consideration use trellises to hang or grow plants along segments of the paths—green walls for decoration and visual barriers. What landscape architect Prentiss French calls the "ornamenting process," however, should not obscure the technical issues of width and gradient. "As with dress," French reminds us, "planting can ameliorate the appearance of a bad framework, but it can never make it into a genuinely good one."

Add to path design the more recent challenge of skateboarding, which fluent and well-designed paths attract like the proverbial flies to the honey pot. Notes Queen's University campus security (1999): Many reported incidents "are the results of phone calls from staff, students or

Highly prized are network systems that separate pedestrian traffic from vehicular, this being a campus landscape objective that should be given priority in campus development.

faculty complaining they cannot study, work or write because of the noise of skateboarders. As well, skateboarders like to skate and jump off concrete walls and planters, causing property damage that is unsightly and expensive to repair. If you have ever sat on a concrete bench that has been waxed and used by skateboarders, you will know the impact this activity has on clothing; especially light colored clothing."

Some Choices

Six kinds of path imagery will now be cited to illustrate variety and amplitude in landscape designs: the picturesque, the traditional, the dominant spine, the composite, the symbolic, and the contemporary. These are calculated, excogitated works; thus not included in the overview are the informal paths, visible and usually decrepit, carved into the landscape by faculty, staff, and students in locations where planners and designers too often have failed to see the likely shortcuts.

Of the picturesque, Addison's Walk at Oxford University merits first mention for several reasons: age, continuity, and the influence the design has had on generations of advocates and admirers of "nat-

ADDISON'S WALK / Oxford University
Arguably the most influential of the early informal, picturesque campus walks. Modified several times in response to changing topographic conditions and the maturity and suitability of the ground covers and trees, it remains a paradigm and icon of campus landscape beauty.   *Graphic:* Author's collection.

THE DIAG / University of Michigan
An epitome of paths shaping the prototypical American campus, the Diag's importance is recognized in a century of campus stewardship and administrative leadership, which in recent years has encouraged the university to develop a variety of world-renowned campus landscapes.   *Graphic:* Courtesy of Frederick W. Mayer.

ural gardening" in university settings. The quotes here and below are from the famed eighteenth-century esthetician Joseph Addison. His daily perambulations through the Magdalen College grounds and along the campus waterside paths were said to inspire his rejection of the then fashionable formal French landscape concepts and the fussy Dutch arrangements of trees and shrubs. He deplored greenery that was scissored and scalped into "Cones, Globes, and Pyramids." Wrote Addison, "I would rather look upon a tree in all its Luxuriancy and Diffusion of Boughs and Branches than when it is thus cut and trimmed into a Mathematical Figure . . . and cannot but fancy that an Orchard in Flower looks infinitely more delightful than all the little Labyrinths of the most finished parterre."

Addison's essays in *The Spectator* gave generations of Oxford poets and pundits cause to "form the Imagination" as they wandered through the "verdure of the Grass, Embroidery of the Flowers and the Glist'ning of the Dew." The lovely scene in 1999, in appearance ripe with an ancient landscape outwardly stilled by unchanging time, is not a natural campus landscape discovered and conserved but actually an artificial work of art constantly adjusted to site realities and use. The original sixteenth-century causeway and Addison's paths have been

CAMPUS WALK: SPINE VERSION / Rochester Institute of Technology
The Stubbins Associates walk a decade after the original planting; good landscape effects take time to mature.
Photo: Author's collection.

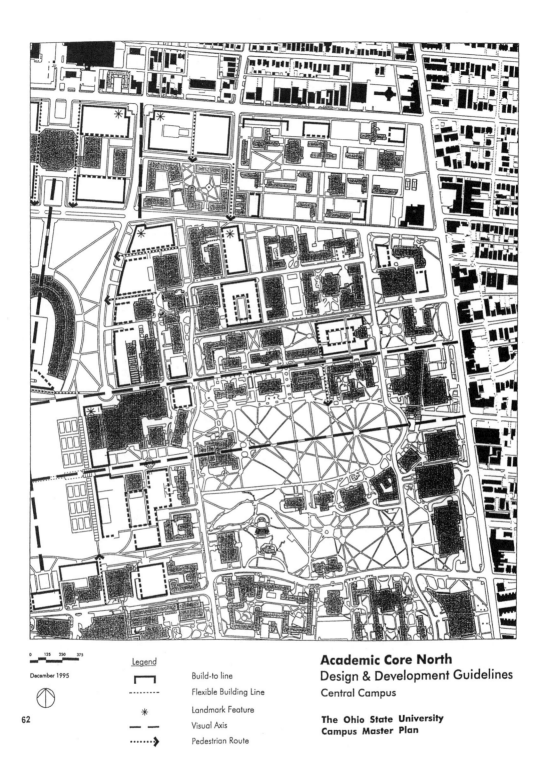

0   125 250 375

December 1995

62

Legend

⊓   Build-to line

----------   Flexible Building Line

✳   Landmark Feature

— —   Visual Axis

·······▶   Pedestrian Route

Academic Core North
Design & Development Guidelines
Central Campus

The Ohio State University
Campus Master Plan

WALKS AS DESIGN STRUCTURE / Ohio State University
Sasaki Associates' strategic objective: locate new walks to optimize views and vistas into and from the historic central campus landscape.   *Graphic:* Sasaki Associates, Inc., for the Ohio State University.

altered several times for flood control, security, and unobstructed walking. In the past decade oaks and red alders have replaced beech trees, which were difficult to maintain on sloping banks. Though as contrived as a Disneyland scene, Addison's Walk is a stroll through a memorable landscape experience, authentic in spirit if not in kind.

The "Diag" at the University of Michigan, an honored central campus crosswalk system, is a historic example of traditional path designs that inform and mark many American campuses. At Michigan the importance of paths as campus design structuring devices is easily recognized in the university's archival plans and graphics, where they can be seen to help configure a prototypical American open-quad concept. Shade trees line the paths and the bounding perimeter street in a predictable order; lawns and trees are the iconic interior landscape; simplicity in design treatment is de rigueur.

Paths can be charged with symbolic and emblematic import. Brick being the material associated since the seventeenth century with campus design at the College of William and Mary, several paths through the woods separating campus precincts there are paved with brick. Trinity College (Connecticut) celebrates graduation with a cavalcade along its triumphant "Long Walk." Here can be seen a remnant of history, a piece of a larger formal quadrangular design, never completed, with its straight-line paths axial in homage to Oxbridge precedents.

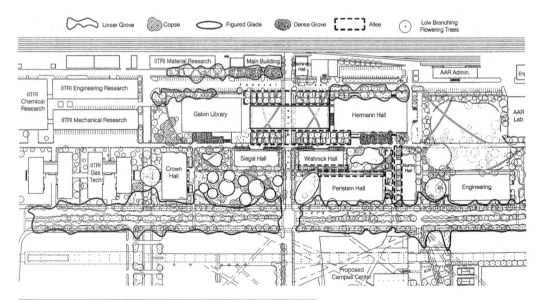

CONTRAST, MODULATION, AND COMPLEXITY / Illinois Institute of Technology

Six kinds of landscape expression are utilized to connect the pieces into a visual entity and to add, says designer Michael Van Valkenburgh, "an expressive character of landscape to play against the more solemn beauty of the campus architecture." The plan calls for about 1,200 new trees, many of them along and embracing the campus walks. *Graphic:* Courtesy Michael Van Valkenburgh.

University of Massachusetts, Amherst

BECKONING VISTAS / Kingsborough Community College
Paths, buildings, and landscapes can be sequenced and composed to draw attention to major destinations along the routes as well as for visual interest.   *Photos:* R. P. Dober

Though truncated by the necessity to provide a site for a library, Howard University's "Long Walk," coincidental in name with Trinity's, is also replete with symbolism and rich with memories of campus purpose and place. Also a scene of commencement processions, once forbidden territory for freshman—a rule enforced by upperclassmen—and now a secondary route through campus, the path remains a visible reminder of institutional aspiration and achievement.

The Main Mall at the University of British Columbia exemplifies the dominant spine—a long, landscaped mall or promenade essentially limited to pedestrian traffic. The western end of the major path at UBC is punctuated with a rose garden constructed over a parking garage. A crescent-shaped drop-off for buses and taxis terminates the eastern end. Gardens and landscapes are positioned along the spine. As one walks the main path the esthetic experiences unroll like an oriental scroll, with impressions that are often subtly different in appearance from day to day with the changing weather and light. Particularly pleasant is the area that visually connects the new library and the old with an open courtyard whose stone walls are mute reminders of the textured facades of the university's earlier buildings nearby. For its combinations of all-season greenery, lighting, flags, sculpture, surface treatment, intersecting paths, and spatial sequence, the main walk at the Rochester Institute of Technology is a good example of a shorter version of the dominant spine concept.

The composite path system is well represented at Ohio State University. The first buildings were grouped (some later critics say scattered) around an oval and adjacent secondary green space. The oval had paths situated in a faux Beaux Arts concept, with a dominant visual axis connecting the main library and the administration building and auditorium. Paths in the adjacent green space were less formal. As growth occurred outside the historic central area in the twentieth century, linear paths were introduced with T-square regularity. The 1995 campus design guidelines (Sasaki Associates) use the path system and building frontage, new and added, to orchestrate an intricate site-sensitive landscape strategy, balancing respect for the historic landscape with the need to accommodate significant growth with a lattice of straight and right-angled paths. At the Illinois Institute of Technology, the T-square campus design is animated with a richer palette.

Library Walk at the University of California, San Diego, is a casebook example of contemporary path design, noteworthy in its gestures to conventional landscape concepts that have been reinterpreted with the flair and fashion that the cognoscenti would associate with modern California landscape design. On approach, the straight-line path leads the eye to the temple of knowledge, the main library. During passage the wayfarer will experience a mini arbor on one side of the route and sculpture gardens on the other. The decorated paving is

Sweet Briar College
Photo: Sweet Briar College.

West Texas A & M
Photo: R. P. Dober.

edged with minimalist rectangular stones, each inscribed with the
year of a graduating class.

Orchestrating visual sequences along campus paths is akin to the
art of cinema. Foreground and background, close-ups and panoramas,
space opening and closing—many of these perceptible and delightful
impressions of campus landscape while in motion or at rest can be
predetermined. Skyscape and landscape can be melded with dramatic
results. The best will take a predictable end-of-the-path view and add
a surprising vista. Maggie Roe's work in training trees, pleaching for
spatial effects, represents some landscape ideas not yet fully present
on American campuses. With the advent of computer-aided devices
designers can construct three-dimensional simulations of their ideas
for path design and adjust accordingly. When the computer technology is not available, the mapping of site features discussed on page 58
will help inform path designs that recognize site realities and possibilities in the planning stages.

Few campuses have a single uniform path design system, though
several have attempted to establish landscape design criteria in the
expectation that uniformity will please the eye and make more discernable the overall campus design structure. The older the campus
the more likely it is to have diverse architecture. The truism is applicable to the path systems, especially in detailing. Appearance, stability,

ALONG THE WAY / Pennsylvania State University
Superb scenic effects can be achieved when path designs are integrated with adjacent buildings and landscapes, as in Sweet Briar College's delightful composition of arcades, terraces, and seating areas (*page 127*). The view of the coarse, sparse, and forbidding building at West Texas A&M would suggest an opportunity to raise the quality of the campus landscape in an area visible to the public—a quality well illustrated in EDAW's Pennsylvania State University project. *Photo:* Pennsylvania State University; Dixi Carrillo/EDAW, Inc.

initial cost, and continuing maintenance form an equation that must be solved for satisfactory designs. The selection of paving color and texture, curbing, and scale can be likened to writing a major symphony, with each instrument contributing a singular sound as well as a collective voice.

PLEACHING AND VISUAL EFFECTS

Maggie Roe's exploratory designs for pleaching trees along campus walks. Such could bring back into fashion modern versions of late Renaissance landscape design. *Graphic:* Author's collection.

As noted earlier, surface choices are plentiful—macadam, concrete, granite, brick, pounded earth, crushed stone, river-washed and glaciated gravel, and occasionally an exotic material so different from the customary that it announces that one is entering or passing through a special place. The mix and changes of materials can give clues to direction or safe passage, interdict entry, or arbitrarily paint the surface three-dimensionally to the designer's whim and fancy. One surface can be separated from another with thin strips or wider designs of a contrasting material and shape, or with metallic or stone trim, set flush, indented, raised. The corners can be utilitarian, rustic, or shaped as an art object. Eccentric combinations should be questioned if visual continuity is the desired goal.

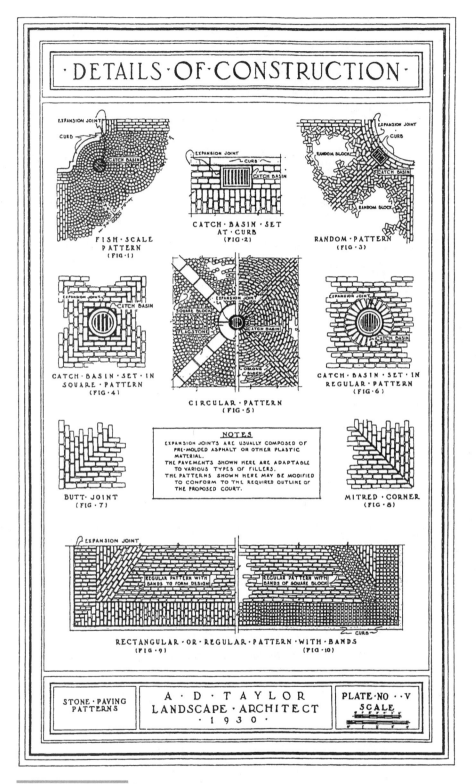

CLASSIC DETAILS

Detailing sheet for paving from one of the early twentieth century's master landscape designers, A. D. Taylor. *Graphic:* Author's collection.

CONTEMPORARY DETAILING / College of Santa Fe
Simplicity supreme: crushed stone, pavers, lane markers.   *Photo:* R. P. Dober.

Simple path components such as curbstones and water channels can vary in length and thickness, be straight-edged and rounded, battered, truncated, or flared. Gratings inserted for drainage can be stylized, suggesting compatibility with buildings and landscapes of a recognizable architectural period. In the right location textured surfaces are artworks; that they are treated as such is evident in construction drawings from past masters. This attention to detail can reinforce the sense of place. Bollards come in many forms: metal, carved granite, cast stone, with and without reflectors and built-in lighting. Size and placement should be treated like in-situ sculpture, though in some areas a readily perceived tank-trap effect might be considered necessary to keep out undesired vehicular traffic. Here metal fixtures may communicate a warning (no entry) better than stone.

The solution at the University of Birmingham has a reasonable balance of function, form, and features. Textured pavement defines the juncture of road and pedestrian paths, a becoming visual contrast with the mounded grass and trees on the other side. The bollards, with inserted lights, are positioned to keep vehicular traffic from parking or entering the precinct, yet the overall design is sufficiently permeable to permit and welcome pedestrians.

University of Birmingham
Photo: Courtesy of Hugh Casson.

CONTEMPORARY DETAILS / University of Pennsylvania
Bollards and paving define where walks intersect with adjacent courtyards and signal vehicles not to trespass.
Photo: R. P. Dober.

Stability and a smooth surface treatment—wrinkled paths being another indictable offense—come with experienced hands detailing and constructing the wearing course, basic course, subbase, formation level, and subgrade. Beware of expedient solutions and budgets. The thickness of each and provision for drainage will depend on existing soil and site conditions and projected use. In certain climes special allowances will be made for snow removal and heavy rainfall.

Some routes must be designed to accommodate joint occupancy by vehicles and pedestrians—building service and maintenance, emergency and security, goods delivery and trash pickup, moving in and out of residents' belongings or scientists' lab equipment or the music department's piano. Here again thoughtful planning and landscape design will mediate potentially adverse conditions.

Activity space along the line and the line itself are interconnected. Numerous teaching-learning exchanges occur at predictable hours

unpleasant	pleasant
depressing	elevating
disturbing	peaceful
unhealthy	healthy
unsuitable	suitable
irritating	relaxing
simple	exclusive
ugly	beautiful
negative	positive
careless	careful
useless	useful
untidy	tidy
heavy	light
nasty-smelling	fragrant
noisy	silent
unfriendly	friendly
dirty	clean
dreary	daring
cold	hot
leaves me unaffected	engaging
agitating	calm
mitigating	activating
impersonal	personal
idle	energetic
harsh	idyllic
irrational	rational
passive	active
conservative	radical
discouraging	stimulating
inadequate	adequate
uncomfortable	comfortable
stale	fresh
worthless	precious
uninteresting	interesting

a **b**

straight ——
rounded ——

STRAIGHT AND CURVED PATHS / Hesselgren's Conclusions
Column A, negative values; column B, positive values. When asked for their preferences between straight, head-on vistas and those arranged in a curving site design, the people questioned showed no preference for one over the other. *Graphic:* Author's collection.

and in different locations. At times path designs must take into account movement that must approximate the accuracy of a flight plan. And, of course, campus life has many casual moments where passage is not so bound to the clock. Conceptually, the design of the walk system can account for both circumstances.

Path design sometimes seems like folklore inflected by custom. Models from elsewhere were accepted and emulated in a language with no words for boredom and dysfunction, nor even a syntax for critical questioning. Welcomed, then, in recent years has been some interesting research published by social scientists who have spent considerable time actually observing and measuring human behavior and spatial perception as people use and walk through various environments. Not unexpectedly, they discovered multiple functional and design interactions. many interdependent. One's use of the route and participation in the activities along the route impact and are impacted by one's esthetic understanding and appreciation of the built environment. The perceptions of being in a particular physical place and one's progress through it (and one's satisfaction or dissatisfaction with the journey) can be influenced by the quality of the designed environment. Documented research of this quality and focus can purge arbitrary designs from the design process. As noted in our Factor X comments earlier, these kinds of investigations throw out some provocative leading questions. Do people prefer straight or curved lines? The Swedish architectural theoretician Sven Hesselgren provides one answer in his punctilious and still relevant book *Man's Perception of the Man-Made Environment* (Stroudsburg, 1975).

Wayfinding is the overall term for this aspect of applied perception psychology. In prodigious works such as Kevin Lynch's *Form of the City* (Cambridge, 1962), researchers have articulated descriptive vocabularies for defining and evaluating elements of the perceived environment, and by implication have outlined ways to design strong images and strengthen the weak. Lynch's vocabulary included *path, edge, district, node,* and *landmark.* Clarity in the forms and routes of movement was given high value, though Lynch himself, and several of his assistants, much enjoyed the visual ambiguity of historic Italian hill towns and dense, unstructured urban areas.

Lynch's studies were conducted with the discipline associated with his home institution, the Massachusetts Institute of Technology. Equally weighty was Gordon Cullen's coeval *Townscape* (London, 1962), informal, more poetic, and less procedural. Both treatises stimulated decades of research and discussions about quality or lack of it in the built and imagined environment. Gradually and productively this kind of insight and information was integrated into the curricula at professional schools and in examinations for licensing.

Orchestrating visual sequences along campus paths is akin to the art of cinema. Foreground and background, close-ups and panoramas, space opening and closing—many of these perceptible and delightful impressions of campus landscape while in motion or at rest can be predetermined.

Christ Church College, Oxford

CONTRASTING STYLES / University of Illinois

As in all campus landscape, there are contrasting choices among paradigm designs. The eighteenth-century Christ Church walks serving the adjacent library exemplify the swirling Palladian approach to path design, the University of Illinois designs the more typical straight-line American campus walk system. The latter example, designed by Sasaki Associates, includes a center-strip bicycle path.   *Photos:* R. P. Dober.

University of Utah

CONTRASTING TREATMENTS / Miami University, Ohio

Excellent and contrasting place-marking landscape treatments. At the University of Utah, the path runs parallel to the building, terminating at a green sitting area. At the University of Miami, rows of cultivated flowers, shrubs, and trees reinforce the direction of the path, straight-line in contrast with the Palladian curvature and jagged edge at Utah. *Photos:* R. P. Dober.

Let us cite some further words now from Cullen's gloss in concluding our comments and recommendations on this component of the typology. His fine eye, thought-provoking essays, and superb graphics revealed how grand gestures and mundane details can be melded into an art of visual choice and manipulated for scenic effect, social ends, and striking images. Thus his praise for undulation in path design; it is "not just an aimless wiggly line; it is the compulsive departure from an unseen axis or norm; and its motive is delight in such proofs and essences of life...it demonstrates the range of possibilities in one situation."

Cullen again: "By attention to detail, by training the eye to see detail, the man-made world starts to grow in interest and quality." Favoring "entanglement" in detailing path design and the physical components that constitute physical surrounds, Cullen believed that "[w]hat to the quick glance have no significance, come to life upon more study." On spatial sequence: "A variation on the closed vista is deflection." The object ahead is sited off center from the expected right-angle view, "thus arousing the expectation that it is doing this to some purpose."

Purposeful orchestration of visual effects can be scored like a ballet. To achieve the frisson of esthetic delight rising from sensing, seeing, and then experiencing the arbitrary and unexpected as one moves through space requires careful planning and a sensitive eye for organizing vertical and horizontal panoramas and scenic continuity.

One danger in choosing the unexpected over the predictable and prosaic, and allowing campus landscape design to rise (or fall) like stagecraft, is ambiguity in circulation design, and in turn a blurred perception of the overall campus design concept. Utilizing Lynchiana, we urge clarity in designing path systems. Applying the Cullenesque, we favor intricacy and complexity in visual effects. Better yet is a clever combination of both. As anodyne for monotony and confusion when locating, designing, and landscaping the ever-present campus walks, the fusion approach is no more a contradictory notion than St. Augustine's blend of reason and faith as a formula for a well-balanced and rational life.

2.7 BIKEWAYS

▶ The bicycle is a silent steed and one which moves much more dangerously and rapidly than either the driving or saddle horse.... If bicyclers are not content to limit themselves to a reasonable speed and to observe the rules of the road, they may be properly asked to ride elsewhere than on the parkway. (Olmsted, Olmsted & Eliot, *Boston Park Commission Report*, 1896)

▶ In the past, the bicycle has not been a major problem on campus. With the increasing concern for ecology and the mounting automobile and parking problems, the bicycle has emerged as the third form of circulation to go along with the pedestrian and motor vehicle. The number of bicycles on campus has risen from approximately 1,500 in 1969 to an expected 3,000 this fall. The University police have stated that the number could approach 5,000. It is apparent that from this dramatic increase that the bicycle must be considered in all future campus planning and design. (University of Minnesota Office of Physical Planning and Design, 1972)

In recent years more bicycles have been sold annually than automobiles, with total bicycle ownership in 1999 over 120 million units in the United States, according to industry sources. Biking on campus is a popular recreational activity and provides cheap transportation. For short trips it is competitive in time, cost, and convenience with automobiles for portal-to-portal travel. Nonpolluting, energy efficient, physiologically beneficial, biking appeals to environmentalists and health enthusiasts. In certain locales expensive bikes are a status symbol. At some campuses biking is deeply rooted in local culture and custom. The University of Illinois, the University of Minnesota, Duke University, and the University of California, Santa Barbara, are notable examples of places demonstrating persistent efforts to encourage and provide for bicycling. Interestingly, the four are situated in dramatically different climate zones, suggesting that bike use is not climate restrained.

Biking on campus can be dangerous. Accidents occur because of speeding, mixing types of traffic, poor right-of-way design, and college-age youth's propensity to ride outside the routes designated for bicycles and to ignore traffic rules and regulations. Education and enforcement may address the human problems. In Massachusetts, for example, since 1971 a bicycle has been "recognized as a vehicle… subject [in the main] to all the rights and responsibilities of an automobile."

Ave Olmsted, who saw some of these conflicts and contradictions early on, when bicycle use soared as pastime and sport at the end of the nineteenth century. As in any landscaped environment where the pedestrian is sovereign and vehicles must serve, not dominate, right-of-way design is a campus landscape opportunity.

Bikeways is the common label given to rights-of-way for general planning and design purposes. As with campus roads, a design hierar-

An optimal situation for the central campus, where pedestrian and bicycle traffic is predictably densest, is a walk suitable for both.

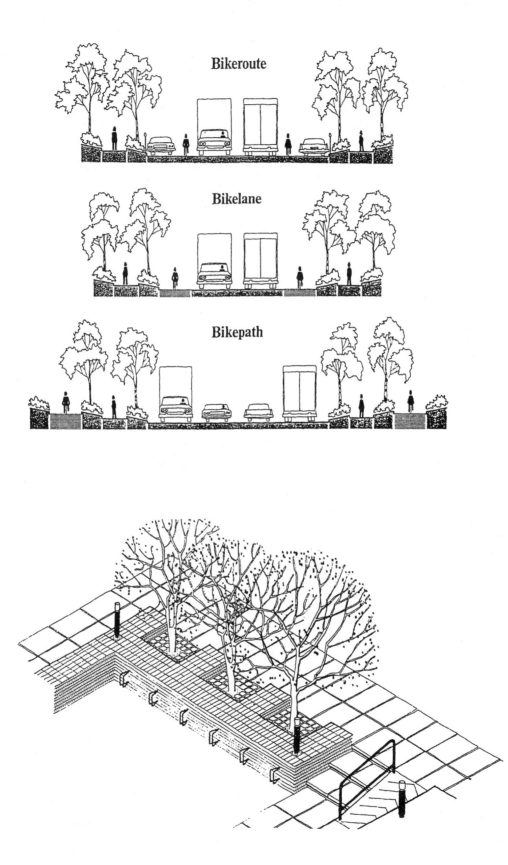

Bikeroute

Bikelane

Bikepath

chy can be established that informs design specificity. Thus, a *bike path* is a route designed for bikes exclusively; a *bike lane* is a segment of the road set aside for bikes, a space comparable to a parking or breakdown lane; *bike routes* are rights-of-way where through signs, lighting, striping, and other signaling devices, it is understood that bicycles and vehicles, or pedestrians and bicyclists, share the same travel lanes. See also the illustration of the University of Illinois on page 136.

Inevitably, most campuses will have all three kinds of bikeways. An optimal situation for the central campus, where pedestrian and bicycle traffic is predictably densest, is a walk suitable for both. In this instance a path ten feet wide with gradients of 5 percent or less would be the minimum criteria. Outside the central campus, where the routes can be *largely* bike-oriented, more generous dimensions can be afforded, with windbreaks, means of creating shadow in the summer sun, lighting for night use, and circulation laid out to make the journey visually interesting. The use of the term *largely* recognizes that bikeways of this character are also attractive to joggers and runners; thus thought must be given to the distances bicyclists will need to view ahead in order to avoid conflict.

At rest, the bicycle is a physical nuisance and visual blight when chained to fences, posts, utility poles, and pillars—anything upright and seemingly permanent—so as to secure wheels and frames from theft. The issue is real, as the value of the bike and its parts has risen, insurance is expensive, loss is frustrating, and bicycle thieves are well equipped with bolt and wire cutters for rapid sundering of the security devices and a quick getaway.

On the other hand, there are elegant and better ways for storing the bicycle, ranging from covered parking areas under surveillance to custom-designed racks, which, while not tamper-proof, have reduced the incidence of bicycle theft and damage. Ground slotted racks, sculptural with their stony texture, make great photographs in a book on campus design but are difficult to maintain, as they are quickly clogged with dirt, leaves, and other debris. Tall bike racks, when empty, are forlorn visual objects. Better and more handsome landscapes can be generated when bike racks are combined with seating and resting areas. Such prominent locations also increase security for all.

On campus, mopeds and motorcycles should be treated as low-speed motor vehicles. Mixing moped and bike traffic on the same

---

BIKEWAYS (*opposite page*) / Design Options
Lane designs can be integrated functionally and esthetically with other campus circulation elements. Bicycle parking areas should be seen as an opportunity for a special campus landscape treatment, not just a storage area. *Graphic:* Author's collection.

right-of-way can be dangerous, although parking mopeds with bicycles may be acceptable for security, traffic control, land use, and appearance.

2.8 THRESHOLD

Many campus walks begin and end at building doorways. The threshold areas are natural gathering places for conversation, conviviality, and participation in the common and corroborative activities that advance and enrich campus life.

Many campus walks begin and end at building doorways. The threshold areas are natural gathering places for conversation, conviviality, and participation in the common and corroborative activities that advance and enrich campus life. Too often architectural designs at the threshold—whether traditional or contemporary architectural styles—fail to recognize or provide for these functions. Worse, they send silent signals that life beyond the doors may be less than satisfactory both esthetically and operationally. See page 128.

There are many reasons to reverse course: programmatic ones, to promote collegiality; philosophical ones, to encourage contact and communication among all the campus constituencies in response to the potential anomie of cyberation; and physical ones, to upgrade the appearance of the campus in areas where the application of limited funds could have best results. In constructing new buildings, in renovating old ones, better landscaping at the threshold will produce a designed environment that has multiple positive results. In existing locations such projects, as part of general campus renewal strategies, may be worthy in their own right. Envisioned is a contemporary response to what institutional designs did so well in the Renaissance, that is, *docere* (teach), *delectare* (delight), *movere* (motivate)—or at the least create places for this to happen informally. Accordingly, substantial landscape designs at the threshold would include benches, paving, trees, planters, signs, lights, and, if architecturally feasible, some protection from the weather at the doorways.

2.9 TERMINUS

Terminus, in a dictionary sense the end of a travel route, is applied in our gloss to the pickup or delivery point for people, goods, trash, and the what-have-you of an active campus. Observationally, in conjunction with thresholds, these are the places where campus attitudes about the built environment and landscape are exceptionally evident. In some places the design of the loading docks, for example, is so poorly handled as to be another indictable offense—indecent exposure. Landscape can remedy some existing deficiencies, but the prob-

DISMAL, DREARY, DEMEANING / No Name University
A central campus area where neither time nor budget has yet been allocated to help remedy or mediate visual pollution at the terminus.   *Photo:* R. P. Dober.

lems usually begin much earlier, when insufficient time is given to siting the building in relationship to approach roads and other structures and service requirements. Drop-off points for vehicles that have to penetrate the pedestrian areas are another test of campus landscape design attitudes. Drop-offs are needed for the handicapped, guests, taxis, and service and emergency vehicles. Here again landscape can raise utilitarian solutions to an art form with attention to surface detailing, curb cuts, plant selection, lighting, and signs.

2.10 PARKING

▶ Every phase of the parking problem has a distinct relation to every other phase. (National Safety Council, 1928)

▶ Parking...must be of such a nature and so located as to permit ready and convenient access. [It] must be located in such places that the vehicle users can consummate their desired ends and reach their objectives with a minimum of inconvenience. The vehicle operators should also be provided with such facilities as to relieve them of all anxiety as to the security of the vehicle and reasonable time limits. (The Eno Foundation, 1942)

▶ There is a school of thought that any action which provides additional parking facilities is preferable to no action at all. The proponents of this view do not go so far as to say that action should be taken blindly, but they do point out that in view of the doubtful value of much information collected in parking surveys it may be better to install facilities where the need is most obvious, and if these do not prove sufficient, to install more. (*Solving Parking Problems,* Department of Commerce, State of New York, 1950)

▶ [I]nstitutions of higher learning resemble cities. They include dormitories, residential areas, classrooms, office buildings, recreational areas, stadiums, auditoriums, hospitals and relatively small amounts of retail area. The campus has parking areas, traffic signals and a road network. And, like cities, traffic and pedestrian problems are complex. Planning for transportation by most metropolitan areas has become an established fact. But as far as many institutions are concerned, there is slight chance for a systematic approach. Each situation requires a different approach or solution. (Wilbur Smith, *Access and Parking for Institutions* [Connecticut, 1960])

▶ [I]t is the university's obligation to either prohibit the use of automobiles by students or to provide adequate parking space for student cars. This is not to say that these spaces need be adjacent to, or even close to university buildings. (University Facilities Research Center, *Parking Programs for Universities,* 1961)

▶ Updating a parking system usually is a costly project for colleges and universities. Careful planning is needed to phase in successful cost-effective solutions that create safe and esthetically appealing environment. (Susan A. Kirkpatrick, *Planning for Improved Campus Facilities* [Virginia, 1992])

Roads and parking form a connected utility system, like water and waste disposal. On too many campuses the waste disposal systems (parking) are medieval, visually the equivalent of an open sewer. And as with an open sewer, disease is rampant—in this instance a visual affliction, *autosprawl,* the unconscionable acceptance of parking in locations and with designs that debase, if not devastate, the campus landscape.

Institutions struggling to attract and retain tuition-paying students may feature safe and convenient parking as a campus asset.

These conditions have been acknowledged since the end of World War II, when campuses began to grow in number and size parallel with automobile use. A perusal of different phases of campus plans at several institutions over a forty-year period indicates a worrisome pattern of indifference, especially the construction of small parking lots where consolidation would self-evidently be a better solution. Well remembered is a 1999 visit to one of America's elite campuses, a recognized landmark in campus design, where of forty parking lots totaling fifteen hundred spaces, half had twenty-five or fewer on-grade spaces. At every turn of the head the glinting metal from the ubiquitous automobile caught the eye. Several times a day pedestrians and cars would

CAMPUS PARKING

Necessary, intrusive, a convenience, a blighting element in the landscape, a reward, an aesthetic liability—there are few aspects of campus development that occupy more time than the vexing issue of campus parking, and the minutes of many meetings are filled with contrasting opinions. *Photo:* R. P. Dober.

play toreador during class changes, as faculty and staff used the lots as shortcuts to campus buildings.

There is general recognition that free-choice, laissez-faire parking never works. Campus parking becomes a vexing, vicious issue. In the central campus it is an expensive use of land. Parking is seen by some as an institutional obligation, by others as a privilege. The challenge of locating and designing sufficient and convenient space is compounded by late-twentieth-century needs: fluent access from adjacent campus roads, signage for safety, lighting for security, computerized gates for control. Further, because of cost restraints, insufficient funds are allocated for the quantity and quality of the paving and landscape materials that define and surround the parking areas. Vacillation in decision making as to amount, location, and design of parking areas is too often accepted as a visionary solution.

As a campus landscape component, parking offers some exceptional opportunities to blend function and art into laudable campus design. What follows is necessarily a generalized approach, there being striking differences in the conditions and considerations that influence the analysis of need and the articulation of acceptable parking proposals. A small college in a rural setting will have requirements and solutions different from those of a major university whose population is large enough to support satellite parking areas and shuttle buses. For the community college student—balancing the time demands of job, home life, and classes—convenient parking could be the critical factor in satisfying educational aspirations. Parking for the handicapped near buildings is mandated by national and local building codes and regulations. The fancied Nobel prize winner may demand a parking space near his or her lab as a contract perquisite. The staff member who gave exceptional service during a particular month might be honored with a designated parking space adjacent to the spaces reserved for the senior officers. Institutions struggling to attract and retain tuition-paying students may feature safe and convenient parking as a campus asset. Campuses with hospitals, sports arenas and stadiums, and cultural centers will have a greater parking demand than institutions with fewer such buildings and activities. Some cities and towns have included parking requirements in their building and zoning codes, often driven by the hope of keeping student parking out of their neighborhoods. In urban areas, the argument that mass transportation is available and hence a minimal provision of parking is acceptable will be questioned if winter weather affects the perceived distance from transit station and bus stop to campus destination.

Given these variations and differing circumstances, there are currently no standard rules for estimating parking requirements that would be applicable in all regions and for all kinds of institutions. As a guide to planning, one might gather current statistics from peer institutions as to current conditions and practices. Include acreage and campus population. From those numbers one may deduce a reasonable target if emulation of peers is an acceptable approach to estimating need or rationalizing an allowance.

As to appearance and the potential positive impact of campus landscape applied to the parking function, one best starts by banning curbside parking and then addressing the pervasive and perverse small parking lots that indifference has allowed to spawn in the central campus. At the least, many of these lots can be moved from visually prominent locations in the central campus and consolidated in another location. As to appearance, if autosprawl is the disease, then a methodical approach to redesign is the cure. Parking maven Susan A. Kirkpatrick's earnest work at the University of Michigan sets a precedent worth emulating. Faced with 230 surface lots "unsafe, confusing, awkward, and unsightly," the university methodically documented the functional and esthetic deficiencies so as to pinpoint solutions in specific locations. Many of these solutions were commonsense measures requiring no more than a disciplined eye, backed occasionally by specialized engineering knowledge. Kirkpatrick's report to the 1991 annual conference of the Society for College and University Planning listed useful suggestions applicable to many on-grade campus parking lots. These included better curbing and drainage; "removing excessive, inconsistent, haphazardly mounted signs; selecting plant materials that are tolerant of drought and urban conditions; and, building walls no taller than three feet to help screen the undesirable portion of the parking lot yet allow security surveillance."

A notice from the University of Wisconsin encapsulates another kind of solution in the face of a further proliferation of smaller parking lots: "We welcome you to the campus and hope you share our feeling for its beauty. Unfortunately, if you come by car you must also share one of our problems: a shortage of parking spaces. We realize these arrangements are not ideal and may cause some hardships...be assured they are hardships you share with [students, faculty and staff] who spend the academic year with them." For Wisconsin, satellite parking and a bus system were an acceptable price for preserving campus landscape. At the other end of the time scale, new institutions, particularly those with heavy commuting populations, have devised campus designs where the central area is largely automobile-free and parking is located along the perimeter. In these areas campus landscape should be generously and extensively planted.

Usually, on-grade solutions are less expensive than open parking decks; and the latter are more expensive than closed parking decks, while parking under buildings tends to be the most expensive solution.

Though attractive in principle to older campuses, placing parking on the perimeter is not easily accomplished because of seemingly immutable building and land use patterns. An insightful 1960 study at the University of Cincinnati diagrammed some of the typical options and consequences for campus parking on constrained central sites. Sloping topography can be manipulated to insert a parking deck, or parking can be placed under a building, or the institution can choose to use scarce central campus land for teaching facilities rather than parking. Left unstated was the possibility of combining all three; but each diagram did made a significant gesture to utilizing campus landscape as buffer or amenity.

Some experts suggest that parking within 1,000 feet of any campus designation would be acceptable in principle. When documenting the factors that constitute a decision-making tree for resolving parking issues, one must also include land available, site character, climate, the degree to which meeting demand is an imperative, the cost of parking solutions, and a realistic evaluation of options and choices.

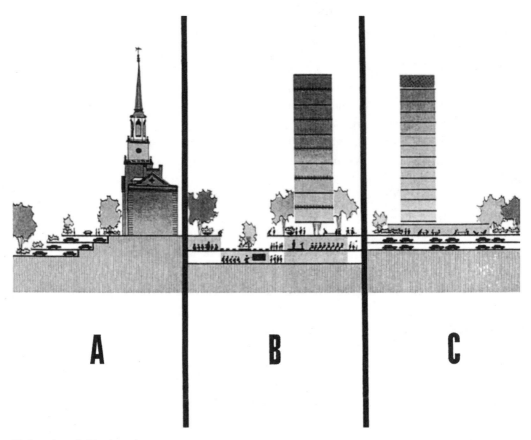

University of Cincinnati
Graphic: Author's collection.

Usually, on-grade solutions are less expensive than open parking decks, and the latter are more expensive than closed parking decks, while parking under buildings tends to be the most expensive solution. When land values per square foot exceed the cost per square foot of on-grade parking solutions by a factor of 3.5 or more, then multiple-level solutions should be considered. For any parking solution the positive contribution of campus landscape should be axiomatic and included in project funding.

Four examples of reasonable parking-cum-landscape follow: an in-close small on-grade parking lot, a deck with a facade that serves as landscape armature, an underground parking garage with garden above, and parking placed under a play field so as to get multiple uses from available land. It also serves as a green setting for nearby buildings, a better solution than a metal-reflecting car pound.

Buffering. Large earth berms (reminding one, perhaps, of Viking ceremonial mounds) serve as a green buffer between the parking lots and the buildings at the University of Odense (Denmark). The green strip is wide enough to dramatize the differences between land use areas: parking, greenbelt zone, building precinct. Bryant College planners propose using a slight change in grade to achieve a similar result.

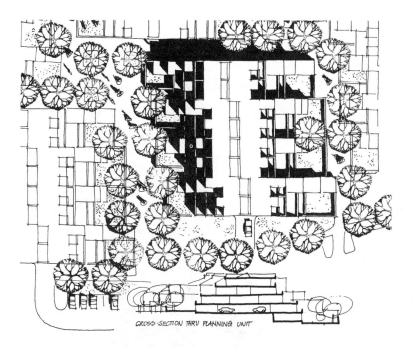

CROSS-SECTION THRU PLANNING UNIT

PARKING ALTERNATIVES / Connecticut College
Variations on a theme (*above* and *left*): using changes in topography to mediate the impact of parking visually and to encourage campus landscape development.
Graphic: Connecticut College; Dober, Lidsky, Craig and Associates, Inc.

GREENBELT / University of Odense, Denmark
A generous greenbelt separates parking from the building zone.   *Photo:* R. P. Dober.

FIELDS AS GREENBELT / Bates College
A variation on the green strip of grass and trees; in this instance play fields are positioned as a greenbelt.
Graphic: Dober, Lidsky, Craig and Associates, Inc.

150

SHAPING / The Cranbrook Institute
In-close parking is accepted, but designed with skill.   *Photo:* Courtesy Stephen Holl.

PEDESTRIAN ENTRANCE PARKING GARAGE / University of Melbourne
A one-level parking deck is covered with a green lawn, and the pedestrian entrance to the garage is marked with a whimsical, place-making set of caryatids.   *Photo:* R. P. Dober.

151

At Bates College play fields are used as the green buffer strip between parking, dorms, and a proposed campus center.

Shaping. At the Cranbrook Institute architect Stephen Holl shapes the in-close parking as a design element in counterpoint to the rectangular buildings. The lighting pole is treated as a sculptural element in the center of the parking lot. The curving arc of the stall area (an inventive alternative to rectangular lots) is reinforced visually by dense landscape.

Layering. At the University of Melbourne (Australia) parking is handled in a one-level garage. The upper surface is landscaped as a lawn with trees. The automobile entrance is treated perfunctorily. The pedestrian side is wrapped in an attractive thick landscape, with an eye-catching place-marking doorway framed by caryatids. A similar scheme is being developed for Westminster College (Utah). In this instance the upper surface is being engineered for play fields. Under-surface parking is cost effective, given the economics of land acquisition for combinations of fields and surface parking.

WESTMINSTER
C O L L E G E

CAMPUS PLAN *for the* 21ˢᵗ CENTURY

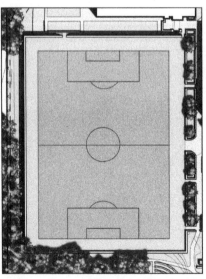

Field Above Grade Parking

FIELD ABOVE GRADE PARKING

In conformance with the Board of Trustees' clear directions, a playfield is maintained in the campus plan on the site of the Hansen Field. A full-sized soccer field can be accommodated, including generous out-of-bounds borders, above approximately 360 parking spaces. The unusual aspect of this proposal is that the field will be raised above a large parking reservoir at, or near, the current grade level of the land. The structure will be open so as not to require mechanical ventilation; it will be fully lit and monitored by video cameras and patrols, as is the Northwest Deck.

The field level will be closer to the level of the west-sloping core campus mall. The field will be more clearly visible from the center of the academic area, extending that landscape as a large green plat. The lower edges of the field will be treated as a low-scaled building with surrounding trees, shrubs, and vines. The grade-level pocket space between the field structure and the Health, Wellness, and Athletics Building offers a special opportunity to create an intimately scaled garden space or sculpture court. This small transitional space would be one through which commuters would pass daily and enjoy in transit, or possibly linger in simply to lounge or to meet colleagues. The design concept of this space is as a threshold to the academic area, a conversion zone where drivers become pedestrians and are welcomed as such to the *sanctum sanctorum* of the College. This will be an ideal location for benches or seating areas along a pathway into the campus.

LAYERING / Westminster College, Utah
A variation on the University of Melbourne concept, with the upper surface designed for play fields. *Graphic:* Dober, Lidsky, Craig and Associates, Inc.

CENTRAL PLAZA: BEFORE AND AFTER / University of Minnesota
Parking relocated to underground garage with surface redesigned as central landscaped plaza. *Photos:* University of Minnesota, Master Planning Office; courtesy Clinton N. Hewitt.

153

Burying. Audaciously and with great skill, the University of Minnesota transformed a small campus parking lot into a multilevel underground garage. What was a car pound on the surface was then transformed into a landscaped plaza in the center of the campus. The design includes a segmented lawn with trees, benches, and light fixtures. A pedestrian tunnel connects the garage to adjacent buildings.

Decking. Countrywide, the general reluctance to date to pay for garages is being overcome by a recognition on some campuses and sites that multideck parking is a necessary solution to autosprawl. Recent projects with commendable designs and landscape features can be found at Central Connecticut State University, the University of Kentucky, the University of Oklahoma, and Princeton University.

SPACES

▶ It has always been difficult for landscape architects to explain, and still more difficult for them to convince the unfeeling person that their art in its natural or imitative forms has an esthetic basis and is in reality the result of design and not simply lending a helping hand to nature.... [W]hat ever beauty might be is largely the result of human effort and intelligence. (Charles Downing Lay, "Space Composition" [*Landscape Architecture,* January 1918])

▶ At the present time it is possible to formulate with some confidence the ideals of American landscape architecture, at least that section represented by the professional practitioners.

The outstanding ideals are three:

1. To make a snug, comfortable, beautiful suburban home.

2. To make a clean, healthful, convenient and beautiful city.

3. To protect and interpret the native landscape. (Frank A. Waugh, "American Ideals in Landscape Architecture" [*Landscape Architecture,* April 1925])

▶ Cultural conventions and customs directly affect what people notice, find interesting, and prefer about the landscape.... [There is an enormous] opportunity to experiment with possible landscapes.... [These require] thoughtful development of methods that reside in the traditions of no single discipline but grow from the purpose of the work. (Joan Iverson Nassauer, "Culture and the Changing Landscape" [*Landscape Ecology,* 1995])

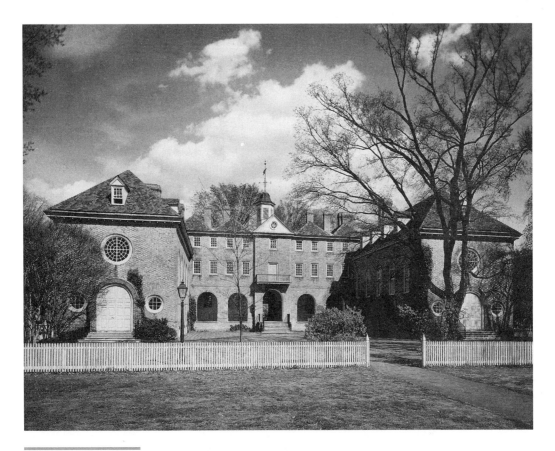

DOMESTIC SCALE / The College of William and Mary
Photo: Thomas L. Williams; courtesy College of William and Mary.

Campus spaces are essentially determined landscape designs. Functionally purposeful and created artworks, they are not, in the main, natural preserves or conservation zones occupied with buildings. The spaces will vary in size and in types of greenery. After examining hundreds of examples of campus landscape images, one could conveniently sort the designs into three categories: domestic, institutional, and monumental. (See illustrations, pages 155, 156, 157.)

The goals applicable to designing a town or neighborhood would seem germane to the spaces of higher education as well. Campuses should be designed to be convenient, comfortable, healthful, and beautiful. Campus design is thus akin to civic design, with its formal or informal disposition of key buildings, open spaces, and circulation; or to variations of urban park design with contained greenery—lawns, trees, shrubs, and other plants—dominating the scene. In the spirit of either tradition conscientious designers, sensitive to environmental issues and opportunities, will (and should) factor existing site features, terrain conditions, and climate into their configuration of

INSTITUTIONAL SCALE / University of Chicago, Ryerson Hall
Photo: Kaufann and Fabry; courtesy University of Chicago.

formal or informal concepts. Decades of observation of flawed campus landscapes would suggest this basic principle should not be taken for granted. It imposes no limits on variations in style or esthetic expression.

Our focus will be today's typical situation. Detailed descriptions begin with the sovereign and dominant campus landscape spaces. Given their importance physically and semiotically, these are grouped in the *heritage* category. Major settings for campus life, the presence and quality of heritage spaces measurably define a memorable landscape experience. We will then define through illustrations and commentary *secondary* and *tertiary* spaces, and end with *wetscapes* and *dryscapes.* The last two are campus landscapes marked by various combinations of water or aridity.

On the horizon are new landscape concepts not yet realized and thus not covered in this book. As twenty-first-century research enlarges and extends our understanding of what Professor Nassauer

MONUMENTAL SCALE / United States Air Force Academy

Spaces—three scales and the resulting campus landscape images. The domestic type, such as William and Mary's seventeenth-century building (*page 155*), can be likened to a manor house with a fine lawn. The second, institutional, encompasses the landscaped settings and large buildings traditionally associated with higher education (*page 156*). Old styles or new, typically there is also a lawn and trees that frame facades. The latter might also be a support for symbolic greenery, such as the ivy on the University of Chicago's Ryerson Hall. Monumental designs are declarative spatial architectural statements, hardly ever picturesque, of which the Air Force Academy may be the best twentieth-century version. *Photo:* USAF News Office.

calls the "possible," new paradigms may be introduced. In her construct, for example, an ecological approach to landscape design would consider not only scientific factors and patterns of human behavior, but also cultural values. "Possible landscapes are landscapes designed in the context of cultural expectations and ecological knowledge. Innovative designs [are] a vision that is beyond the realm of models that rely on existing patterns," says Nassauer. Our typology admits room for such speculation in theory and application.

2.11 HERITAGE SPACES

Heritage spaces function as outdoor rooms for campus rites, rituals, pageants, social encounters small and large, formal and informal meetings and discussions, and unstructured recreation and relaxation (solo and in groups), and are occasionally used as ad hoc outdoor classrooms in good weather.

Heritage spaces provide access to clusters of adjacent buildings, which often frame and form the space. They act as a green lung, establish the nexus for intersecting paths, and serve as the contrasting element in the built/nonbuilt campus design equation. Art and artifact, these are the spaces that leave a strong impression on the visitor. Campus personified, their photogenic images fill the front covers of view books and student recruitment brochures, and are illustrated and highlighted in fund-raising appeals that aim to create in alumni and friends that frisson of warm and heartfelt recollection so necessary for a productive capital campaign.

Heritage spaces often function as cultural conventions. They provide what people have come to expect a campus to look like, though on close inspection that perception is sometimes not real. Harvard Yard seems to the uninformed casual visitor to be a fine example of colonial collegiate life. It is, of course, a place with several centuries of accretion, and its current physical expression, while generating awe and respect for assumed ancient values, has little connection to earlier educational practices and campus life.

As to forms, the descriptive nouns associated with primary spaces are a veritable litany for higher education: *grove, quad, lawn, yard, green, oval, square, plaza, mall.* All these are architecture's admirable companion, the recognized and respected center, the campus signature design, loaded with symbolism. Estheticians may categorize the designs as formal versus informal. Accordingly, the untrained eye would see nature imitated or interpreted, or arranged geometrically with clearly dimensioned designs, with plantings often linear, arrayed, and tiered. When they mature, the best heritage spaces become overlays of site history, exquisite horticultural mixtures, seasonal in color and foliage, plural in detail like a mosaic, often when inspected untidy in spots, used, and a pleasure ground for many rather than a static memorial to a single person or promoter or patron.

Let the Green at Brown University stand in for the many heritage spaces now equally sanctified as the image of a special collegiate place. Around three edges of the Green, generations have constructed examples of the best architecture of their time, or so they believed. Though critical opinions may now rate that architecture differently, few would

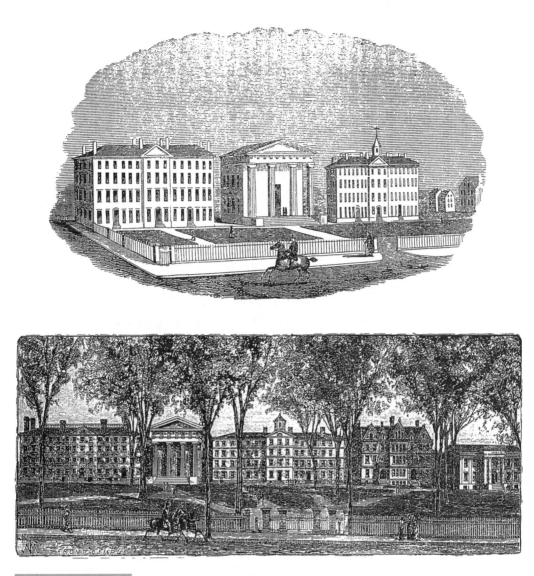

HERITAGE SPACES / Brown University
Historic or new, certain campus open spaces become icons of institutional purpose and presence—heritage spaces, such as the front Green at Brown University. *Graphic:* Author's collection.

deny the quality and power of the Brown ensemble, nor find cause to disarrange the simple landscape pattern in the Green with landscape interventions out of scale or in visual disharmony.

Of other celebrated primary spaces, some seem static and fixed in time, others seemingly amenable to further change. Each instance has its own rationale. With the latest restoration plans (by EDAW, Inc.) Thomas Jefferson's "academic village" at the University of Virginia now takes a significant step into the future as a settled and unaltered icon. The new tree-planting scheme for Harvard Yard remains faithful to the past but recognizes that new greenery must be added as trees mature and die, and such is welcomed as an opportunity to adjust paths and views to contemporary taste and needs.

Classifying Heritage Spaces

Historians and critics often classify campus landscape arrangements as "open" or "closed," "urbanized" or "pastoral." As with all such simplifications, cause-and-effect relationships are instructive in understanding basic differences but do explain all circumstances or variations. The open model is heralded as significantly American. Buildings are dispersed. Those passing along the street could look into the campus, see and be impressed by the layout. Keeping buildings separate also reduced the risk of fire and optimized natural light in the structures, additional reasons cited for the supposedly American preferences. Closed models are said to be European. Early examples emulated monasteries and palace grounds in their formality, such as walled enclaves and courtyards. These contrasting site arrangements and landscapes, "formal" versus "informal," will be discussed further shortly. Regionally one can find other international influences, such as campus plazas in the Southwest, with their Spanish antecedents.

These comments apply to existing campuses, the prevalent situation, and our focus. There are about four thousand existing campuses in North America, with perhaps a hundred more being added in the first decades of the new century. Thus we will look at a group of existing heritage spaces to see how they came into being, appreciate their existence as three-dimensional culture—truly valuable evidence of aspirations and achievements—and, by inductive reasoning, support conservation measures for their maintenance and enhancement. Newly minted campuses will have comparable spaces, some of which in time may become heritage spaces. And, of course, out on the horizon are Nassauer's "possible" designs, which if realized might also be declared heritage spaces by future generations.

Precedents and Consequences

The allure of a respected past and its esthetic verities holds sway when change threatens. Squeeze the essence from thousands of pages of campus histories that document design preferences and decisions and two large drops fall on the surface of compressed conjecture concerning cultural conventions: formal versus informal. As to the latter, whosoever traces the pastoral concept of campus landscape as cultural concept walks in the Olmsted brothers' shadow, and that of their predecessor Andrew Jackson Downing and numerous protean followers. In this approach one accepts the given physical situation and with moderation allows terrain and landscape to dominate a picturesque scene in response to functional necessities. Design here is an adjustment to site realities. Frederick Law Olmstead Jr. wrote, "Whenever this human control over the land and the objects upon it is influenced by desire to make the resulting landscape more enjoyable than it would otherwise be, an element of artistry enters, which often attains the quality of Fine Art." Cited earlier as examples of this approach were the University of California, Santa Cruz, and Wellesley College.

Formality comes in several guises, most clearly in monastically influenced geometric quadrangular schemes or interpretations of Jefferson's extended mall, which can be found at the Yale University Divinity School and Dillard University, and, as noted, numerous schemes influenced by the City Beautiful movement. The latter dominated campus design for decades with its mantralike message of "clothing with beauty of adaptation to purpose [that] which is the strong desire of civic art" (C. M. Robinson, *Modern Civic Art, or the City Made Beautiful* [New York, 1888]).

Residue of philosophies engendered by the 1893 World's Columbian Exposition in Chicago, arguments, articles, and books about City Beautiful, such as Robinson's, resonated with trustees responsible for buildings and grounds. Who would dispute Robinson's observation that universities "rising building by building and gaining steadily in resources and visible splendor [nonetheless] scattered their new structures hit or miss about their grounds"? They displayed "no system, nor orderliness, no idea of gaining an aggregate effect that should be more impressive than any series of individual results could be." And so the "great popular object lesson" from the Chicago exposition, said Robinson, was "the value of cooperation, in placing of buildings and their landscape development as strictly as in their architectural elevation." This procedure "set a goal worth striven for . . . giving an assurance that every step taken now, in accordance with the ultimate vision is wisely taken and will not some day have to be undone." The pitch applied also to civic centers and hospitals, which in plan, form, and occasional elevation seem like campuses' esthetic cousins.

Githens' Compositions

Like baton passing in a relay race, the connection between civic design and campus design was stated and restated as gospel through the late 1930s, such as Thomas Adams noting that "important universities have been well planned in parts" and comparing them, with illustrations, to government and civic centers (*Outline of Town and*

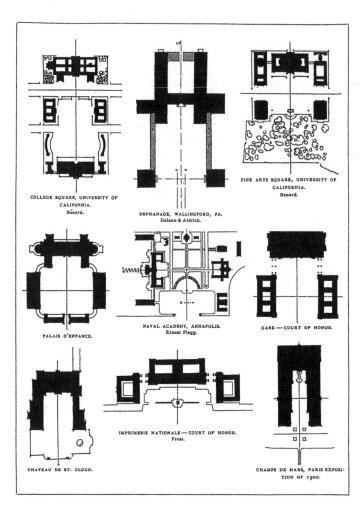

COLLEGE SQUARE, UNIVERSITY OF
CALIFORNIA.
Benard.

ORPHANAGE, WALLINGFORD, PA.
Delano & Aldrich.

FINE ARTS SQUARE, UNIVERSITY OF
CALIFORNIA.
Benard.

PALAIS D'ENFANCE.

NAVAL ACADEMY, ANNAPOLIS.
Ernest Flagg.

GARE — COURT OF HONOR.

CHATEAU DE ST. CLOUD.

IMPRIMERIE NATIONALE — COURT OF HONOR.
Prost.

CHAMPS DE MARS, PARIS EXPOSI-
TION OF 1900.

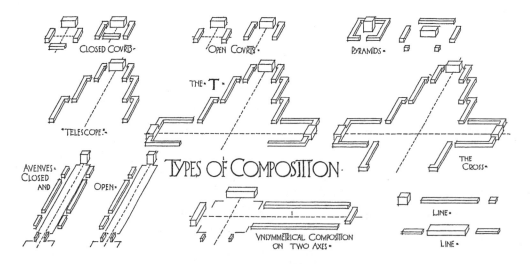

CLOSED COURTS·

OPEN COURTS·

PYRAMIDS·

THE·T·

·TELESCOPE·

THE
CROSS·

AVENUES·
CLOSED
AND

OPEN·

TYPES OF COMPOSITION·

UNSYMMETRICAL COMPOSITION
ON TWO AXES·

LINE·

LINE·

City Planning [New York, 1935]). While civic design ideals were soon buried in the rise of modern architecture, they are now surfacing again and interesting the younger generation. Canadian landscape architect Robert Allsopp intimates that there is growing "recognition that one key to good city form is the pattern and shape of the open spaces that link everything else together." In a commendable editorial stance (*Landscape Architectural Review,* March 1991) Allsopp launched a series of project profiles that would demonstrate how the older ideas were once again relevant, with the banner heading "Civic Design: The Return to Traditions."

Accepting Allsopp's insights, if there is fresh wind carrying new ships to old territory, how useful is that journey to the traveler searching for assistance in generating campus landscape? Alfred Morton Githens' gloss on types of campus spatial composition (*The Brickbuilder,* September 1906) seems to cover most of the formal possibilities, as well as illuminating where the art of landscape then stood in critical reviews and discussions. His exposition is also a good lead-in to the benefits and cautions associated with interpretations of the City Beautiful movement as it was practiced and as it might now be applied.

Githens' essays are infused with the Hegelian certitude that comes with his trade: "We Americans are architectural libertines and have no restricting traditions." Githens wanted some degree of unanimity in collegiate design. "It is hard to see why American buildings should run the gamut of [so many] styles. Each man seems to have his own theory about the expression of modern and local conditions, so each starts anew for himself instead of developing the style used by others before him." Perplexed by the wave of stylistic innovations that flooded journals and the press, Githens agreed that "a campus of some sort seems the natural concept for an American Scholastic group." In an instructive pictorial analysis he offered ten compositional solutions: closed courts, open courts, pyramids, telescope, the T, the cross, avenues closed and open, unsymmetrical composition on two axes, and line. In regard to greenery Githens had little specifically to propose, citing but two examples with campus landscape: the Fine Arts Square at California University (*sic*), and the formal ensembles at the Annapolis Academy (*sic*) with its views centered on the Severn and Chesapeake Rivers.

Within the vocabulary of forms, Githens saw conflict, "war between two styles—Classic and Gothic." The former is a "*scholarly*"

GITHEN'S GLOSS (*opposite page*)
Some examples of Alfred Morton Githen's pioneering effort to categorize campus spaces in the spirit of the City Beautiful movement.   *Graphic:* Author's collection.

plan (his italics), and "seeks the greatest single effect, and as rule, the simpler the composition the more successful... The latter is *natural* [again his italics], masses and skylines are irregular... Surprise is sought rather than classic calm and logic." Githens acknowledged that "[e]ach school has its adherents and strong opponents. Neither camp can see any good in the other and the bitter war goes on. So far, compromises have proved hopelessly inferior to a complete expression of either school." In that battle, apparently, landscape architecture was an innocent bystander. For reasons not clear from scanning the professional literature, the profession seems to have allowed architects to occupy the high ground. Of approximately 650 articles, reviews, and editorials in *Landscape Architecture,* volumes 1–25, before and after Githens, Harvard University librarian Katherine McNamara listed but four on "college, university, private school grounds."

On the other hand, the ability to deal with design fundamentals, such as Githens' disciplined spatial taxonomy, may not necessarily indicate good and prescient judgment on related matters. Wrote Githens, praising closed site compositions in certain locations, essentially monastic quadrangular designs: "Any country college is a community of its own; the less communication with the outside world the more college spirit is fostered." And architect Alfred Granger, former president of the Illinois American Institute of Architects (AIA), expounded on site design (1931): "If the institution is co-educational, the women's dormitories with their dining hall and kitchen should be separate from the men. In this case the best location for the chapel is between these dormitory groups where it can occupy a dominating architectural position as the center of spiritual life." On the other hand, who would quarrel with this Granger dictum? "[C]ourts and quadrangles attractively planted and entered through archways or cloisters, at once create an atmosphere of quiet beauty conducive to study and contemplation."

Today's reader might imagine Githens' manual was a useful starter kit for a Beaux Arts competition, like today's electronic "wire frame" for generating computerized three-dimensional landscape images. For the "deconstructionist," the drawings that accompany Githens' text are revealing, a few with a gesture to landscape, most without. How architects viewed campus landscape then and how they view it now is edifying; perhaps it is a reflection of training, or interest, or understanding how collegiate buildings and grounds intermesh. One recalls two recent site plans from an architectural competition at an eminent university. Both are the work of honored designers. One leaves the landscape space surrounding the new building unrealized, the other suggests reasonable solutions (see page xxiv).

Landscape Reinforcing Structure
and Shaping Primary Spaces

When cast in unalterable physical forms, the static City Beautiful philosophy becomes a straitjacket more germane, one thinks, to designing a cemetery than to designing a campus. When accepted in principle—a vision of the future, periodically adjusted to emerging reality, with each part contributing to a comprehensive scheme—then the City Beautiful approach is generally beneficial in terms of function and form. Further, the esthetic called for collaboration among all those involved in developing the built environment: architects, landscape architects, artists, engineers, and those who have "made a special study of the general science and art of city-building."

If one understands the City Beautiful limitations, the movement has much to offer campus landscape designers today. For example, clarifying and ordering the disposition of primary and secondary spaces, the spatial sequence and experience, and the use of landscape elements to structure a comprehensible design concept within heritage spaces would be featured. These design principles will be illustrated in four plans that espoused these principles at the height of the style: a state capitol, a town center, and two campuses.

The Morell and Nichols 1920 plan for the state capitol grounds in Bismarck, North Dakota, was intended to be developed "in an unusual way, which may be stimulating in similar work in the future." Although the plan was never fully implemented, several of the ideas are pertinent to themes in this book. "Unusual" meant four things, all extraordinary for that time and place. The quotes above and below are excerpted from Wm. Hay Williamson's article "Recording History in Landscapes" (*Landscape Architecture*, January 1921). We have rearranged his sentence order to suit our narrative, and make some judgments that may not have been his intention.

The North Dakota state capitol landscape leitmotif was an intertwining of history and ecology. The plan for the proposed capitol grounds aimed to be a celebration and "commemoration of events of North Dakota history, the preservation of monuments and legends from the past, and the setting forth of the resources of plant beauty of the state for easier comprehension of the people" (the last is an idea now prominently featured at the Iowa state capitol).

The North Dakota design concepts included a simulation of the ways settler and Indian shared the same crops. The region's first citizens were honored with the replica on the capitol grounds of a tribal totem, "an enormous effigy of a turtle formed of boulders laid down on the prairie near Bismarck by Indians centuries ago." From the

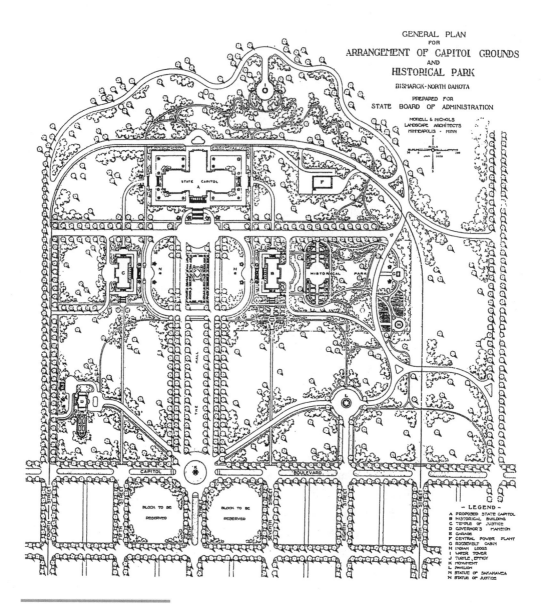

MORELL AND NICHOLS / North Dakota State Capitol
An extraordinary design for a new state capitol, by a firm that had an extensive campus landscape practice. Ideas still suitable for incorporation in current campus plans: regional plant selection, something blooming year-round, topographic sensitivity, and site history. *Graphic:* Author's collection.

BEAUX ARTS EXEMPLIFIED (*top opposite page*) / Eaton Rapids Junior College
F. A. Cushing Smith's imaginative City Beautiful scheme for a civic center, incorporating a junior college. The college site sits at the end of an axial composition, embraced on two sides by parks. Obviously, the automobile had not yet encumbered the layout with utilitarian necessities. *Graphic:* Author's collection.

BEAUX ARTS WITH GREEN NECKLACES (*bottom opposite page*) / St. Joseph's Seminary
Another Cushing exercise, an enticing air view of a campus never built; a loss of what surely would have become an American classic: oval, mall, quad, terrace, lawns, and recreation fields in lovely sequence. *Graphic:* Author's collection.

166

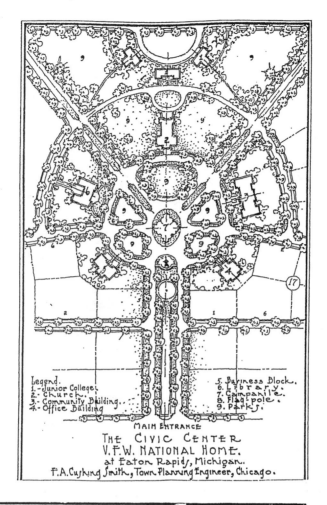

Legend.
1.- Junior College.
2.- Church.
3.- Community Building.
4.- Office Building

5.- Business Block.
6.- Library.
7.- Campanile.
8.- Flag pole.
9.- Parks.

MAIN ENTRANCE

THE CIVIC CENTER
V.F.W. NATIONAL HOME.
at Eaton Rapids, Michigan.
F.A. Cushing Smith, Town Planning Engineer, Chicago.

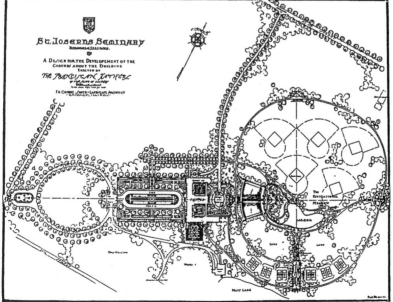

ST. JOSEPHS SEMINARY

Queen's University Campus Plan

An Approved Development Plan for the Mid and Long Range

DU TOIT ALLSOPP HILLIER, 1994

Queen's University is an established and relatively cohesive grouping of buildings and landscapes located within an urban context. Future development is constrained by heritage buildings and landscapes, and by community resistance to expansion.

The Campus Plan establishes strategies to consolidate the existing campus, optimize land use efficiency, preserve heritage features and enhance the character of the campus. Mid-range needs would be accommodated primarily through infill and intensification. The grounds of the campus would be improved both in association with building design and through independent landscape projects.

The Plan identifies where expansion should occur to accommodate long range development needs, and outlines building patterns that would help integrate campus and community and retain valuable historic buildings.

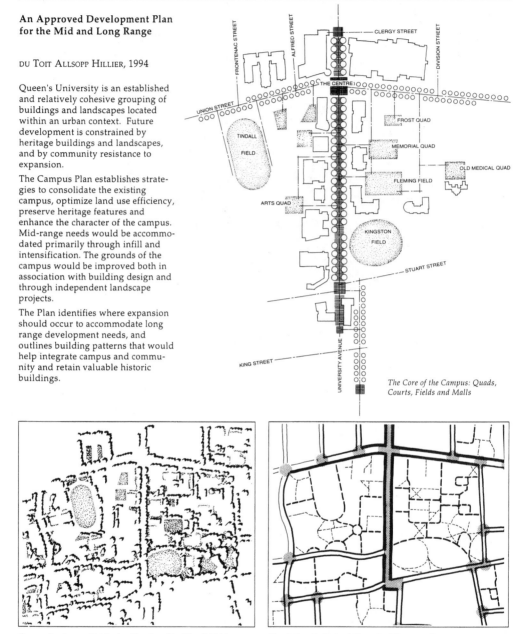

The Core of the Campus: Quads, Courts, Fields and Malls

Campus Landscapes: Reinforcing Structure, Providing Delight

Circulation: An Ordered Network of Movement Routes

Queen's University, Ontario   *Graphic:* Courtesy du Toit Allsopp Hillier, Toronto.

heights the plantings would unfold downhill ecologically, starting with local pines and junipers on the ridge. "Gradually descending the slope will be native oaks and ash, terminating at the southern end of the grounds with native poplars, willows and similar trees liking more moisture than those indigenous to the higher ground.... Every tree,

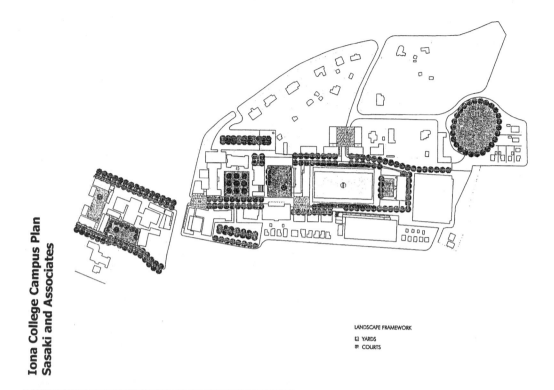

Iona College Campus Plan Sasaki and Associates

LANDSCAPE FRAMEWORK
🔲 YARDS
▦ COURTS

LANDSCAPE FOR SPACE CONFIGURATION / Iona College

At Queen's University, Roger du Toit organizes and reinforces the campus spaces with plant materials. The structuring device is applied to the path system in a contemporary version of the City Beautiful methodology. At Iona College, designed by Sasaki Associates, the landscape framework defines the yards, courts, oval, and paths. *Graphic:* Courtesy of Sasaki Associates.

shrub, flower, plant and blade of grass on the entire grounds will be native American, native Dakotan. The groups of shrubbery will be adapted to the plan, from the extreme to the high hills to the lowland of river bottoms. Likewise the formal flower beds will be various species of native flowers in succession from spring to autumn."

For some today, the overall physical development policy itself would be as attractive as the specific design and planting concepts. "Plans for the [state capitol] buildings are now being prepared. They will be adapted to the grounds, rather than the grounds to them." The drawing conveys that conviction. The landscape elements outline and configure the capitol spaces, their boundaries, and the space sequence.

F. A. Cushing Smith's utopian schemes for Eaton Rapids, Michigan (where he labeled his job "Town Planning Engineer"), and St. Joseph's Seminary (where the credit line on his work is "Landscape Architect") convey graphically how some civic design ideas are related to campus development. In the former scheme five community buildings and mini parks encircle a campanile. A junior college sits at the head of an axial composition that, overall, anticipates community life with few automobiles. In St. Joseph's Seminary Smith linked the full range of Beaux Arts space concepts into an unrivaled campus landscape pastiche. From west to east in axial sequence there were an oval, mall, courtyard, quad; even the athletic fields and tennis courts were arrayed to convey an image of syncopated symmetry.

The three drawings illustrate well how landscape planting gives skeletonlike structure to the broader campus design concepts. The arrangements also help outline and give emphasis to the shape and sequence of the primary spaces, an approach relevant on some campuses today, as indicated in the Sasaki Associates campus plan for Iona College and du Toit Allsopp Hillier's work at Queen's University.

The selection of plant materials for this kind of structuring is an art unto itself. Trees can be powerful regional place markers, such as evergreens in the Northeast, palm trees in the arid Southwest. Tree selection may be influenced by functional objectives (shade), visual effect (branching that frames or hides views), massing (some trees cluster better than others), ecology (dependence on a single species may be disastrous), and maintenance and replacement.

Caveats and Cautions

If the design cycle is again turning toward degrees of formality, some caveats and cautions need mention. Many campuses and campus sectors inspired by the City Beautiful movement are now treasured enclaves, such as Cope and Stewart's West Campus dormitories at the University of Pennsylvania and the main campuses at the University of Chicago and Stanford University. Less convincing in application were the attempts to bring to Napier, Illinois, a civic center concept for a college campus that in all other respects would seem to deserve Olmsted treatment, or landscape architect Arthur A. Shurtleff's geometric concepts for the topography at Mount Holyoke College, circa 1921.

It was, thought Shurtleff, a good time for women's institutions to avoid "the confusion of building developments which overcame most of the colleges for men between 1801 and 1890." He wrote that in his scheme for Mt. Holyoke, "[n]o effort is made to astonish or to present some striking feature." He would set aside the "Victorian ideas of the picturesque [that] encouraged a scattered formation." The irregularities would be corrected by straightening out nascent quadrangles with new and remodeled buildings. All capital investments were aimed at resolving a "confusing" layout. The pragmatic was melded with the esthetic, such as replacing roads and pedestrian networks. The college paths "are to be made as direct as possible and in some cases wide enough to accommodate emergency use by fire apparatus and ser-

Trees can be powerful regional place markers, such as evergreens in the Northeast, palm trees in the arid Southwest.

Arthur A. Shurtleff
Landscape Architect

CITY BEAUTIFUL IMPOSED / Mt. Holyoke College
Arthur Shurtleff's rendering of how Beaux Arts quadrangles could be developed and inserted into the college's
historic, pastoral, picturesque layout.   *Graphic:* Author's collection.

vice trucks, the latter especially at the opening and closing of college
when a great amount of baggage and supplies must be handled."

Shurtleff's air view drawing is a persuasive representation of his
objective. The revitalized campus looks as if two flatland City Beautiful axial Yale quads were glued to the Mt. Holyoke terrain. To Shurtleff's credit he gave the college excellent advice on replanting "decrepit
trees, the creation of new groves for shade and picturesque effect,
the development of interesting plantations of shrubbery and flowers
along the valley immediately east of the college." He persuaded the

trustees to relocate the power house, build a new chapel and infirmary, consolidate and extend the athletic fields, and transform a redundant gymnasium into a classroom building. He anticipated the coming of the auto age, declaring, "As far as possible, vehicles are to be kept out of the quadrangles" (*American Landscape Architect,* January 1930). Ironically, the Mt. Holyoke principles were directly opposite to his views about landscape and campus development at Wellesley College, where the picturesque was a dominant theme.

Shurtleff's report picks up and broadcasts several background themes evident in the early Depression days, a cultural condition that may have dampened the war of styles and their impact on promoting heritage spaces in any guise. Expounding in an article entitled "Convenience and Beauty in the Grouping of Buildings on a College Campus" (*American School and University,* 1931), landscape architect Arthur H. Carhart said an appropriate master plan for the grounds "considers primarily and directly efficiency, good organization of elements, basically sound design for use." Style, formal or informal, is not the issue. "Convenience, efficiency, low maintenance, fullest adaptation of the site to use are primary objectives.... Beauty is inherent in the design when these objectives are reached."

Mixed values, mixed signals, mixed plans are ever a danger to creator, patron, and the created. Another example of an ideal pursued as cultural convention but seen in different ways by those affected by the designs is Charles Platt's plan for the south campus at the University of Illinois. A noteworthy concept from the 1920s, informed by the university's landscape supervisor, Ferruccio Vitale, the plan was intended to address the results of what Karl B. Lohman, associate professor of landscape architecture, called American higher education's "worst period of architectural decadence." In words that may seem equally germane for our age, Lohman linked the "inharmonious" with "changing National tastes, changing administrative and educational policies, and alternating financial ups and downs" (*American Civic Annual,* 1930).

The Platt concept "will stand for centuries as monuments of good taste and far vision," wrote architect Alfred Granger, also reviewing the scheme in 1930. The "landscape planning" of the central spaces will help bring "polyglot architecture...into some sort of harmony with the new [and the campus] will have much the same charm in the prairie country as have the courts and quadrangles of Cambridge in the flat fens of England."

Interestingly, or ironically, Lohman saw a different cultural emphasis when commenting on the same scheme. It is "a style which was used by the early builders of America and which is closely intertwined with our American traditions...a domestic, livable character.

Without being stiffly formal or monumental the buildings [and land-scapes] have achieved dignity, scale, vigor, fitness, and beauty." One place, one plan, two polar interpretations as to intention and meaning.

Time, Taste, Continuity

The impact of time on the grand concept can be benign or bruising. The University of California, Irvine, campus plan (1962) was a bold-stroke concept that superimposed six clusters of buildings in a geo-metric arrangement on rolling southern California farmland. Like spokes in a wheel, clusters were pointed toward and joined at a hub, in this instance an arboretum. The combination of formal and informal landscapes and parking on the periphery gave priority to pedestrian movement throughout the campus. As in Central Park and Radburn, New Jersey, vehicular traffic was separated from pedestrians by bridges and short tunnels. The central space would contain viable trees, gath-ered worldwide to celebrate the university's connection to the larger world. The design envisioned a lake, informal grove, and amphitheater. Presumably one would gaze across the park to the other sectors.

A photo from a site visit in the 1960s evokes this sense of open-ness. The campus design structure is palpable. A site visit thirty years later and comparable view discloses blankets of thick foliage in many directions. The design concept is obscured. If a perceptible sense of place is the desired outcome, Irvine has lost it. If an exceptional and extensive range of landscape experiences is favored, then the trade-off has been productive. Furthermore, apparently the diminishment of the first form and its mandated style has encouraged some adven-turesome architecture. With project-specific landscapes done in Cali-fornia style, Irvine has become a must-visit venue for seeing and enjoying late-twentieth-century institutional design.

In contrast, the buildings and grounds concept at the Harvard Uni-versity Graduate School of Business, conceived as a distinctive precinct design, not only has survived the possible ravages of changing taste and time but has thrived, admitting some peculiarities in architecture but ever faithful to the Olmsted brothers' landscape design. The original Collegiate Georgian *parti* was set by McKim, Mead & White, winners of a design competition that included French Provincial and Neoclas-sic solutions for seemingly desolate tidal river marshland. Parentheti-cally, the bait that attracted potential donors to commit to relocation, thus launching the competition, was a relatively crude drawing that showed the proposed business school teaching and administration buildings spread out like the College Yard (as Harvard Yard was then labeled) and four dormitories surrounding a large nondescript quad.

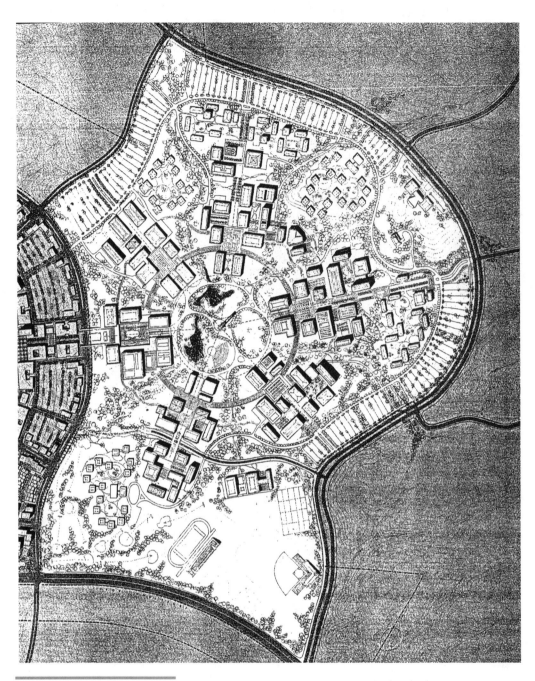

START-UP CONCEPT, 1963 / University of California, Irvine

A formal geometry is overlaid on a mix of quads and gardens, the centerpiece being an arboretum.   *Graphic:* Author's collection.

UNIVERSITY OF CALIFORNIA, IRVINE, 1967 / UNIVERSITY OF CALIFORNIA, IRVINE, 1999
The central open space has been filled with a lush landscape and the geometry of the founder's concept blurred by new attitudes about appropriate architecture and landscape. *Photos:* R. P. Dober.

There was little mention of landscape, nor were there clues as to site design objectives.

The competition instructions covered all aspects, however. The $40,000 investment in prizes and Harvard's reputation drew attention worldwide. The McKim, Mead & White scheme was vetted in January 1925, with groundbreaking in June 1925. The first dormitories were occupied in October 1926, and the original educational and library building complex was finished in February 1927. The enterprise was a fine example of facility planning and fast-track construction, faithful to the first conceptualization, although the final scheme did not include a chapel or a model factory, as some had hoped. These latter buildings were unnecessary and not wise, ruled a senior administrator. But he was willing to set aside sites for undesignated growth, holding land that secured the school's future physically. As it turned out, seven decades later a new chapel, a creative blend of indoor and outdoor landscape, graced the school grounds.

The original landscape was slower to develop because of inadequate funds and a terrain that had not yet settled or dried sufficiently for planting. After three years passed, both conditions were rectified. Succeeding generations became responsible stewards of the Olmsted principles: open quads and small courtyards laced with an exceptional variety of regional plant materials, human in scale—a comforting landscape of heritage spaces. The latest plan (1996) situates new housing so as to keep open a lawn that frames picture-postcard views from the dining hall—one of the great campus design vistas in North America. A proposed campus center is positioned to forge one edge of a new quad, spatial growth by complimentary accretion. Baker Library is expanded southward to maintain its traditional river frontage. As it should in principle and implementation, the composite view of the 1996 development plan illustrates a unified landscape concept, though in fact the ensemble has grown and will grow in several stages.

Irvine modified significantly (some would say rejected) its founding landscape design concept because it did not reflect newly perceived and (presumably for Irvine) better architectural concepts. The Harvard Graduate School of Business was able to incorporate some new tastes in building style with a set of heritage spaces that to date can continue to accommodate those inevitable transitions in architectural taste. Further, where reasoning and funding can prevail, some of the buildings that are architectural misfits will be removed or altered in accordance with the plan. As to the campus landscape, the desired outcomes are firmly stated in the business school's 1996 campus development policy and campus plan: "The campus landscape is recognizably vital to the character of the existing campus. The extension

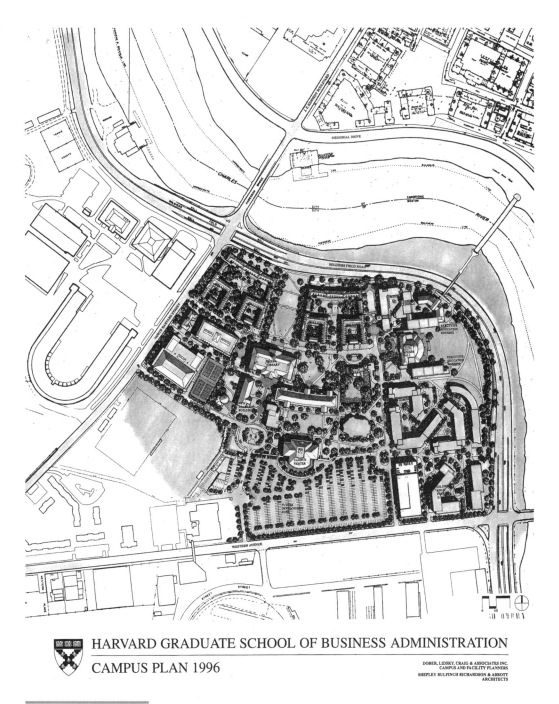

1996 CAMPUS PLAN / Harvard University Graduate School of Business Administration
A new quad is added to one of New England's most outstanding landscaped precincts, exceptional in the continuity of the landscape concept, the visual sequence from space to space, the Charles River vistas, the variety and quality of the plant materials, and maintenance.   *Graphic:* Dober, Lidsky, Craig and Associates, Inc.

and perpetuation of focal open spaces and distinctive plantings is a design imperative."

Another aspect of time's impact on primary spaces involves plant growth and longevity. Under the guise of financial prudence, some imaginative schemes have foundered because the trees selected for the start-up were too slight and slender for the desired effect. Being incomplete, the designs became orphans. Left unattended, they withered. Other schemes have matured but then disappear through poor maintenance and ignorance as to when and how to replace the greenery. John C. Loudon's memorial to Humphry Repton (c. 1830) summarizes the dilemma of maturation for the creators and the created: "Unfortunately, the monumental works of the landscape gardener are not like those of the architect, which live to future ages, and become a lasting record of the taste and genius of the contriver. Time makes unrelenting havoc with designs, which, in living materials during the [first years] may have afforded unmixed satisfaction. Young trees will outgrow their situation, while old ones will be uprooted by age or accident [falling] into decay, or be neglected by their owners... leaving no trace of the master hand which first laid the foundation of future improvement."

Heritage space features: More often than not, these are combinations of grass, trees, shrubs, planting beds, limited paving, sculpture, seating, lights, and signs. Even the most urban and site-constrained campus will embrace some version of the formula as an iconic gesture to membership and participation in the community of higher education. Witness the courtyard at Manhattan's New School for Social Research, the blanket of grass at the Victorian College of the Arts (Australia), and the eye-catching greensward at Santa Fe Community College (New Mexico), a soft emerald isle beguiling in contrast to the desert colors, soil, and vegetation surrounding the complex.

The seesawing of taste and preference colors historic accounts, particularly in the past century, when the number of institutions increased exponentially, leading colleges became full universities, architectural theory and practice dramatically transformed accepted esthetic canons, and functional requisites enlarged the number of building types. Campus landscape followed these movements (with some exceptions), seemingly more humble in terms of claiming a new and advancing cultural position. If the professional journals are reliable indicators of aspirations and accomplishments, most of our current forms of primary spaces generally existed by the 1900; not so with architecture. On the other hand, where architectural styles run up and down the escalator of prevailing styles cyclically defined, developed, disseminated, dismissed, rediscovered, there appear to be fewer debates about campus landscape other than chronology and formal-versus-informal concepts. Campus greenery in any guise seems to be a situation taken for granted, comforting and acceptable to all.

Contrasting Spaces

Are there fundamental differences in these two kinds of three-dimensional art—architecture, which seems to require innovation or novelty to survive as art, and landscape, with its self-perpetuation and recycling of older ideals? Architecture changed with technology: relatively cheap steel and glass, the elevator, the telephone, air-conditioning, computers. Landscape has fewer comparable impacts. Arguably, historical examples that are energized with enlightened contemporary variations are splendid templates for primary spaces when they achieve recognizable excellence. And especially blessed are those campuses where one can see and enjoy contrasting concepts of heritage spaces, as in the University of Minnesota's St. Paul campus. The confluence of Cass Gilbert's formal quadrangle, a landmark in campus design, and the Olmsted-inspired informal landscape to the north is a splendid three-dimensional history of changing tastes and visual experiences.

New College (Oxford) is one the oldest and best examples of linked contrasting spaces. Founded in the late fourteenth century, it is believed to have been the first Western institution of higher education built to a comprehensive plan. The centerpiece is the Great Quadrangle with its time-honored grassy oval. To the west is the formal Cloister, also fourteenth century, dominated by a large holm oak

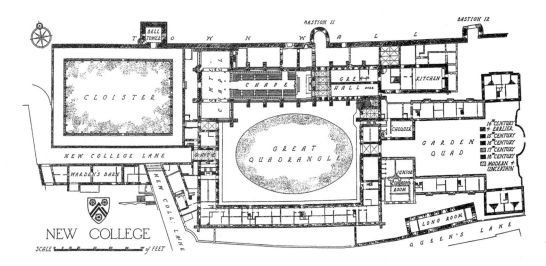

CONNECTED SPACES / New College, Oxford
Cloister, Great Quadrangle, Garden Court—five centuries of landscape development, unsurpassed examples of collegiate landscape beauty. *Graphic:* Author's collection.

POTTER'S PLAN / Union College

The power of an original concept gains respect from later generations: E. T. Potter's faithful gesture toward completing Joseph-Jacques Ramée's scheme. In a Victorian style two city halls are joined to a chapel. Clusters of trees surround the focal building. The emphatic architectural composition, little of which was built, seemingly divides the lawns from the forest beyond. The lawn remains today; the forest is now a low-density residential neighborhood. *Source:* Author's collection.

that shadows most of the space. The Garden Quad was transformed several times, and its history parallels changes in English landscape styles. It was built first as a conventional open quad; an artificial ziggurat-shaped mound and geometric lines of pyramidal trees were later inserted in the sixteenth-century formal fashion. In the eighteenth and nineteenth centuries the mound was softened and disguised by thick plantings. Some straight-line walks were replaced in part by Romantic-style serpentines, and the walls, once fortifications, turned green with mold as a background for seasonal flowers.

Of early American campuses, Union College (Schenectady) provides a superb example of contrasting heritage spaces and a good tale of changing tastes and enduring concepts. Abutting are a formal green carpet and a 10-acre heavily textured botanical garden and arboretum. The first is the benchmark open space in Joseph-Jacques Ramée's formal campus plan; the latter is Jackson's Garden. A landmark in campus design, the calibrated Ramée scheme is the collaborative effort of a visionary college president (Eliphalet Nott) and the immigrant French architect. Around 1813 the two devised their scheme for transforming swamp and sand hill, ravine and pasture into a pancaked plane, U-shaped campus design. Dramatic in simplicity, the heritage space has buildings on three sides, with the visual center punctuated by a domed structure reminiscent of James Gibb's Radcliffe Library. To the north, on undulating terrain, the eponymous Isaac W. Jackson, from 1831 through 1877, created a 10-acre plantation. Site features today include a running brook (kill), formal garden, meadow, and amphitheater. The delightfully textured mix of botanical gardens and cultivated groves is being restored (1999), suitable homage to the oldest continuous garden of its type in American higher education.

More recently the college has added a third heritage space to the ensemble. The campus center building was redesigned and extended to take advantage of the views into Jackson's Garden. Three landscapes were added: a lawn and terrace, an herb garden, and a wild-flower garden. Events and activities in the center can spill out and over into an extraordinary collegiate landscape environment. This is in

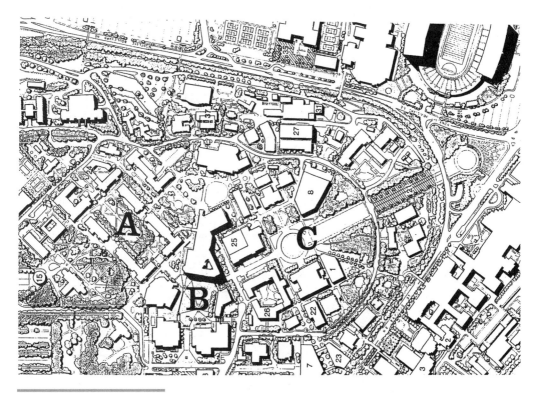

CONTRASTING SPACES / University of Washington

Why not contrasting spaces? A campus is an educational institution, and a variety of spaces in different styles can be read as a three-dimensional textbook of fads, fashions, and local history. At the University of Washington one can see and appreciate a cross section of landscape concepts. (A) the traditional quad; (B) an irregularly configured plaza; (C) a remnant of a City Beautiful mall. *Graphic:* University of Washington; courtesy Pam Stewart.

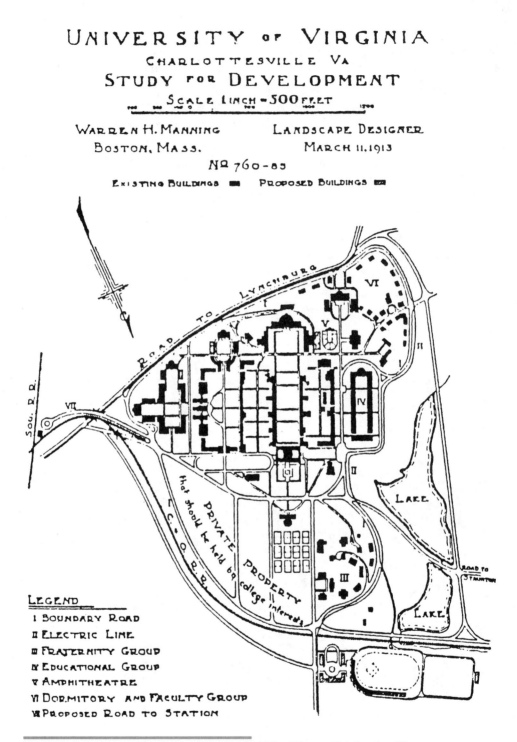

UNIVERSITY OF VIRGINIA
CHARLOTTESVILLE VA
STUDY FOR DEVELOPMENT
SCALE 1 INCH = 500 FEET

WARREN H. MANNING   LANDSCAPE DESIGNER
BOSTON, MASS.   MARCH 11, 1913

Nº 760-83

EXISTING BUILDINGS ■■   PROPOSED BUILDINGS ▥

LEGEND
I BOUNDARY ROAD
II ELECTRIC LINE
III FRATERNITY GROUP
IV EDUCATIONAL GROUP
V AMPHITHEATRE
VI DORMITORY AND FACULTY GROUP
VII PROPOSED ROAD TO STATION

BEAUX ARTS AT CHARLOTTESVILLE / The Warren H. Manning Plan
Graphic: Author's collection.

keeping with one of the defining functional characteristics of heritage spaces—they are infused with multiple uses and are not just static stage scenery for architecture. Thus the Union College ensemble of heritage spaces supports educational programs (outdoor classroom, arts display, testing area for student soils engineering and botanical experiments) and campus life (college center functions, informal social gatherings, picnics, ceremonies, general rest and relaxation).

Institutional reality: The older and larger the campus the more likely it is to have a group of contrasting primary spaces, usually because tastes change, as at Minnesota, and the start-up design cannot accommodate growth. The reality can be negative or positive, depending on the location and quality of the original design, the degree to which the subsequent spaces are equally meritorious, and the man-

IMPRINTING FASHIONABLE DESIGN / Harvard College, 1960
Warren Manning's 1913 proposal for imprinting a flatland axial Beaux Arts concept on Thomas Jefferson's rolling terrain at the University of Virginia (see *left*) is an interesting example of fashion ignoring site realities and history. Thus commendable is the Sasaki, Walker landscape concept for Quincy House, Harvard College. Clearly and cleanly a modern aesthetic, the design is an intelligent interpretation of Collegiate Georgian (a gesture to local tradition), urban Cambridge (a welcome open space on an impacted site), and New England greenery (the planting choices reflecting climate and changes). *Photo:* Gotthscho-Schleinser, Inc.; Author's collection.

ner in which they are purposively linked to generate an attractive sequential landscape experience.

Contrasting heritage spaces may be grouped in clusters or arranged like a necklace. The University of Washington central campus area is commendable, with three kinds of primary spaces within several hundred yards of each other: a residential quad, a formal mall, and a plaza whose configuration conjures an image of an ancient Tuscan hill town. Each space has a distinctive landscape treatment. At the University of Pennsylvania the main campus walk (see page 133) offers glimpses into a string of visually interesting heritage spaces.

The contribution of circulation design (paths and roads) to the shaping, positioning, and perception of heritage spaces was discussed earlier. When they are well formulated, the linkages and connections between heritage spaces will raise the quality of the overall campus landscape from the top tier to the nonpareil. Interestingly, in this respect not all honored places have been successful. The Claremont Colleges possess a full range of landscape types, but their primary spaces are not yet linked into a single areawide design concept. Jefferson's heritage space at the University of Virginia, icon and template for many campus landscape schemes, seems to defy visual and physical connection to adjacent spaces. Landscape architect Warren H. Man-

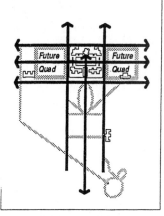

Original axes (1891)

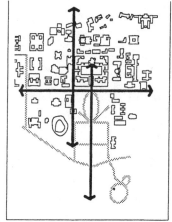

Buildings have blocked half the original axes (1988)

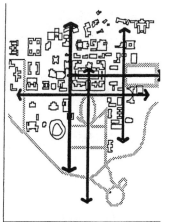

The Near West Campus Plan proposes restoring one of the original axes and creating a new one (2000)

ADJUSTING TO SITE REALITY / Stanford University

Site demolition allows the university to restore some of the original (1891) spatial concepts. Lesson: Campus landscape strategies should reflect site realities, and good results may require some capital investments in removing visual impediments as well as adding new landscape components. *Graphic:* Stanford University; courtesy Phil Williams.

ning's 1913 efforts are revealing. On paper his proposed expansion east and west from Jefferson's Lawn, with its combinations of closed and open site compositions and connecting paths, would seem sensible were the terrain flat, which it is not. The drawing exposes the basic flaw in Jefferson's scheme, a self-contained jewel situated on a site whose terrain limits fluent and immediately perceptible additions and connections. Fortunate, then, is Stanford University, where the original landscape scheme, delightfully informed with primary spaces, highly axial in composition, could be extended in spirit without topographic impediments. The original design was somewhat blurred by later construction, which the latest set of landscape guidelines addresses. Actions include removing a major structure (the Physics Tank) to open views northward, additional portals and gateways to connect the earlier-generation heritage spaces, and a new axis to the west leading to a contemporary set of primary spaces.

The ideal of contrasting and connecting primary spaces, informed by local culture and traditions, can be introduced at the policy level as well as in site-specific proposals. At the broadest scale of campus design, the University of Wyoming expects to make a campus design asset out of the pronounced differences in two contrasting heritage spaces and their different landscape expressions. At first glance, Wyoming's West Campus would appear to have the most attractive spaces and architecture, with East Campus being "merely an area of leftovers." On closer inspection those impressions hold true. West Campus is defined, say the local campus planners, by a strong perimeter that includes rows of cottonwoods. These convey a message that the precinct is a "cloistered environment, turning inward as opposed to outward, a perspective very much in line with the philosophy of a campus as an educational community unto itself." East Campus is a "very amorphous and ambiguous space." The West Campus landscape is the pedestrian's domain; on East Campus the automobile reigns. Future landscapes (existing heritage spaces preserved and new spaces added) in each geographic precinct will reflect a territorial duality. West Campus, a "garden of education," will have a landscape that "engages students in the action of learning, while setting up barriers to ensure outsiders cannot disturb this process." Promoting "visitor interaction," the East Campus landscape will surround and enhance facilities devoted to "entertainment and public events." The unfolding development is being explained and furthered by a university Web site labeled "A Dialogue Between Two Separate but Equal Landscapes," helping gain support for historic preservation funds (always difficult to raise) and site locations where new landscapes would be most beneficial.

2.12 SECONDARY SPACES

Acknowledging some degree of ambiguity in definitions—campus landscape being more art than science, and every campus being a distinctive place—nonetheless it is useful to separate primary spaces from secondary ones. The division is one not of size, specific design, or artistic merit, but of recognition that heritage spaces in their fullest expression have greater visual and symbolic impact on the campus design than secondary landscapes. The latter forms would include minor quads, courtyards, terraces, and the perceptible landscape zones that surround and extend architecture. Admittedly there is also an overlap in definition with gardens, which we treat below extensively. The overlap may be explained by degrees of horticultural expression. Secondary spaces have some landscape features. Gardens, with their many variations both functional and visual, are the apical forms of campus greenery.

Historically in Western architecture, courts and courtyards in castles, palaces, and monastic colleges provided light to the surrounding building interiors, and privacy and shelter from unwanted intrusions. Most accounts of the evolution of campus architecture and landscape pay proper homage to Oxford and Cambridge, at one time literally, as in Bryn Mawr College's 1907 library. Less celebrated antecedents are some continental examples, of which the Alhambra (Granada, Spain) would rank high in responsiveness to topography, climate, and local ecological conditions. Parenthetically, the variations in the shape and landscape treatment of the spaces that make up the Alhambra composition should be of great interest to contemporary landscape architects seeking to animate their designs with contrasting expressions inside a determinable and perceptibly bounded area.

Yale University's Hewett Quadrangle gains attention as a secondary space within which a sunken courtyard, with a sculptural work by Isamu Noguchi, provides light to interior rooms. The patterned marble courtyard floor holds a stone circle, pyramid, and cube, the artist's symbolic gestures to passing time and chance. At Stanford University—memorable with abundant and extraordinary campus landscapes—a recently developed sunken courtyard (1996) is equally abstract in landscape features, but the interpretation is less mystical. "Magical realism," says *New York Times* critic Lisa Germany (March 21, 1999) in praise of architect Ricardo Legoretta's designs for the Visual Arts Center of the College of Santa Fe. The courtyards and their visual sequence are like "a medieval city, developed piecemeal over the years." The colors and textures of the walls framing the spaces, rust red and pink, were inspired by the designer's memory of the region at dawn and dusk.

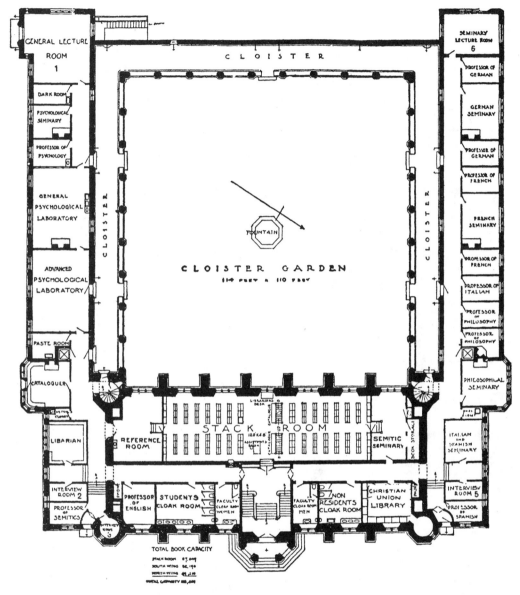

CLOISTER GARDEN, 1907 / Bryn Mawr College

Oxbridge comes to Pennsylvania in this stylized interpretation of a monastic university landscape design. The cloistered area is a 12,000-square-foot garden of grass, a green carpet for a fountain given by the class of 1901. Honored on its opening day for its plan and design and listed today as a meritorious historic building, it was not a concept that set a standard for peers who favored less enclosure in their campus designs.   *Graphic:* Author's collection.

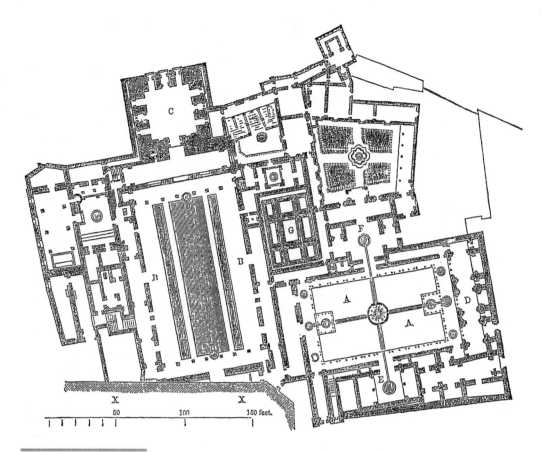

X   X
50   100   150 feet.

NEW PRECEDENTS? / The Alhambra
The impact of historical forms from Cambridge and Oxford can be found in numerous late-nineteenth-century architecture and landscape. Examining current trends, one would surmise that places such as the Alhambra, with its exceptional and eccentric layout of gardens and courtyards, may offer ideas of consequence to contemporary designers. *Graphics:* Author's collection.

The ensemble belongs near the top of the list of great late-twentieth-century campus landscapes. The courtyard at Claremont-McKenna goes stylistically in a different direction, contemporary Spanish Baroque, loaded with place-marking hints of and gestures to regional history. That which was commands attention. Princeton University describes the plaza dedicated to the class of 1941 as an evocation of its Gothic tradition, but also in its detailing and greenery an "example of the urban landscape formed by the newer architecture and plantings on the campus." Another connection between civic design and campus design?

For Indiana University, landscaped collegiate courtyards are rich in the cultural values that inflect and inform the purpose and physical forms of higher education. In a poetic exposition, *Islands of Green and Serenity* (Indiana University, 1991), the university declares itself to be a "place of many smaller places." Praising the landscape theme at an alumni dinner in 1982, university president John W. Ryan said nature must rule "to soften the edges of concrete and stone and to embrace the whole campus in the loveliness" of bountiful landscape. The Indiana campus design is praised today as "a series of courtyards, some formal, some open. The campus is not seen from any one place but reveals itself gradually as a progression of changing outlooks."

The Indiana campus landscape theme is a mosaic of visually different secondary spaces—not a hodgepodge, one appreciates, but an encyclopedia of fashions and styles. In contrast, the landscape for the new campus for the Benemérita Universidad Autónoma de Puebla (Mexico) was conceived from the beginning (1977) as a series of connected courtyards and small plazas. The design reflects and honors the local architectural and landscape traditions that have given Puebla high ranking for its vernacular civic design. The palette includes paving, water, plants in containers, and sun and shadow effects where buildings and spaces intersect. Never fully built to the original specifications, left decaying in the politically tumultuous decades that followed, the campus design landscape concept was revived and extended as part of a campus revitalization plan in 1994.

HEWETT COURTYARD / Yale University
Gestures to passing time and chance via Isamu Noguchi's stone carvings.   *Photo:* R. P. Dober.

MAGICAL REALISM OR MINIMALISM? / College of Santa Fe
One of those rare works of art that can be enjoyed for metaphorical allusions, or as an interpretation of regional design influences, or as an awesome and breathtaking spatial experience of unexpected but convincing combinations of form and color: an ensemble nonpareil. *Photo:* R. P. Dober.

The design of secondary spaces affords substantial opportunities to install campus landscapes that mark, in significantly different ways, time and place—designs that transcend the bland, formula-driven, and repetitive. There are exalting choices when considering strategically a campus landscape design motif, say Apollonian versus Dionysian. The former may be characterized as geometric, linear, rectangular, controlled, organized, transparent, muted, hard-edged, and (*pace* New His-

COURTYARD: REGIONAL STYLE / Claremont-McKenna College
Regional themes used in place marking.   *Photo:* Sasaki Associates.

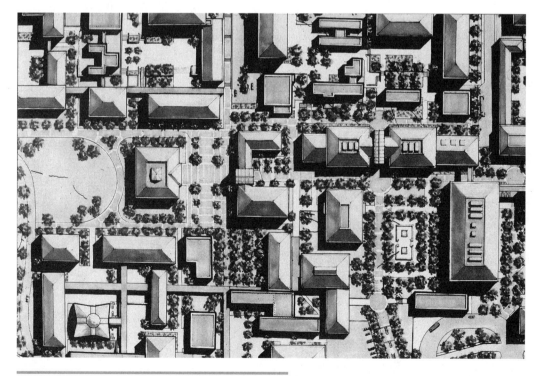

RESTORATION AND ENHANCEMENT PLAN / Benemérita Universidad Autónoma de Puebla
Courts and quads were restored, extended, and added as part of a campuswide landscape revitalization strategy.
Graphic: Dober, Lidsky, Craig and Associates, Inc.

torians) formal. The opposite would be loose, picturesque, soft-edged, and polychromatic, not easily perceived or understood in a glance. Preferment? One remembers with delight student studio debates on the merits of Rothko versus Mondrian. How splendid to have choices.

For the searching eye, there are ample opportunities on most campuses to install secondary landscapes. Seeing "leftover" space between buildings, "a dreary, empty yard with an uneven floor of asphalt accommodating broken bicycle racks and a few old cars," the principal at Upper Canada College (Toronto) found funds to transform a campus design esthetic liability into an award-winning landscape asset. As a place-marking gesture, the quadrangle floor is paved with local Credit Valley sandstone. At the University of Utah library expansion, the roof level becomes a landscaped terrace, with bountiful cityscape and campus panoramas.

The alert campus planning office will keep track of such landscape opportunities, such as the proposals illustrated in MIT's East Campus strategic development plan. Far from grandiose, they communicate the desire to create places that people are likely to use in the course of the day (attractive and convenient) and experience visually while passing

Prince Philip Quadrangle

Upper Canada College, Toronto

Quadrangle Redevelopment

DU TOIT ASSOCIATES LTD., 1979

This "leftover" space between buildings was, in the words of the principal, "a dreary, empty yard with an uneven floor of asphalt accommodating some broken bicycle racks and occasionally a few old cars". It has now been transformed into an attractive urban quadrangle. Flooring is Credit Valley Sandstone with seating steps facing south. Lightly leaved locust trees catch the sunlight and provide dappled shade.

The quadrangle was opened by HRH Prince Philip during the 150th anniversary of the school. Construction cost was $50,000.

WASTE LAND REGAINED / Upper Canada College, Ontario
Wasted and obsolete space reclaimed for a courtyard with a design good enough for royalty.   *Graphic:* Courtesy du Toit Allsopp Hillier, Toronto.

LIBRARY TERRACE / University of Utah
A landscape opportunity afforded by the library expansion. *Photo:* R. P. Dober.

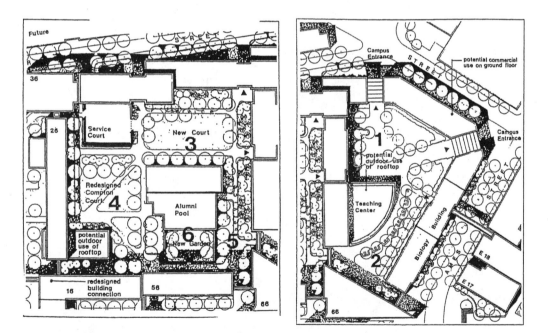

PLANNING AHEAD / Massachusetts Institute of Technology
Landscape is a rare art in that its fullest expression may never be seen by its creators. A cluster of convincing landscape concepts is defined and illustrated in the sector plan as part of the overall physical development strategy. The drawings (Wallace, Floyd Associates, Inc.) help the institute's constituencies and the city understand MIT's qualitative campus landscape goals and objectives. The exciting and forward-looking mix includes courts, gardens, terraces, and rooftop landscapes. The specific concepts and drawings are a casebook example of anticipatory design. While the concepts may not be constructed as shown, they also serve as an informative graphic programmatic statement of desired design intentions and directions. *Graphic:* MIT Planning Office.

EXEMPLAR, OUTSIDE / Pomona College
An index to high-quality design: benches, paving, trees, shrubs, a fountain, and lighting, all semienclosed, accessible from a major building, and located at the intersection of two major campus walks.   *Photo:* R. P. Dober.

EXEMPLAR, INSIDE / Rochester Institute of Technology
An indoor gardenlike courtyard, adjacent to the campus union, and particularly delightful in the gray months; a space type too often missing on the American campus.   *Photo:* R. P. Dober.

through the spaces. The proposals also optimize land use with the suggested rooftop greenery. Concepts of this quality, expressed as strategy and adjusted to emerging resources and needs, belong in every institutional campus planning portfolio. They make visible the possible and, as benchmarks, alert those who are making capital investment decisions to the existence of criteria, standards, and directions worth taking.

Of concepts realized, the residential courtyard at Pomona College and the campus center atrium space at the Rochester Institute of Technology illustrate how high aspirations for secondary spaces can be achieved with reasonable budgets.

2.13 TERTIARY SPACES

Viable campuses have landscaped nooks and crannies and outdoor areas that provide opportunities for individuals and small groups to participate in the less formal aspects of collegiate life. Refuges for some, social transaction areas for others, the spaces may be adapted for these purposes by chance, or may come into existence as purpose-built and carefully located functional landscapes.

Purpose-built tertiary spaces may range from gazebos to a large planter, indented wall, or an outdoor staircase alcove—each custom-

TERTIARY SPACE OPPORTUNITY / No-Name College
Photo: R. P. Dober.

NOOK AND CRANNY SEATING / University of Michigan, East Campus
Photo: Courtesy JJR.

designed also for seating. Seating is the prime function of tertiary spaces, and the forms and features seem unlimited as one scans the campus for places and the product literature for examples. It has been said that architects know they have gained prominence when manufacturers produce windows that emulate the designer's invention, if not patent. For landscape architects the equivalent tribute might be benches, for there appears to be no limit as to choices in style, configuration, and materials. Not all are well designed, so buyer beware. Some are hard to clean of debris and dirt, or the seats are pitched so rainwater can't drain, or they are uncomfortable in height, width, or backing. The selection and use of a single design type can help unify the landscape visually. And there would still be the possibility, occasionally, for some unusual bench or seat design that in contrast to the predictable enlivens the campus scene with an eccentric piece suitable for an educational institution.

Some seats can be clustered into a tertiary landscape, like furnishing an outdoor living room. Those situated off major paths tend to get the heaviest use. Where such is likely, some kind of paving under the seating avoids mud and puddles and adds to the appearance of being in a designed space. Add to the enclave some lighting, signs, and trash baskets and one can realize a high-quality campus landscape solution, functional and attractive. Such might be walled in or fenced by hedges. Any and all are excellent for commemorating or memorializing a person, graduating class, or event. See also pages 54–76 for some additional design and human behavior issues, and page 194 for illustrations.

2.14 WETSCAPES

▶ There is nothing of the kind lovelier in England. The velvet turf, the ancestral elms and hoary lindens—the long vistas of ancient avenues—the quiet river—graceful stone bridges—old halls of grey, red or yellow—the lofty pinnacles of King's College Chapel o'ertopping all. (A. E. Reeve, *Cambridge Chronicle* [Cambridge, 1859])

▶ Of all the elements that combine in the perfect garden or landscape design none are more important than the judicious use of water areas. (George Dillistone, *Landscape and Garden* [London, 1936])

▶ Fall Creek and Cascadilla Creek gorges are defining features of Cornell.... Crossing them on a daily basis is a significant experience for many in the Cornell community. They give access to a powerful image of wilderness within an increasingly controlled urban landscape. (John Ullberg [Ithaca, 1992])

———————

Wetscapes is a term devised to describe landscapes that are essentially marked by the use of water. The designs range from those crafted by hand or machine to natural features captured and contained as macroscale campus landscape imagery. Forms include rivers, streams, creeks, lakes, ponds, and monumental fountains. Small or large, they may function as a vista or setting, something to see near or far; or from their shore they may present a view to another horizon. In some instances the fountains serve as a contrapuntal element in an architectural composition, or are freestanding sculpture with elaborate lighting, conceived as minimalist art with an arching spray rippling a sheet of water. The fountain at Imperial Valley College delights with its splashing sounds and cooling effect. Reflecting the realities of an arid region, the palm trees integrated into the area design afford some shade and complement the campus landscape theme. Some wetscapes may function also as recreation areas, for example, for crew, canoeing, sailing, or swimming, or for walking, running, or biking around the lake or along the riverbank.

Campus design histories are rich with significant examples of wetscapes. Early engravings of American campuses included water features. Often the draftsperson would show an idyllic pond in the background or foreground—features that on further research have proven to be a promotional illusion, probably to make the site fashionable and attractive to the public, or maybe simply the designer's chimera. Of works completed, our favorites would include the lakes at Worcester College (Oxford), Carleton College (Minnesota), and the University of Miami. Here some unlikely sites were turned into beauty spots.

The Worcester site was a "swampy, evil smelling" remnant created when the Oxford Canal was cut across the college property. A "virtue out of a necessity," writes historian Mavis Batey, describing the transformation (*Oxford Gardens* [Avebury, 1982]). In the early nineteenth century 3 acres of muck were deepened, formed, filled with water, and edged with trees to create an epitome of the picturesque campus landscape style. The Lyman Lakes (Carleton College) were first dredged in the 1920s by a physical plant director, D. Blake Stewart, from an overflowing pasture and brook, and later reshaped and embellished. The classic oxymoronic "untrained professional," Stewart had a good eye and an intuitive feel for melding topography and plant materials into picture-postcard scenery. With the landmark Lyman Lakes formed, he eventually went on to extend the lakeside greenery to the college arboretum, rerouted a campus creek to create athletic fields, and generally was responsible for changing what appeared to many as a windswept cow pasture with college buildings into a landscaped campus.

About the same time Blake was beautifying Carleton College, Miami was excavating and shaping a Florida version of Minnesota wetlands as a focal element in its embryonic development scheme. Seventy years later the university lakeside continues to be improved visually by relocating parking from its edges and by constructing better footpaths around the lake perimeter. The water theme is evoked with numerous campus fountains, including an eye-catching water spray positioned as a vertical element in Lake Osceola itself.

Among America's best example of high-quality contrasting spatial expressions, the University of California, Berkeley, campus is like a tasting menu, with a sample of landscape designs likely to please every palette. Two branches of Strawberry Creek, downplayed in earlier plans that promoted Beaux Arts site designs, are now armatures for pleasing rusticity. Winding their way through the undulating topography, the creekside landscape, with its "native vegetation and naturalized species forming dense woodlands," is featured in the 1990 Long Range Development Plan as a substantial contributor to the "unique character of the campus." Notable new campuses have developed significant water features as place-making campus landscape elements. These kinds of designs require careful engineering for gradients and enclosures, expert knowledge for viable planting at

Notable new campuses have developed significant water features as place-making campus landscape elements. These kinds of designs require careful engineering for gradients and enclosures, expert knowledge for viable planting at the banks, and a painterly eye for rendering either the soft-edged picturesque or the hard-edged design.

A SPECTRUM OF WATERSCAPES / University of Miami

Above, a water spray animating Lake Osceola (a heritage space) as art and aerating the water for viability; *below,* campus fountains, water used as a landscape theme.   *Photos:* R. P. Dober.

the banks, and a painterly eye for rendering either the soft-edged pic-turesque, as in the case of Furman University (South Carolina), or the hard-edged design, as at York University (Great Britain).

Expert George Dillistone divides water-related landscapes into three categories: lakeside or natural ponds, steams and watercourses, and "artificial construction where some retaining medium other than natural earth has to be used for conserving water." Of "formal pools and basins, it is really a simple matter of respecting the architectural design and creating invisible receptacles of sufficient area" for the de-sired play and movement of light, shade, and reflection. For nature captured, where necessity and opportunity so indicated, he would fill out the scene with plants that "thrive" in their unique ecological zone, and in that species selection and planting plan avoid the "disastrous sense of incongruity."

Frank Waugh (*Landscape Architecture*, April 1931) offers some in-sights for those who would like to take a pond or lake from an esthetic experience to an instructive exemplar of water, soil, and plant succes-sion. Waugh was concerned that landscape architects in their search for beauty "seriously, needlessly, and unintentionally contravened" natural plant groupings. The designer's interest in varying textures, colors, sizes, and shapes could be well met in the "naturalistic" ap-proach, thought Waugh. He outlined eight planting types, which could stretch from the middle pond or lake up the banks and beyond. These were: wholly submerged vegetation, floating leafed plants, marsh plants, marsh meadow, marsh shrub, swamp forest, and climax forest. Versions of Waugh's water-related planting schema, when adjusted for differences in regional plants and site conditions, could be explicated as an example of site history or folded into the natural sciences or environmental studies curriculum as an outdoor lab.

The Charles River basin (metropolitan Boston) is a photogenic example of buildings and landscapes viewed as a regional design, arguably the world's largest macro-scale campus heritage space, wet or dry. Several building clusters at Boston University, Harvard Uni-versity, and the Massachusetts Institute of Technology are designed and sited for river views. Looking inward from the riverside, there are attractive vistas of variegated architectural and landscape styles. The campuses are linked with an automobile-free network of riverside paths and bike routes. River recreation is available all year: crew in clement weather, ice skating when the water freezes deeply. With the completion of a regional water treatment project, the river will be safe and healthy for casual and supervised swimming.

A century in the making as a university setting, the Charles River basin is an accretion of now pleasing happenstance. The fortuitous is also present in its contrasting counterpart, the Backs at Cambridge University, England. The contrast is to be found in both forms and features: the Charles River urbanized versus the pastoral River Cam, whose flow of water past six English colleges and their abutting lawns and gardens is an ensemble without equal. And all this, again, from the least promising beginnings, as Doreen Brockhouse records in her informative essay "The Cambridge Backs" (*Landscape and Garden,* summer 1938). "It must be remembered that the college enclosures at first had little to do with creating beautiful surrounding." The riverside was "utilitarian [and development] was at the mercy of many conflicting authorities." From swampy ground, fish ponds, grazing land for horses, "huge pigeon houses, which brought in money for dung sold as manure…came the happy mingling of the two arts of architecture and gardening." While the effect was serendipitous and unplanned, she writes, people of "vision and great taste and culture were not lacking, and although there is no record of coordinated activities, the sum total of their labours is this beautiful unified picture."

2.15 DRYSCAPES

Arguably, campus landscapes could be organized into three groups, greenscapes, wetscapes, and dryscapes, and an interesting pictorial essay could be written and illustrated with the components in the trilogy displayed in all their contrasting beauty. For our taxonomy a few notes on *dryscapes* will have to be sufficient, using two examples to stand for many.

Xeric is the technical term for landscapes in arid areas, where plants are selected for their viability in such an extreme climate. Several campuses in the American Southwest, notably the College of Santa Fe, Pueblo Community College, the University of Arizona, and New Mexico State University, have developed landscapes featuring xeric themes. They highlight crushed stone, geological specimens, cacti, and related plants. The compositions are superb place markers, especially when arrayed with differing colors, textures, and exotic forms against buildings whose facades and materials also are derived from regional architecture.

For stylistic rather than environmental reasons, some campuses have courtyards and plazas designed largely devoid of any greenery. Textured paving, bounders, stones, and metal are featured. Of several dozen seen recently, the dryscape courtyard at Western Kentucky State University would rank high on any list of paradigms.

Xeric is the technical term for landscapes in arid areas, where plants are selected for their viability in such an extreme climate.

XERIC LANDSCAPE / University of Arizona
Photo: R. P. Dober.

DRYSCAPE: DETAIL, LIBRARY TERRACE / College of Santa Fe
Photo: R. P. Dober.

GROVES, GARDENS, AND FIELDS FOR EDUCATION, ENTERTAINMENT, AND ENLIGHTENMENT

▶ Before long several of the schools drew themselves apart in special buildings, and even took their most familiar names, such as the Lyceum and the Academy, from the gymnasia, in which they made themselves at home.... Gradually we find the traces of material provisions, which helped to define and perpetuate the different sects. Plato had a little garden...in the shadowy groves of the Academy...there lived his successors, [gathering] pupils...who listened...as they walked under the trees, and who even had their little huts built there to live as near might be round his garden...a tiny glebe at first...but wealthier friends of learning added from time to time to the domain. (W. W. Capes, *University Life in Athens* [London, 1877])

▶ The original conception of a botanic garden was that literally implied by the name...[later] these institutions developed along broader and more inclusive lines, and a botanic garden is properly defined as a scientific and educational institution whose purpose is the advancement and diffusion of knowledge. (*Encyclopaedia Britannica*, 14th ed.)

▶ In medieval Europe, the immediate ancestor of our own civilization, the first scientific study of plants centered about their medicinal uses.... [H]erb gardens of the monasteries, in which learning survived during the "dark ages," became used for the instruction of future physicians: they were perhaps the first botanic gardens. (W. H. Rickett, *The Garden Journal*, September-October 1956)

▶ I have a dream for this garden. When a person is tired, or anxious, or in quest of beauty, may they enter and come forth refreshed to meet the problems of the day. (Lorraine Miller Collins, donor, Earl Burns Miller Japanese Garden, California State University, Long Beach, 1996)

The comments on the typology will now cover eleven campus landscapes whose functions are informed and shaped by educational goals and objectives. This section of the typology also gives opportunity for some expanded comments on the factors and circumstances that make these and related landscapes particularly relevant for sites devoted to higher education.

We begin with landscapes that are designed to use plant materials for scientific and esthetic purposes. The former include discipline-based studies such as botany and dendrology, outdoor laboratories for the natural sciences, and training grounds for horticulturists and landscape architects. As to esthetics, some campus landscapes are intended to be works of art through their horticultural display; others are the binding space within which artworks are inserted, a kind of outdoor museum, typically for sculpture. As one can readily appreciate, in this category the dividing line between science and art is often blurred. The very selection and arrangement of botanical specimens of scientific and educational purposes can create visual effects of great and enduring beauty. There are also significant differences in magnitude and scale and in degrees of intention, relevance, and permanence in designing and constructing these kinds of landscapes. Our list includes botanical gardens, horticultural gardens, arboreta, natural preserves, and nature walks and trails. Gardens for art, special theme gardens, amphitheaters, and site history are then discussed, followed by play fields and recreation, and finally interior landscapes. The next to last recognizes the educational importance of these greens, where organized and informal sports promote a sound mind in a sound body. Inside greenery gets attention because new technologies offer exciting opportunities for shaping dramatic spaces and keeping plants viable. For purposes of carrying out an assessment and evaluation of an existing campus, or to outline concepts for inclusion in a new campus, the eleven items should cover most circumstances when applying the topology matrix. When conditions and factors require some modification in definition, so be it. Such would be a tribute to the complexity and diversity in landscapes that seems evident at campuses honored for their greenery.

2.16 BOTANICAL AND HORTICULTURAL GARDENS

We begin with landscapes for science, honoring an important starting point in the development of Western universities. Renaissance gardens in Padua, Uppsala, Leyden, and Oxford were notable for their acquisition, interpretation, and dissemination of scientific knowledge of drugs, herbals, and spices, and for their contributions to economic botany in the Age of Discovery. Early events at Padua have a contemporary overtone. The herb lore saved from monastic days, plants obtained through diplomatic exchanges and conquest, and a commune willing to pay for a status-conferring facility were melded into a university curriculum and campus design that drew scholars from around the world. As a result, this backwater town—a Venetian satellite and a minor place when compared to Florence or Milan—gained political stature and economic strength. The synergy was reminiscent, one observes, of contemporary regions seeking status and financial benefits by promoting and building joint university-corporation biotechnology centers in campus locations.

Today, outdoor campus-based science functions typically take the form of botanical and horticultural gardens and arboreta. The first are specialized landscapes encompassing a bountiful span and supply of plant materials. Arboreta are agglomerations of woody trees, shrubs, and vines, usually emphasizing dendrology. Generally, acting like museum curators, those responsible for these landscapes obtain, label, and interpret collections, which in this instance are of plants. These are grown for study and display, and provide living material for teaching and research. As much as possible the curators try to replicate the nurturing conditions associated with the specific plants. Art and science support each other. Display is the art and viability the science. Ponds for aquatics, rock gardens, a grove of trees with a background of shrubs— these are simulations of nature; carefully done, they are uplifting as

SARAH B. DUKE GARDENS / Duke University
Photo: R. P. Dober.

esthetic objects in the campus landscape as well as discipline-specific educational and investigative material. When the collaboration of designer and natural scientist works well, the results yield some magnificent campus scenery. Of exemplars, the Sarah B. Duke Gardens (Duke University) and the 39-acre living plant museum at the University of California, Riverside, illustrate two contrasting concepts, the horticultural garden and the botanical garden—functionally overlapping in purpose, different in forms, varied in features.

The Sarah B. Duke Gardens were started in the 1930s from a 50-acre pine forest valley adjacent to the university's West Campus. Popular tourist site, photogenic backdrop for wedding pictures, tranquil respite from quotidian university routines, informal playground, and of course, superior horticultural collection—the aquatic garden, rose garden, memorials, planting beds, open-air theater, classrooms, and support buildings offer something for everyone and anyone drawn to the site.

The art of gardening is epitomized in landscape architect Ellen Shipman's terraced gardens and the adjacent lily pond and plantings by F. H. Leubuscher. The gardens' commitment to education is expressed in many ways. Installation of garden artifacts and changes in plant arrangements become occasions for teaching not only garden art but also cultural history. The 1990 construction of a memorial sundial, a custom-crafted centerpiece sited in the Duke iris garden, gave cause for the curators to lecture visitors on the development of timekeeping devices as well as garden ornamentation, including a trope on variations in sundial inscriptions. The forcing of eight thousand tulips to bloom in concert each spring can be explained in budget sessions as longitudinal horticultural research, but the display is best remembered by many Duke University visitors for the dramatic splashes of color. Gardens of this quality and purpose require an institutional commitment to continuous care and unglamorous maintenance, a commitment not fully understood or easily gained when annual operating budgets are under siege. The Duke story includes endowment income for the gardens and periodic fund drives. The 1996 restoration plan addressed circulation and operations problems, clarified some of the planting schemes, and added another generation's share of plants and trees to the celebrated collections.

In size smaller than the Duke gardens, the 39-acre botanical garden at the University of California, Riverside, has more the profile of a natural setting than of a cultivated enclave. Where the Duke layout might be likened to a large plantation, the visitor experience at Riverside is influenced by the rugged terrain and the contrasting ecological zones. Within walking distance of the central campus are alder, cactus, red alder, and sequoia landscapes, mammal and bird sanctuaries, rose and herb gardens, a geodesic dome housing the cycad collection, and a bridge over a fish pond. The pond itself is alive with moisture-loving cattails and papyri, turtles and sunfish, dragonflies and reptiles. These and other features were started in the 1970s and then linked by an "outdoor classroom" trail. Beginning at a gatehouse and herbarium, the route carries one from a "low desert" zone to the more florid upper canyon and back. At several dozen points along the rail placards and information boards explain the site's significant natural features.

Surprisingly, of the four thousand American colleges and universities less than 10 percent have botanical gardens and arboretums. Why this should be so is puzzling in an age when ecology and the quality of the natural environment are central subjects. As we will see, extensive acreage is not required. The quotidian campus landscape can be arranged as an arboretum, if only by labeling trees with their botanical names and adding some local specimens not yet represented. Why should such opportunities be neglected? Ironically, hundreds of titles describing garden history and garden design can be found in architectural and design libraries, but few deal with campus examples of landscapes centered on science. The index in Norman Newton's magisterial compendium *Design on the Land: The Development of Landscape Architecture* (Cambridge, Massachusetts, 1971) has no listing for arboreta or botanical gardens, and no cross-references to such at colleges and universities, Arnold Arboretum excepted. The raw ore for a refined and valuable design history of campus landscape remains relatively unmined.

For the ardent proselytizer of additional and extensive campus landscape, aiming to encourage the further greening of higher education, what follows now are some additional descriptions of landscapes for science in the United States, beginning with antecedents and precedents and ending with some enlightening projects recently conceptualized. Plants, research, teaching, campus landscapes—of the value this linkage holds there should be no doubt, whether on today's campus or among the antecedents. These kinds of landscapes are well rooted, metaphorically and literally, in American higher education.

Inspiring Precedents

The value of university botanical gardens economically was identified by Presidents George Washington, Thomas Jefferson, and James Madison when they advocated creating a national botanical garden for Washington, D.C. Washington's ideas are thought provoking. Rather than construct a marine hospital on one of the squares designated in L'Enfant's plan for the new capital city, Washington favored locating thereon "a botanical garden [which] would be a good appendage to the institution of a university" (1797).

Later (1814) the first architect for the Capitol building (Dr. William Thornton) pressed Madison to support funding for such an enterprise. Citing Washington's idea, Thornton said the garden "would also be requisite in the establishment of a school of arts." Bolstering the argument of economic benefit, he also pleaded, "Every dollar laid out in forwarding such an institution would be well spent. The advantage would be incalculable, and the plants, trees, grapes, etc., distributed throughout this extensive country would everywhere be considered as blessings . . . for in the midst of incalculable riches we are poor, through miserable ignorance" of the nation's natural resources. Not then realized, the fundamental policy issue (national support for education and research with horticulture as a focal interest) was eventually met more fully with establishment of the great American agricultural and mechanical colleges and universities.

The legislation that launched these enterprises was, of course, Abraham Lincoln's Land Grant College Act of 1862. Proposed by Senator Justin Morrill in 1857 and authorized as an example of a beneficent central government during the desperate years of the Civil War, the act gave federal land to the states to sell or support colleges devoted to the agricultural and mechanical arts. In some instances, Cornell University being prominent, the assistance was given to private existing institutions. In the less settled regions, new campuses were developed.

"Aggie" architecture and landscape came in two forms, as institutions sought attention and status in the late nineteenth century. Some adopted architectural styles Old World and imperial in their iconography. Boxlike, functional brick and stone structures were embellished with classical motifs or paste-on Georgian details, or were given mansard roofs and towers that would seem more in place in Victorian Manchester than in an American rural setting. Sketch plans would show buildings arranged in rectangular regularity into quads that acknowledged monastic origins and East Coast fashions. Typically the complementary landscape would be a lawn and trees, sometimes sloped, but more often than not anticipating a machine-flattened topography.

Reality took a different course. Comforting to some institutions more rural than urban in their outlook, the less formal landscape concepts were most often adopted as the populist landscape theme. These were loose and strung-out site compositions, with architectural plums prominent in a seemingly casual and shapeless green pudding. The sedate formal concepts were squashed by sparkling picturesque compositions. The best designs, nature contrived, were magnificent. In this group pictorial and picturesque, pleasant and provincial Michigan College (now Michigan State University) could claim preeminence.

Michigan College was "undoubtedly one of the most beautiful examples, in some respects the very best example, of the type of landscape characteristic of the American college of the 19th century," Frederick Law Olmsted reported in 1915. Through "judicious planting and care" the Michigan College site had become a paradigm of the "pastoral approach" to campus design, with the "noble trees and broad expanse of turf...no self-contained quadrangles...[instead] "a pleasant part of a spacious open country." Expansion plans by successive campus planners have aimed to strengthen this idealized, value-charged landscape concept.

Coloring and carrying forward our account, Harold W. Lautner's recapitulation of Michigan College's later growth (*Landscape Architecture*, 1952) underlines the influence the horticulture faculty had on the local ethos. As early as 1865 courses were given in "landscape gardening." By 1884 the coursework, teaching modes, and educational intent had jelled. The college catalog stated: "Landscape gardening is treated as a fine art...principles are discussed at length and abundant illustrations are drawn from the picturesque views upon the college premises." Horticulture as a science was also woven into the landscape gardening degree requirements. "All these subjects are illustrated in walks which the professor takes with his class over the beautiful and extensive grounds of the college." In this respect the campus was an arboretum. Students could see and appreciate the linkage between science and art, and were quick to take pleasure in their knowledge. One remembers with appreciation subtle discussions at the drafting tables about landscape concepts, decades ago, among those trained in the Michigan tradition (with a strong grasp of botany and plants) and those from the Harvard University mode, where the historic botanical garden had succumbed to urbanization and the arboretum was miles away.

As a servant to the agricultural and food industry, Michigan College's involvement in basic research and information dissemination earned the school international rank. Throughout these decades professorial involvement in campus development became as influential as it was pervasive. The matching of the academic programs with the professional responsibilities for campus beautification reached a historic climax during the unprecedented expansion at Michigan College following World War II. The college's Department of Landscape Architecture and Urban Planning then argued for a more direct role in campus development. It cited how it had been teaching "the individual and social values of the landscape...[by putting] this art and science into practice" at the local level. Stated Lautner later, "The College administration could see no reason why a teaching department qualified to teach landscape architecture could not also be capable of coordinating and directing all the college's effort in the general area of landscape architecture in the classroom and on college property." Theory and practice were merged, and the science and art of campus landscape was given the entire campus as its laboratory.

The "Aggie" heritage also includes other campus landscape components: arboreta and horticultural and botanical gardens specifically evolving from research and community service, but also a sense of landscape being part of the campus tradition that has roots in a farmer's ethos and respect for land and nature. The combination of a compressed contemporary central campus wrapped in acres of experimental plots and less dense campus precincts is, of all extant comprehensive campus landscape concepts, the most truly American in origin.

Other Places and Personalities

Skimming campus archives, one discovers that apparently many of the existing older American campus landscapes came into being thanks to eccentric and single-minded professors and groundskeepers who visited European gardens, exchanged plant materials and seeds, and dedicated themselves to improving the appearance of the college grounds.

The informal and picturesque campus landscape is not exclusively the domain of the larger public institutions. Designs at Michigan State University and Smith College are two branches of the same tree, whose trunk is Frederick Law Olmsted. The titan of nineteenth-century American landscape designers, Olmsted was consulting for several Massachusetts institutions (Amherst, Mount Holyoke, and the Massachusetts Agricultural College) when Smith invited his firm to guide its expansion plans. Accordingly a collegiate version of the metropolitan Boston park system was superimposed on the Northampton grounds in 1892. The picturesque ensemble of ponds, groves, patches of ground cover accented with specimen trees, and controlled views and vistas responsive to topographic changes was laced with curving walks and roads and gardens.

With the appointment in 1894 of a skilled botanist (William F. Ganong) and a groundskeeper trained at Kew Gardens, England (Edward J. Canning), the college began to adapt the Olmsted vision to the Smith resources, campus life objectives, and educational mission. The emerging concept had two major objectives: to transform the entire campus into an arboretum, and to provide "the most thorough, vivid and economical [scientific] instruction for different grades of students," wrote Ganong in *Forest and Garden*, December 1887. His vision and mission became the educational banner behind which successive generations would march. The "botanical or educational aspect of this Garden has first place [but it is not] to be inferred that its aesthetic side is neglected [and] it may yet come to pass that there will be something of that charm which makes the gardens of Oxford almost sacred ground."

Arguably and ironically, the vicissitudes and cyclical disinterest that have afflicted arboreta and botanical gardens historically can be overcome when the beginning vision is sound and fundamental, as in the Smith chronicles. Exceptional gardeners at Smith left for better positions but were replaced by those with equal or better experience. An attempt to impress a fashionable, formal, geometric design on the looser picturesque landscape was rejected in 1914. The greenhouse is now recognized as a landmark example of functional architecture. Over two hundred trees lost in the hurricane of 1938 were replanted with a superior selection. A rock garden, for a time decaying and neglected, was restored. Dated and disheveled flower beds were replanted to conform to and illustrate modern taxonomic theory and practice. Presently the college includes in building project budgets special landscape funds, believing these are opportunities to add inspiring landscapes to the Smith scene, infusions responding to Gagong's dictum "Constant improvement through experiment."

The Davidson College Arboretum, another instructive exemplar, originated in an 1869 faculty motion to the board of trustees "to make the Campus in its contents represent in time the forest growth of the State, and if possible, the general beauty of the region." These kinds of initiatives, of which there is no adequate history to date, are scattered through the annals of American higher education. Some progenitors were people of enormous stature and fame, such as Ezra Cornell, whose presidency left his eponymous university with a treasured campus landscape tradition.

Of recent faculty initiatives, Professor Nalini Nadkarni's work at Evergreen State College is likely to produce a landmark campus landscape—an accessible forest research laboratory to study trees from bottom to top. The canopy level will include an overhead walkway from the college library through a segment of the forest, with an intermediary stop at an "observation pod." The program and place reflect Evergreen's reputation as an innovative leader in environmental studies. "An important message we will impart," writes Nadkarni, "is that all forests, not just pristine wilderness areas, make significant contributions to the health of our planet."

As homage to many that have labored to green the academic precincts for science and art, and to illuminate what can be done in seemingly adverse circumstances, the work of three less well known personalities is instructive. Let Harry Lindberg, the landscape gardener at the University of Kentucky circa 1925, exemplify the many unsung staff. With tractor and shovel he converted 9 acres of campus waste land into a botanical garden, work that included digging two pools for aquatic plants. With the assistance of the Lexington Garden Club and local nurseries he secured and planted what was at the time the largest collection of hybrid rhododendrons in the state. From the California Department of Forestry he obtained an Italian cypress, a handsome tree that was said to have been grown from seeds found in the Garden of Gethsemane. To serve as place markers (campus design elements that give visual and emblematic distinction to a particular locale), Lindberg built a rock garden, walks, benches, and piers at the garden entrance from local limestone. His influence today can be felt in the new and the expanded arboretum.

Byron Thompson (Oklahoma State University, class of 1933) spent thirty years transforming the grounds of his alma mater "from bareness to beauty." The school's centennial history describes his first

BYRON THOMPSON'S TRIUMPH / Oklahoma State University
Photo: R. P. Dober.

COKER'S GARDEN / University of North Carolina
Photo: Karen Berchtold.

impressive efforts: seven hundred trees and twenty thousand plants for shrubbery and flowers installed in a three-year period. Demonstrating a productive blend of horticulture as science and art, experimenting with fertilizers, soil conditioning, and grounds maintenance practices, "coaxing greenery of all kinds from the tight clay and hardpan of Payne County," he produced an exceptional range of campus landscapes. Thompson's formal gardens fronting the campus center and the main library terrace have few equals on any campus.

Coker Arboretum, University of North Carolina, exemplifies the work of another dedicated and visionary professor. Chapel Hill's first professor of botany and chair of the university's first Buildings and Grounds Committee, William C. Coker transformed a 5-acre marginal pasture into a mini arboretum. The plant collections from overseas, particularly East Asian trees and shrubs, were matched with their North Carolina counterparts. Designed as an outdoor classroom in the 1920s, the arboretum is now enveloped by the built-up central campus. As a nature preserve, it welcomes not just students and faculty observing the scientific aspects of the garden but also those seeking a pause in the demanding life of a striving university. Like ripples from a stone thrown in a pond, Coker's influence radiated outward.

The university now operates 600 acres of arboretum and garden lands with four major themes: "plant diversity, human dependence on plant diversity, the resulting need for conservation, and the critical role of research in botanical gardens and universities for solving modern problems and increasing human quality of life."

These examples from recent history undergird our conjecture that life in the twenty-first century will create both the interest and the need to expand and enhance campus landscapes, and that garden and arboreta designs, extended and new, will be funded as essential projects. Recent events at Ohio State University further substantiate this judgment about multiple-action concepts for greening the campus. OSU's 1998 landscape strategy includes 11 acres of special-purpose gardens, extensive tree planting along an abutting highway, filling in of the 1,600-acre campus with trees so it fully qualifies as an arboretum, and a new campus gateway. The latter is landscape architect William Johnson's "greenway zone—a signature space where automobile, sports facility, and arboretum become partners in creating a new entrance to a great university." The highway planting scheme, for example, used plant materials suggested by faculty who wanted to illustrate the visual aspects of plant succession (landscape design department) and the viability of central Ohio's ornamental plants (horticulture department). A local resident is donating a thousand trees (1998); another is giving $1 million for campus landscape improvements (1999).

Page 218 outlines a strategy for sizing arboreta and their cousin designs, botanical and horticultural gardens. The plea, again, is to search for and find opportunities to enrich the campus landscape with functions that combine science and beauty, which, large-scale or small, can add so much to the built-environment serving higher education.

2.17 ARBORETA

▶ Their Groves (whenever they planted any) were always regular, like unto orchards which is entirely wrong; for when we come to copy or imitate nature, we should trace her steps with the greatest Accuracy that can be. And therefore when we plant Groves or Forest or other trees, we have nothing more to regard than the outside lines be agreeable to the Grove, and that no three trees together range in a straight line; except now and then by chance to cause variety. (Batty Langley, *New Principles of Gardening* [London 1728])

▶ A piece of ground, a few dollars, a love of trees and nature and beauty, a collector's instinct, and an interest in science [will jump-start] an arboretum.... An acre is ample for 20 to 25 specimen trees and many beautiful shrubs. Five acres is plenty for a really representative collection. (*Yearbook of Agriculture*, 1949)

▶ The amount of land sets a practical limit to the planting and suggests the type of planting. If only five acres are available, one cannot waste much space with large trees, or if he wants large trees he must limit himself to a certain group of them just as a stamp collector limits himself to stamps of a certain nation. (Fred Lape, *A Garden of Trees and Shrubs: Practical Advice for Planning and Planting an Arboretum* [Ithaca, N.Y., 1965])

▶ Major arboretum directions in the next few years are to make the arboretum more enjoyable for people and to expand educational and research programs. To do that we plan to improve physical facilities, add new curricula, expand interpretive displays and trails, continue research on cold-hardy and disease resistant plants, conduct research on consumers' landscape design preferences, and find better ways to inform people of research results. (Peter J. Olin, director, Minnesota Landscape Arboretum, 1986)

The traditional role of arboreta, with their emphasis on woody plants (trees, shrubs, and vines), is typically expanded on campus to include other kinds of plant life and to operate as a scientific, educational, and cultural resource in the community. Typical college and university arboreta functions include growing, testing, and showing the best regional plants; introducing new varieties; supporting science teaching and research; disseminating knowledge through publications and programs; encouraging economic development of all aspects of greenery; and providing outdoor recreation. The activities and collections may be dispersed throughout campus, be designed as enclaves in or adjacent to the campus, or be large enough to sustain themselves as a special-purpose campus.

McMaster University (Canada) serves as steward for a 2,400-acre conservation and natural area abutting the main campus. In collaboration with the Royal Botanical Gardens, the university's life science and engineering departments conduct multidisciplinary research in habitat manipulation, wetland restoration, and biodiversity. Adjacent to the central campus, the megascale environment gives McMaster a substantial surrounding green context that informs the university's physical image and sense of place as well as provides extensive outdoor laboratories.

The Minnesota Landscape Arboretum was launched in 1958 as an operating unit of the Department of Horticultural Science and Landscape Architecture (University of Minnesota). The 675-acre tract west of the Twin Cities includes native species and plants from around the world. The attractive site design features impressive stands of trees, theme gardens (roses, herbs, perennials, hosta), residential landscape design demonstration areas, an education center, a conservatory, a library, and a gift shop. Here in one place is a three-dimensional encyclopedia of landscape art and science.

The University of Alberta operates a 180-acre reserve, the Devonian Botanic Garden. About half the land is a natural preserve of pine trees and wetlands. The remainder is a series of cultivated landscapes, including one composed as a Japanese garden. A garden illustrating Chinese landscape principles is in the planning stage (1999). The site operations are subsidized in part through fees charged to wedding parties and tourists and through sales from a gift shop.

The Utah State University Botanical Gardens occupy a self-sufficient 7-acre zone with a visitor and education center and greenhouses surrounded by collections devoted to roses, perennials, lilacs, a mini arboretum, and a native landscape garden. Here is proof that a limited amount of land can be arranged to support that which its director proudly calls "a place of serene beauty" overlaid with a facility for research, teaching, and community service.

The University of Central Florida's arboretum concentrates on ornamental and native plants associated with the geography and natural features in the campus environs. The original 12-acre plot, established in 1983, had been enlarged to 80 acres by 1998. The natural habitats provide a campus landscape in sharp contrast with the nearby field house, engineering complex, parking lots, and large man-made floodwater retention lake. Inside the arboretum one can follow a trail that was mapped out and labeled to demonstrate the natural sequence of oak hammocks, sand pine, and cypress dome. In a short span of space and time, one can observe a living testimony to the web-of-life theory, that is, the mutual interdependence of living organisms and its impact on biodiversity. The pass-through conveys structured information for those walking under professorial direction, as well as provides incidental and unexpected encounters with nature for those strolling for exercise and leisure. Nature's reality being more impressive than any digital version, both experiences are educational. Since its inception the arboretum has also helped train specimen collectors who have identified and supplied over six hundred local species to the university biology classes, a productive jump start on establishing and filling a local herbarium.

Combinations of research in plant viability, instruction, training, and recreation can be found among institutions in each tier of higher education. "Scholarship with applied experience" is the Delaware Valley College mission. The Henry Schmieder Arboretum special collections include daylilies, beeches, dwarf conifers, a hedge demonstration garden, and an herb garden. These outdoor laboratories advance teaching and research through "the display of common and unusual plants in pleasing combinations and ideascapes." The student center is located in one of the display gardens. The center includes a shop where the public can purchase horticultural books, souvenirs, refreshments, and seasonal plants and produce grown by students and staff.

Durham College of Agriculture and Horticulture (England) operates out of Houghall. The estate has a historic set of planting beds, a water garden, an arboretum, and a woodland garden. The heritage complex is used to instruct students in the horticultural sciences and arts. The theories taught in classroom lectures are thus strengthened by practice, especially by being able to see and tend and manipulate high-quality landscape. In the same spirit, learning by working with exceptional examples, the horticultural gardens at Sandhills Community College (North Carolina) include a formal rose garden, trellised enclaves, and hedges and lawns that would brighten the eyes of Henry James and Edith Wharton. In addition to giving students a science-based understanding of horticulture, the college prides itself on turning out groundskeepers who can maintain public buildings, particularly those in our nation's capital.

Requisites and Action

Given the importance the life sciences, ecology, and environment ethics will have in the twenty-first century, might not a national effort be launched to increase the number and quality of campus-based botanical gardens and arboreta? Such landscapes would increase and enrich, casually and formally, encounters with science, and for some people would encourage further engagement and exploration of scientific methods and principles. Whether stimulating awareness or motivating learning substantively through hands-on experimentation and problem solving, landscapes for science should be considered fundamental components in a campus plan. Envisioned are campus landscapes that attract attention for their beauty, arouse the emotions and the intellect through their content, awaken an interest in horticultural cause and effect, and lead to a substantive understanding of the natural world and our place therein. As to their importance as outdoor labs for practicing scientists, scholars, researchers and their students, that function too should be self-evident from our descriptions above.

In these respects, Swarthmore College's landscapes are notable. Emphasizing the scientific objective, the garden's first director, John C. Wister, preached in 1930 that "colleges seldom have utilized their grounds for educational ends. They might just as well be an integral part of the educational plant—an outdoor extension of the laboratories of botany and horticulture…and an education in esthetics." By 1998 arboretum staff and college science faculty had selected, grown, and tested over five thousand different kinds of plants, mostly ornamentals. Swarthmore has become a green college precinct that treats the main campus as an arboretum interspersed with special theme gardens. The ensemble of oak-lined walks and adjacent lawns from Parrish Hall, draped downhill to the railroad station, is a campus landscape deserving of landmark status. And the college's capture and restoration of Crum Woods, adjacent to the cultivated campus, provides visual contrasts most beguiling (the built versus the nonbuilt) in this sector of metropolitan Philadelphia.

How much land is required for arboreta and botanical gardens? Let us put to one side the college and university enterprises that involve a significant commitment in acreage, large staffs and significant

SCIENCE DEMONSTRATED; PLEASANT PATHS AND PLACES / University of Rome
Demonstrating the combination of greenery for research/instruction and horticulture-as-art is one of the cherished traditions evident in arboreta at leading colleges and universities. *Photos:* R. P. Dober.

Swarthmore College

budgets. These custom-designed campus landscapes, emphasizing the botanic and natural sciences, will require special and particular development for which local determinants will prevail. For the rest, our scanning of the existing literature and site visits suggest that 5 to 7 acres would provide sufficient land for a viable arboretum, and 3 acres would be sufficient for a splendid botanical garden and greenhouse. Alternatively, as at Connecticut College, Davidson College, and Hofstra University, the entire campus can be declared and tagged as an arboretum; and sites as small as 1 acre can be designed and planted as a workable and/or botanical garden.

As Donald Wyman cautioned in his forward-looking "How to Establish an Arboretum or Botanical Garden" (*Chronica Botanica,* summer 1947), these places must be "carefully planned, well financed, and competently administered." While the Wyman manual dealt with opportunities and conditions everywhere, his advice is clearly applicable to campuses. First, the best plans come from mutual, collaborative endeavors. The planning should be entrusted to a committee representing various interests and experience. Germane to academic life, though perhaps unintended, was Wyman's observation that "[l]arge committees move more slowly than small ones, but somehow all ... should be heard prior to the time the actual site is decided upon and the plan is completed."

The concepts will be influenced technically by size of the site and its configuration, the selection and placement of materials in accordance with scientific guidelines, climatic factors, and terrain analysis. These matters require professional judgment. Again Wyman: "[A]ll should be critically considered from the standpoint of landscape design...much money can be saved and many disappointments avoided by doing the right thing at the right time," not least being the preparation of judicious estimates and ensuring the commitment of capital funds and projected annual operating costs.

As to site location, Wyman proposes "a local spot of beauty, of historical significance." Better, we think, would be a campus site lacking beauty, if viable scientifically—thus replacing the dismal, unpromising, and ordinary acreage with a new campus landscape. Such would be in keeping with the spirit and achievements of the epical James Chester Raulston (1940–1996), a professor of horticulture. With a student crew, in 1976 he transformed an 8-acre patch of derelict land at North Carolina State University (Raleigh) into a world-class arboretum. Within two decades the collection numbered about seven thousand woody plants, many grown from seeds gathered by Raulston and former students.

In scale, location, and total effect, the arboretum at Indiana University is exceptional. An obsolete stadium was removed and the grounds cleaned and planted with a representative collection of regional trees. One side of the greensward is adjacent to the central library (providing excellent views from the windows) and another edge is near the art museum. The third side blends into recreation fields and the fourth is framed by a city street, with a gateway that directs pedestrians into and through the terrain. The visual experiences along the paths include architectural panoramas, pastoral scenes with brook and bridge that would suit Humphry Repton, glimpses of outdoor recreation, memorials, and highest-quality specimen trees—all this in the central campus, not a peripheral venue.

2.18 PRESERVES

Some campuses have significant natural resources—preserves, in our typology—adjacent to or inside their boundaries. The Duke University Forest is a specific campus land use and landscape area recognized as such in the campus plan. Cornell University has identified significant geologic formations that are central campus design features, visible but undeveloped, important three-dimensional scenery. Glen Ellen, adjacent to Antioch College, is utilized as a natural resources laboratory and recreation area. Some of the groves at the University of California, Santa Cruz, fit this category. The forest land that surrounds the University of British Columbia affords a spectacular entry experience for those approaching the main campus. Carleton College owns a piece of the uncultivated prairie, awesome in its landscape simplicity, significant as a tangible cultural reference point in classroom discussions about settlement patterns or the ethics of ecology, accessible and stimulating for student and faculty botanical research. One suspects many campuses have landscape remnants with comparable features that could serve similar functions.

2.19 Nature Walks and Trails

The educational purposes of plant life on some campuses is met by labeling specimens, charting their location, and providing maps for walking through and seeing biodiversity. The 1.5-acre arboretum at De Anza College (California) displays in a compressed area twelve state plant communities. One enters this domain from a path behind the college tennis courts.

The walking trails and adjacent landscapes at the Kalmia Gardens of Coker College (South Carolina) are structured in 30 acres to demonstrate the succession of plant life from a black-water swamp to a beech bluff. In between lie "laurel thickets and a pine-oak-holly uplands."

Of this kind of campus landscape, the Davidson College example is superior. Over sixteen hundred major trees can be found on campus, accessible by foot and described in a brochure that identifies the species along several well-defined walks through the central campus. The informative tagging includes Latin and common name, hardiness zone, and mature height. The collection features five kinds of trees that were once all but extinct on the North American continent, found again in Asia, brought back to the States, and reintroduced in the arboretum. One seems particularly appropriate for a campus: *Koelreutria paniculata,* which in the Chinese tradition marked the graves of scholars.

2.20 Gardens for Art

Acknowledging the desired presence of art campuswide, gardens for art are a specific topological element, most likely involving sculpture positioned within a formal or informal landscape setting. Campus land-

University of Wisconsin   *Photo:* University of Wisconsin.

scapes are themselves art forms, of course. Picturesque landscapes are painterly compositions. On some older campuses the blend of buildings sculpted with bas relief and/or set in geometric landscapes are superb examples of the classic tradition; few are better than the student union enclave at the University of Wisconsin (Madison). And how prescient and relevant to this aspect of our exposition on campus land-

ART AND LANDSCAPE / Wayne State University
Sculpture and landscape integrated with building and site, yielding exceptional designs. *Photo:* Courtesy of Wayne State University.

scape is Henry Moore's injunction "Sculpture is an art of the open air." His cast bronze interpretation of primal figures anchors one end of the Brown University Green.

Premise: Most campus landscapes would benefit from a mix of singular aesthetic objects positioned in space to amuse, inform, direct the eye, and/or climax a spatial sequence. The examples shown on pages 223–228 illustrate current practice. These include memorials to revered campus administrators; the numbers-as-sculpture that help mark the location of the mathematics building at Ohio State University; the monumental faux book on the library lawn at the University of California, San Diego; and the Wayne State University formal courtyard design punctuated by a single statue. The Keynon College dancers and the statue of Will Rogers at Texas Tech University, also illustrated, show how sculpture can transform a prosaic grass plot into a visually interesting scene. Some designs treat the entire campus or a campus sector as a sculpture garden.

Keynon College
Photo: Keynon College, Office of Public Affairs.

Scalewise, in between would be the Reiman Gardens at Iowa State University and Stanford University's New Guinea Sculpture Garden. The former is a 14-acre multipurpose horticultural demonstration area near the Iowa gateway. It includes the Penkhus Campanile Garden, where a carpet of annual flowers embraces a sculpturelike interpretation of the central campus clarion. The newly crafted pillar chimes hourly and provides background music for garden events.

The Stanford site is an oak and cedar grove that in 1994 became the locale for a group of New Guinea carvers and local landscape

LAWNS AND SCULPTURE / Texas Tech University
The commonplace converted into sprightly campus scenery via sculpture on a grass plot.   *Photo:* Author's collection.

architects to conceptualize and construct a cross-cultural design "not possible in the traditional western museum exhibits." Like gardens for science, education was a compelling objective. "Through this process [creating indigenous South Pacific art on a sophisticated Silicon Valley campus] the collaboration resulted in concrete expressions that visually challenge the constraining narratives of art/artifacts, authenticity/inauthenticity, and primitivism that are often forced onto nonwestern artists," wrote the sponsors.

The Stanford programmatic theme—"challenge the traditional"—is also applicable to conceptual art, where landscape garden art and other materials are intermingled to give a fresh meaning to the phrase *mixed media*. The accustomed and the unexpected are opposing forces that should be welcomed on campuses, where ideas are expected to be debated, deconstructed, and declaimed as part of higher education's mission. On the horizon are some interesting possibilities, with the definition of campus garden as art being extended in a new direction. The central library at the University of California, San Diego, has a wrap-

Ohio State University

around landscape that demonstrates how an unconventional blending of architecture, sculpture, and plantings can create a dramatic sense of place.

Less adventuresome in their making, but nonetheless very attractive in their results, are sculpture gardens adjacent to campus art galleries and visual arts centers. Just as the botanist can send the student to the arboretum to study a tree trunk, the art history professor can direct his or her class to visit an exemplar. Of its kind, few are better than the Franklin D. Murphy Sculpture Garden at the University of California, Los Angeles. Designed by landscape architect Ralph Cornell, "a man obsessed by the beauty of nature," the garden replaced a "dusty parking lot [with] a rolling, expansive and hospitable setting, without benches but with freeform seating areas which could be both sculpture and pedestals for bronzes." More than sixty pieces by artists ranging from Alexander Archipenko to William Zorach animate and inform this "feast of three-dimensional material," a 5-acre university garden extraordinary by any standard.

The Sheldon Sculpture Garden at the University of Nebraska serves comparable functions, a composite of trees, lawn, and sculp-

University of California, San Diego
The sculpted numbers near the entrance to the mathematics building at Ohio State
University and the cast metal book on the sloping library lawn at the University of
California, San Diego, use waggish contemporary art as emphatic place markers.
Photos: R. P. Dober.

ture intended to "document and reflect the finest American art of
this century"—and perhaps its fate, one may add. Ironically, both
the Murphy and Sheldon gardens contain sculptural pieces from
demolished Louis Sullivan buildings, gestures to the ethics of environmental conservation. The Nebraska garden design fills the space

between the Sheldon Art Gallery (designed by Philip Johnson in 1963) and the historic Architectural Hall. It is one of seven gardens that beautify the university's city campus, each with special collections that are "incorporated in the campus landscape, making best use of the building environment for aesthetic and educational pur-

Westminster College of Utah

poses." The gardens are paradigmatic responses to consultant land-scape architect John Ormsbee Simonds' mandate for the Lincoln campus: "One plans not places, or spaces, or things; one plans experiences."

If an entire campus can be developed as an arboretum to serve science, might the entire campus landscape also be conceived as a large-scale sculpture garden? Some examples at both ends of the continent (University of Massachusetts, Boston, and Western Washington University) would affirm that this objective could be achieved with relative ease and visually attractive outcomes. For esthetic aspiration to be translated into achievement, however, such efforts require a firm policy, a campuswide commitment, and occasionally energy and persistence equivalent to basketball's full-court press.

Case example: Western Washington University in Bellingham. Since 1957 the administration has allocated 0.5 percent of its building budgets for art. With funding supplemented by donors interested

CLASSICS AND MODERN INTERTWINED / University of Oklahoma
At Westminster College a contemporary design (plaza and fountain) is situated in the foreground of a classic view of the college's landmark building, with a gesture to a lawn framed with trees. Contemporary buildings embrace a classic closed courtyard composition at the University of Oklahoma, with a Renaissance fountain honoring the beginning of modern engineering. *Photos:* R. P. Dober.

Though not so adventuresome in their making, very attractive in their results are sculpture gardens adjacent to campus art galleries and visual arts centers. Just as the botanist can send the student to the arboretum to study a tree trunk, the art history professor can direct his class to visit an exemplar.

in contemporary work, WWU has acquired an awesome assortment of monumental sculpture distributed throughout the campus. The picturesque campus site, overlooking Puget Sound, is dotted with pieces, many intentionally confrontational, including some that on closer examination are quite waggish. The plaza adjacent to the university concert hall is crowned with a 40-foot abstract work by sculptor Mark di Suvero entitled "For Handel." Lloyd Hamrol's jumbled "Log Ramps," puzzling to many when first installed, is now understood to be an iconic gesture to the region's lumber industry. In a wispy minimalist design concept from Robert Morris, steam clouds from the central cooling tower are directed into forms that vary with the daily climate, wind, and temperature. However, for all its delights, those expecting the overall WWU campus landscape design to have an integrative appearance, such as UCLA's Murphy Garden, will be disappointed. Plop art, some would argue; but few would deny the visual impact of the Bellingham site as a four-star esthetic campus landscape experience.

As we move upward on the list of campuses worth visiting for landscape inflected by art, the University of Oklahoma's collection includes a sobering tribute to the American Indians who first occupied the region, statues of influential presidents and deans, and a stirring reminder of women's contribution to early settlement. The last, particularized by local lore, is expressed in a sculpted shepherdess and sheep situated in a small garden with the kind of comfortable seating and green ambiance that are a refreshing treat on a large university campus. Each example also contributes to site history, a landscape taxonomy described later.

2.21 AMPHITHEATERS

▶ The first element to remember is the planning of two correlated spaces: the stage space and the auditorium. The two should be sloped towards each other. The rake of the stage should be kept slight (about one in twelve is practical); that of the auditorium can be slightly more, but must never be so violent as to make the seating uncomfortable.... If the ground is naturally heavily sloped it is better to terrace it slightly to correct this tendency and yet to utilize it for good vision of the stage. (Horace Shipp, "The Charm of Open Air Theatres" [*Garden and Country*, autumn 1937])

▶ [T]he garden theater should not call undue attention to itself, but should provide, ideally, an unobtrusive yet comfortable acoustically and visually convenient setting for drama, music or the pageantry for which it is designed. (Albert D. Taylor, "Notes on Garden Theatres," [*Landscape Architecture*, fall 1939])

Outdoor theaters are historically and architecturally interesting landscape components. Classic examples from Greece, Rome, and the Renaissance are exceptional collaborative works of the highest artistic merit; indeed, even when left by antiquity in skeleton outline, they are often used as illustrations in synoptic works describing the best aspects of these earlier cultures. The collegiate versions—the word *amphitheater* being the common descriptor—serve as seating for ceremonies such as graduation, outdoor exercises, and pageants, as well as theatrical and musical performances.

Most campus amphitheaters are modest in form and features and are inserted into a natural slope or a bowl shape in a created terrain. Faithful to its antecedents, a simple model layout such as Swarthmore

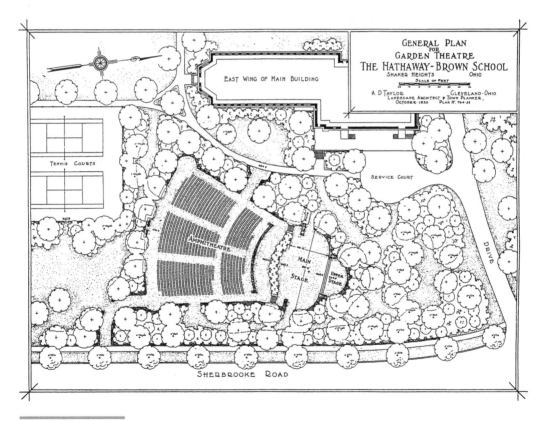

AMPHITHEATER / An A. D. Taylor Paradigm

At a school with a campus setting A. D. Taylor's design for a garden theater illustrates the scale and character of a landscape component that should be welcomed at many colleges and universities. See page 97 for a contemporary interpretation at Bates College.   *Graphic:* Author's collection.

College's surrounds the amphitheater with a belt of greenery and land-scaped paths that add to the experience the frisson of traveling to and from a special place. A workable facility requires about 30 square feet of total space per spectator seated. This total includes the stage and wings and service areas, orchestra or equivalent areas, seats, aisles, and entrance and exit areas. Diagrammatically, the design would approximate a raked rectangle, with the length about twice the width, with the seats facing north. With this orientation neither those in the audience nor those on the stage will face the glare of the setting sun. Location considerations include proximity to parking for the handicapped, water and sewage lines for toilets, and electric service for supplementary lighting. A thick, embracing greenery helps shut out unwanted noise beyond the site and adds texture and color to the overall design.

2.22 SPECIAL THEME GARDENS

Shakespeare inspires the art of the collegiate garden, "where oxlips and the nodding violet grows." Vassar College and Northwestern University both have landscaped enclaves where the plant selection is linked to the Bard's quotable passages. Of the two, Jens Jensen's work at Evanston is the exemplar for several reasons. In scale, 70 by 120 feet, it is the kind of landscape design that demonstrates that limited acreage is no barrier to devising and inserting a garden masterwork into unpromising terrain. In profile, his two-tiered hawthorn hedging provides a sheltered green zone that embraces a path textured with plants and shrubs chosen from Jensen's carefully determined list of species suitable for northern Illinois. Gardener, nurseryman, park superintendent, Jensen had full command of the horticultural palette. Glowing in its vernal garb, the Northwestern University garden is also visually enticing in the dormant months, a time when many campuses need landscape most.

Back to the University of Nebraska, where the Cather Garden pays tribute to the university's eminent graduate Willa Cather. In her protean Pulitzer prize–winning writing she uses the beauty of the state's landscape to set the stage for her region-specific novels. Her imagery communicates some of the fear and trepidation felt by early settlers when encountering both the savage aspects of nature, raw and unrelenting in its expanse, and the awe experienced in the face of its beauty. In the fall visitors are reminded by placards in the garden to see the slanting rays of a sunny day turn the bluestem ablaze, matching Cather's mnemonic of the "red grass that made all the great prairie the color of wine-stains."

A memorial with literary overtones, the Cather Garden features western American rural flora. The collection of native grasses, wildflowers, shrubs, and cottonwood trees does homage to her life and illustrates her writings. Informative placards alert the visitor as to what was lost when the nineteenth-century prairie was plowed under for cultivating corn, wheat, and other cereals. The depletion included the indigenous people's plants, used for food, medicine, and domestic purposes—a loss well chronicled in the garden. On the positive side, the curators point out that the flora is retrievable, grows well in the Nebraska soil, and "shrugs off the wind that howls [*pace* Cather] between the buildings."

Special theme gardens are superb examples of local culture expressed in campus landscape, especially as counterfoils to the blandness induced by global design trends that are interesting as fashion but lack the spirit of authenticity.

Our archives include a picture postcard from Lincoln, 1908. The University of Nebraska library is featured with the surrounding landscape, some of which was planted as botanical specimens, a panorama that Cather probably enjoyed. Today nearby is the Maxwell Arboretum, a 5-acre setting for the university library, as well as a display area for testing and interpreting seven specific collections: oaks, hostas, viburnums, lilacs, rhododendrons, prairie grasses, and perennials. The last of these were installed to show how Nebraskans can use ground covers to anchor as well as beautify soil on steep slopes. Planted by the eponymous Earl G. Maxwell (1864–1966), many of the trees border a meandering creek that runs through the arboretum. If Cather is the poet of the Nebraska landscape lost, Maxwell is the author of the landscape created. As state forester, he is said to have dispersed twenty million trees to ranchers and farmers. The silhouette of one of his favorites, a burr oak, appears on the university logo. With a sense of particular place enriched with reverential local lore, romance, and pragmatism conjoined with descriptive plant selections, all transposed into campus gardens, Nebraska can claim to have a campus landscape design strategy worth emulating.

Of therapeutic theme gardens, two now cited serve this function well, albeit differing in form, features, location, and style. The McCosh Infirmary Garden at Princeton University is a small, heavily planted gem confined by ivy-covered brick walls, offering seclusion and respite for patients and staff. The restorative powers of plant life, scientifically documented by mental health experts, gave reason to construct and plant the rooftop landscape at Stanford University's Lucile Packard Children's Hospital for patient and staff enjoyment. Health-related also, the Medicinal Herb Garden at the University of Washington is interesting as a landscape foil for the new grandiose Chemistry Building and as a resource for "herbalists, medics, and botanists of all levels." The plot's beauty and beneficial application may be reminiscent of the early monastic universities. However, as indicated on warning signs, visitors picking samples should "consult a qualified health professional for advice on using medicinal herbs." The garden is not intended to be a "guide to self-medication."

Special theme gardens are superb examples of local culture expressed in campus landscape, especially as counterfoils to the blandness induced by global design trends that are interesting as fashion but lack the spirit of authenticity. Accordingly we advocate their preservation and conservation and would encourage the development of additional examples. Notes landscape architect William H. Tishler: "They provide the setting and continuity for the people, events, places and artifacts which have contributed to the changing scene of human experience and they represent an important link in our history" (*Landscape Planning*, vol. 9, 1982). An overview of theme gardens at Clemson University now follows as a lead-in to our plea for the development and expansion of a particular campus landscape component, which we label *site history*.

2.23 SITE HISTORY

Our premise: Every campus has a natural history as well as a cultural one. Identifying, transforming, and interpreting aspects of that past via various kinds of campus landscapes is a campus design objective to be encouraged. Using Clemson University as a case history, we illustrate additional examples of creating new landscapes under some less-than-promising circumstances, note the linkage between site-specific landscapes and education, and underline the theme of landscape as site history.

Clemson was established in 1889 as a technical and scientific school; the founder's endowment included a plantation, farmlands, and forests. The start-up 44-acre botanical garden tract has grown into the celebrated 278-acre South Carolina Botanical Garden. Some of the first acreage was reclaimed marginal land, including an abandoned dump. The Clemson scene now includes eighteen special horticultural collection areas, named after donors, distinguished university professors, or unique functions. The Therapeutic Horticulture Garden demonstrates how landscapes can be designed for the physically challenged. The Braille (Natural Features) Trail was constructed for the visually impaired. Partially funded by industry, the Bernice Dodgens Lark Wildflower Meadow is used as a trial plot for wildflower sod. Another plot promotes horticultural techniques applicable in water-short regions.

Landscape students use the Clemson gardens for design projects, employing topographic maps prepared by students enrolled in courses on land survey for agricultural mechanization. Art students practice

To see and sense the contrast between cultivated landscapes and the ancient natural setting is an uplifting esthetic and educational experience. All campuses should find, keep, and interpret some aspect of their founders' site.

HOLDEN CHAPEL / Harvard University
Photo: Harvard University.

landscape drawing and devise sculptures inspired by the differentiated landscapes. Students in entomology collect insects and biology students gather water samples and plant species, while forestry students learn tree classification.

The Clemson mix of heritage buildings and landscapes is outstanding; here history in three dimensions offers hope for those concerned about homogenized campus design. Through university action, Hanover House (1716) was saved and moved to the main campus in 1941, and moved again to the botanical garden, where its original agricultural setting (a French Huguenot farm) has been replicated. Pioneer cabins, a grist mill, and farm implements are located in Clemson's Pioneer Garden. The adjacent plots display herbs, flowers, and vegetables grown by the first settlers.

MEMORIAL COLUMNS / Westminster College, Missouri
Site history whole and in fragments: Holden Chapel (*previous page*) was originally designed for worship, then adapted for chemistry and recently as the headquarters for the college choir. The reminder of events past serves as a vista ending element in Harvard Yard. The Westminster columns are remnants of the 1853 building, destroyed by fire in 1909.   *Photo:* Westminster College.

Might not other colleges and universities consider beautifying their grounds with a few examples of community architecture and related structures and artifacts that are in danger of demolition or destruction? As authenticity disappears into twenty-first-century cyberspace, a campus landscape element comprising historic houses and gardens could be a pleasant place for seminars, or might house offices for visiting scholars and artists and others concerned about preserving and interpreting these three-dimensional documents of an earlier era.

Germane to this idea and illustrating possibilities elsewhere is the site history enclave at Imperial Valley College, California. The region's oldest train station was relocated to the campus to serve as an art galley. The site is landscaped with local plant materials, displays of historical farm equipment, a segment of the plank road that carried crops across the California desert from farm to railhead, and Victorian street lamps saved after downtown gentrification. A mini version with the same purpose (site history) can be seen at the entrance area of Northern Oklahoma State University's main academic building. The farm machinery is set up like sculpture, a three-dimensional memento of institutional mission (training farmers and cattlemen), while the collection of geologic specimens and plant materials filling the site is a reminder of the region's natural character.

The preservation and interpretation of natural preserves and nature trails and the adaptation and reuse of older and obsolete campus buildings are, of course, good examples of macro-scale site history. Small-scale concepts can also communicate site history, as in these examples: (1) the classical columns seen on lawns at Westminster College (Missouri) and the University of Washington (both vestiges of tragic fires); (2) the armillary sundial at Miami University, Ohio (celebrating the fiftieth anniversary of a local fraternity); (3) the alumni garden and carillon at New Mexico Highland University (focusing on a century of academic achievement); (4) the Paul Robeson sculpture at Central State University, Ohio (recognizing cultural affinities); (5) the remnant of an old Roman fortification integrated

SITE HISTORY/TERTIARY LANDSCAPE / Northern Oklahoma State University
Machinery, artifacts, and plants are assembled into a tertiary landscape, a reminder of regional history and the university's founding purpose. *Photo:* R. P. Dober.

ARMILLARY SUNDIAL / Miami University, Ohio
Sculpture and site history combined in a commemorative work celebrating the fiftieth anniversary of a campus fraternity.   *Photo:* L. J. Dober.

into the boundary landscape at Lancaster University (UK); and (6) the
section of the corral wall relocated from the nearby abandoned Fort
Bascom (used 1863–1870) and employed to screen a campus service
drive at West Texas A&M.

In Cambridge, England, town and gown have collaborated in preserving and interpreting Coe Fen. Informative placards describe the
history of the wetlands and how they were engineered to create the

PAUL ROBESON MEMORIAL / Central State University, Ohio
History and cultural affinities expressed in a superb example of a tertiary space and wall defining the landscape area.   *Photo:* R. P. Dober.

FORT BASCOM WALL SEGMENT / West Texas A & M University
A piece of local history saved and relocated to campus to serve as a screening wall for a physical plant service dock.   *Photo:* R. P. Dober.

magnificent settings for the university colleges. One can walk through and experience firsthand the squishy terrain, see the drainage channels, and walk ahead to the edge of the built-up college precincts. To see and sense the contrast between cultivated landscapes and the ancient natural setting is an uplifting esthetic and educational experience. All campuses should find, keep, and interpret some aspect of their founders' site for comparable reasons.

2.24 PLAY FIELDS AND RECREATION

Of collegiate sports and related recreation, a few paragraphs must do for a subject deserving book-length treatment. The educational value of participating in team and informal activities has never been questioned. The responses to the functional objective (promoting sound mind and sound body) in terms of campus landscapes vary considerably. Land available (urban versus suburban institutions) will constrain tight layouts or permit generous ones. The number of people seeking time and space is obviously a design factor, as are the range of sports

The Lacrosse Field of Play

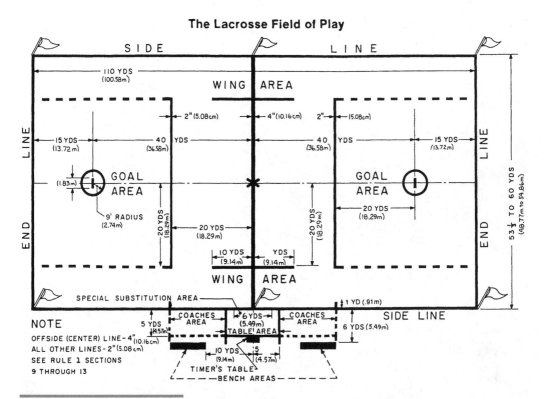

THE RULES OF THE GAME / Dimensioning Play Fields
The number of play fields is dictated by land available; size and configuration are determined by the rules of the game. *Graphic:* Author's collection.

TIGHT SITE/MULTIPLE USE / Worcester State College, 1999
Land limitations and heavy demand produced an all-weather, multipurpose play field that is scheduled eighteen hours a day.   *Photo:* R. P. Dober.

offered and the college or university's participation in spectator sports. The last of these may reflect regional cultural expectations, some of which are induced by traditions (homecoming and institutional rivalries) and increased by climate (which in benign areas extends the season available for play). In recent years laws (Title IX, for example) and sociological changes affecting expectations have increased women's participation in sports. Everywhere there is a renewed interest in health and fitness among students, faculty, and staff.

Recent development at Winthrop University (South Carolina) is indicative of demand and trends. In the late nineteenth century students helped operate the college farm, which supplied products for the dining hall. In the past decade the 324 acres of agricultural plots and pasture have been redeveloped into a campus landscape asset, including seven athletic fields, a recreational lake, and a cross-country course. Large stadiums and significant amounts of outdoor fields serve about two hundred institutions that are involved in so-called big-time athletics. For the others a typical set of outdoor facilities would include a cluster of grassy surfaces suitable for practicing and playing soccer, field hockey, football, lacrosse, softball, and baseball. In addition, there are usually tennis courts and outdoor recreational basketball courts, a running track with accommodations for field events, and sometimes acreage permitting a golf course. The size and dimensions of the play areas are set by competition standards. When not assigned to team activities, many of the areas are used for informal play. Occasionally, for extended utilization, artificial surfaces replace the natural grass.

In the main, we argue, most play fields and recreation areas, while attractive as green open space, do not realize their full potential as campus landscapes. Envisioned are designs along the edge of the fields (a linear arboretum or botanical garden, for example) or a string of pleasant places to sit and enjoy the games or surrounding ambiance. Inevitably, sports fields draw spectators, so there are also substantial opportunities to create landscaped parking areas to replace the dreary sheets of asphalt too often seen in these sectors of the campus.

2.25 INTERIOR LANDSCAPES

On the horizon, we think, will be a renewed interest in creating significant amounts of landscaped open space in campus buildings. Such

PROMENADE / Charlotte, North Carolina, Airport
These concepts and technologies are applicable to college and university interior landscapes.   *Photo:* L. J. Dober.

spaces increase the opportunity for participation in campus life, provide informal gathering areas for extending classroom and laboratory experiences before and after scheduled meetings, and add spatial and visual dimensions that may help "deinstitutionalize" ordinary college and university buildings. The technology now available for constructing affordable large-span spaces and installing energy-conserving building systems can yield some spectacular results. Envisioned is a collegiate concept that would meld the best aspects of the atria at the Gardner Museum (Boston), the Ford Foundation (New York City), and the Charlotte (North Carolina) airport. Emphatic and dramatic designs are to be favored, but even a modest gesture will be welcomed, especially in northern regions during the winter months. Interestingly, most indoor plants specified by experts in such situations come from tropical areas.

The components of interior landscapes include small and large trees, ground covers, vines, and hanging plants. Size, texture, and color can vary considerably. As in the outdoors, plants can be chosen to characterize the region, utilized as emblems, and/or displayed to celebrate holidays and seasons. Selecting and placing plants for their projected height and spread are significant matters, for unlike the outdoors,

PETTENGILL HALL, 1999 / Bates University
Designed by SBRA, this exemplifies twenty-first-century collegiate interior landscapes.   *Photo:* R. P. Dober.

where there is room for unexpected expansion, interior spaces are less yielding. Greenery bent or misshapen because of space limitations is the horticultural equivalent of a cardinal sin. Most plants located near drafty doorways and next to heating and air-conditioning vents will not survive. Hanging planters should not be sited where they offer a physical challenge for students to test their agility or the structural integrity of the planters—again, location, location, and location are the keys to an attractive and secure planting scheme.

Proper lighting and climate control are essential to landscape viability. Lighting requirements (intensity, duration, and radiant energy) will vary with plant choice. In response to seasonal and diurnal changes and plant types, various combinations of daylight and artificial lighting will be necessary. Climate control criteria include temperature, relative humidity, and air quality. Viability also requires disciplined maintenance, especially pruning, which in shaping and forming interior greenery is an art unto itself. Experts (such as the Associated Landscape Contractors of America) recommend hand watering in contrast to automatic systems. The former gives opportunity for finding and eliminating insects and removing trash. The latter, with its valves, pipes, and gauges, is considered too easily vandalized.

PLACE MARKING AND PLACE USING

The tenor (sense of place), thrust (desired direction), and texture (reinforcing detail) of campus landscape as a comprehensive design concept will be well advanced by a coordinated use of signs, lighting, and site furniture, including seating.

2.26 LANDSCAPE ELEMENTS

A coordinated sign system is essential to clarify location and inform traffic direction, as signals of welcoming gestures to visitors and all who use the campus, and as symbols of site occupancy. As graphic art, the sign system can elevate mundane scenery to a higher level of esthetic interest. An appropriate sign system begins at the surrounds and ends inside a building at somebody's office door. Sign size and configuration, color and typography, and sometimes the campus seal or related image are the basic elements seen in award-winning signage programs. Sign locations and sizes reflect projected viewing distance. Clarity at different viewing speeds (walking versus driving) should be given high priority. Type fonts can suggest institutional values, for example, trend-setting Helvetica versus traditional Garamond. Occasionally the standardized system might permit an exception, such as signs on and inside a historic building, or a graphic designed to identify a special place, caution, or direction.

2.27 LIGHTING

Lighting is a landscape art unto itself, for the most stale and prosaic landscapes can be transformed into uplifting scenery through theatrical effects. Lighting has several functions on campus: to provide a safe and secure environment; to illuminate areas used at dawn and dusk, and in the dark; to make visible wayfaring signs and signals; and to accent and embellish buildings, greenery, and related landscape elements.

Just as campus roads and paths can be designed and orchestrated in a hierarchy of significance, so too can lighting systems. The choice of fixtures, light intensity, cones of coverage, and color can be arranged to send clues as to desired behavior and the appropriate activity: *stay out, danger, enter, welcome, stay, use.* A well-conceived lighting pattern would also engender an esthetic atmosphere that complements and helps blend architecture and landscapes into landmark campus design. Poorly chosen and located fixtures will create unwanted glare or shadow, or communicate a sense, perhaps, of a campus closed down or semioccupied.

The use of the term *orchestrated* in the preceding paragraph was deliberate. Lighting components can be likened to a group of symphonic instruments, each having a particular characteristic. Thus there are spotlighting and silhouetting, up-lighting and down-lighting, lighting from wells and wall insets, customized luminaries, and plain-vanilla streetlights. Each involves a conscious choice for a desired outcome; coordination of all is a desired goal. Stanchions, light poles, and fixtures can also be selected and used repetitively to structure and reinforce the legibility and direction of path and road systems, as well as define campus and precinct edges and boundaries. Where possible, design consistency is preferred so that the campus doesn't appear to be a manufacturer's demonstration area of styles and materials.

Lighting has several functions on campus: to provide a safe and secure environment; to illuminate areas used at dawn and dusk, and in the dark; to make visible wayfaring signs and signals; and to accent and embellish buildings, greenery, and related landscape elements.

CAMPUS LIGHTING AS ART / University of California, Berkeley
The fundamentals of an appropriate campus lighting plan can be found at the Haas School of Business courtyard. The scheme includes glowing light from the windows, down-light from wall sconces, and up-light from
planting beds. The tapered pole fixtures, in a historical style, can be found throughout the campus, such as the
library terrace, thus reinforcing the sense of place.   *Photo:* R. P. Dober.

2.28 SITE FURNITURE

Site furniture includes kiosks, gazebos, ash urns, trash receptacles, flag-poles, mailboxes, outdoor telephones, and seating (the last of these will be addressed subsequently). Here again, selection and location can create a functional and attractive setting in which the individual elements are composed with foresight; when treated casually and randomly, however, they convey the impression of institutional indifference about the built environment. The latter seems unnecessary given the simplicity of the task: to establish and implement guidelines for the purchase and installation of the components. Such could be the role of a campus

COORDINATED SITE FURNITURE / University of Kentucky, 1999
The design concept for the landscape is reinforced by a coordinated collection of site furnishings. *Photo:* R. P. Dober.

amenity committee, a representative cross section of the campus community charged with the responsibility of setting campus design goals and objectives and encouraging and furthering their realization, including campus landscapes.

2.29 SEATING

Of all site furniture elements, we think outdoor seating is the most important. The subject has been discussed several times, and seating has been identified as an essential item in campus gardens, along the campus walks, and at the building threshold. Just as the Consumer Price Index (CPI) tracks the condition of the national economy, so an equivalent Campus Participation Index would measure the vitality of campus life. One aspect of the collegiate CPI, we suggest, is the number of places outdoors where people can sit for solitude and contemplation or gather for spirited engagement with others. Dispersed outdoor seating for approximately 20 percent of the campus population at one time would be a healthy CPI index number.

As to specific location, type of seating, and enveloping ambiance, there are few constraints on creative solutions. Single seats under a

LIBRARY PLAZA LANDSCAPE / Northern Highlands University
Variation on the theme: site furniture, lighting fixtures, banners, seating alcove, presidential sculpture, and a historic tree—the ensemble arranged as a landmark campus landscape.   *Photo:* R. P. Dober.

tree or tucked behind a wall, grouped around a fountain, arrayed along campus paths, situated in flowered enclaves, located at the edges of heritage greenery—such have been illustrated earlier. If the esthetic experience called campus landscape begins in the surrounds, then where one sits and enjoys the campus landscape in all its multitudinous magnificence or simplicity would seem to be the logical conclusion for our taxonomy of design opportunities.

LANDSCAPE AS PLACEMARKERS / Pike's Peak Community College
Contemporary architecture fitted to a sloping terrain is configured to form a climate-responsive courtyard. Plant materials serve as iconic reminders of the region's natural landscape, as do the stone walls, designed to provide comfortable seating for those participating in campus life.   *Photo:* R. P. Dober.

INDEX

Lasdun, Denys, 20
Lautner, Harold W., 209
Lawns and trees, 9, 119, 124
Lay, Charles Downing, 76, 154
Legoretta, Ricardo, 186
LeNotre, 44
Leubuscher, F. H., 206
Leyden University, 204
Lidsky, Arthur J., 55
Lighting, 244, 245
Lindberg, Harry, 212
Linear paths, 126
Lohman, Karl B., 172
Loudon, John C., 178
Lyman Lakes, Carleton College, 198
Lynch, Kevin, 76, 135

M

Magdalen College, Oxford University, 121
Maintenance, 52, 75, 81, 134, 170
Manning, Warren H., 69, 182
Massachusetts, Amherst, University of, 125
Massachusetts, Boston, University of, 229
Massachusetts Agricultural College, 210
Massachusetts Institute of Technology, 40, 192, 200
Massey, Raymond, 23
Maxwell, Earl G., 233
Mayer, Frederick W., 121
McCosh Infirmary Garden, Princeton University, 233
McHarg, Ian, 39
McHenry, Dean E., 23
McKim, Mead & White, 33, 173
McMaster University, Canada, 215
McNamara, Katherine, 164
McPherson College, Kansas, 99
Melbourne, University of, 151
Meyer, Elizabeth, 18
Miami, University of, 198, 199
Miami University, Ohio, 137, 237
Michael Van Valkenberg Associates, Inc., 64, 78, 106
Michigan, University of, 121

Michigan, East Campus, University of, 195
Michigan State University, 209, 210
Microclimatic considerations, 6
Miller, John, 49
Minnesota, University of, 18, 20, 96, 139, 153, 179
Minnesota Landscape Arboretum, 215
Mitchell, Collin W., 39
Mopeds and motorcycles, 141
Montpellier, France, University of, 48
Morell and Nichols, 165
Morrissey, Michael, 83
Moshe Safdie and Associates, 102
Mount Holyoke College, 170

N

Nadkarni, Nalini, 211
Nassauer, Joan Iverson, 154
National Safety Council, 143
Natural preserves, preservation and interpretation of, 237
Nature walks and trails, 221
Nebraska, University of, 226, 232, 233
Neutra, Richard, 17
Nevelson, Louise, 50
New campuses, 82
New College, Oxford, 179
New Mexico, University of, 15
New Mexico Northern Highlands University, 237, 248
New Mexico State University, xviii, 48, 201
New School for Social Research, 178
Newton, Norman, 207
Nichols, A. R., 31
Noguchi, Isamu, 186
Nolen, John, 39
North Carolina, University of, 213
North Carolina State University, 220
North Dakota State Capitol, 166
Northern Illinois State Teachers College, 37
Northern Oklahoma State University, 237
Northwestern University, 40, 232
Norton, Charles Eliot, xxv
Nott, Eliphalet, 180

Wise, Herbert C., 11
Wister, John C., 218
Worcester College, Oxford, 198
Worcester State College, Massachusetts, 241
Wren, Christopher, 99
Wyman, Donald, 219
Wyoming, University of, 185

X

Xeriscaping, 16

Y

Yale University, 32, 93
Yale University Divinity School, 161
York University, Canada, 33, 34, 36

Z

Zurich, University of, 28